Classroom-based Research and Evidence-based Practice

Classroom-based Research and Evidence-based Practice

A Guide for Teachers

Keith S. Taber

SAGE Publications
Los Angeles ▪ London ▪ New Delhi ▪ Singapore

SAGE Publications Ltd
1 Oliver's Yard
55 City Road
London EC1Y 1SP

SAGE Publications Inc.
2455 Teller Road
Thousand Oaks, California 91320

SAGE Publications India Pvt Ltd
B 1/I 1 Mohan Cooperative Industrial Area
Mathura Road, Post Bag 7, New Delhi 110 044
India

SAGE Publications Asia-Pacific Pte Ltd
33 Pekin Street #02-01
Far East Square
Singapore 048763

Library of Congress Control Number: 2006937884

British Library Cataloguing in Publication data

A catalogue record for this book is available from the British Library

ISBN 978-1-4129-2322-4
ISBN 978-1-4129-2323-1 (pbk)

Typeset by C&M Digitals (P) Ltd, Chennai, India
Printed in Great Britain by The Cromwell Press Ltd, Trowbridge, Wiltshire
Printed on paper from sustainable resources

Contents

Preface

This is a book about teaching and learning, primarily intended for teachers who are also learners.

In writing the book, I am setting out to support teachers (and those preparing for teaching) in developing their skills in critically evaluating research reports, and in planning and carrying-out their own small-scale school (or college) based research. I am assuming, in particular, that many readers will be getting their first taste of classroom enquiry – usually (but not always) in terms of the projects undertaken on University courses. The book will be particularly useful to:

- those undertaking PGCE courses;
- those setting out on higher degrees (MEd, MA or MPhil) involving classroom research; and
- classroom teachers who have identified enquiry into teaching and learning as a focus of their individual or departmental development plans.

I am particularly aware of the needs of students ('trainees') undertaking initial courses of teacher education, such as the Postgraduate Certificate in Education. PGCE courses require students to undertake academic assignments that demonstrate critical reading of research literature, and most courses also include at least one project-based assignment that involves undertaking small-scale enquiry (research). The rationalisation of higher education qualifications in recent years means that any qualification labelled *'postgraduate'* is by definition at master's level, and this has put an onus on Universities to clearly demonstrate that the *Postgraduate* Certificate in Education involves a level of academic scholarship equivalent to the start of a masters degree course. This is leading to universities increasingly seeing their PGCE as the first part of a masters degree, and has led to an increased scrutiny of the way the students ('trainee teachers') respond to both published research and evidence collected during their own school–based placements.

The distinctive focus of educational research must be upon the quality of learning and thereby of teaching. With few exceptions, the classroom, the transaction between teacher and learner in all its complexity, are what research should shed light upon.

(Pring, 2000: 27)

The book is about teaching and learning, and it is about educational research: both areas where a great deal has been written. Teaching and learning are obviously core professional concerns of all teachers, and there are good reasons for many PGCE projects to be based in these topics. These are key areas that student teachers need to learn about; they are central to the new teacher's development, and in terms of a student research project, they are 'do-able'. That is not to say that there are not other very important areas of educational research, such as (for example) educational leadership and school organisation, but these are usually more difficult topics for the student teacher to tackle.

It is not the purpose of this book to tell the reader everything there is to know about teaching and learning – a comprehensive review of such a large topic would require a much more substantial volume. Nor is this book a handbook of education research methods – that would be another heavy tome. The present volume offers an introduction to both areas – an introduction that should help equip the reader to be confident in critically reading the primary literature, and in appreciating the nature, limitations and possibilities of small-scale, practitioner, classroom research. This volume invites the reader to engage with issues around teaching and learning, and with educational research. It will provide a useful overview for all readers, but I hope many will be enticed to explore both of these areas further.

Keith S. Taber
Cambridge

Section 1
Learning about
Educational Research

This book is organised into three sections. This first section, learning *about* educational research, introduces key ideas that anyone who wishes to be informed about research in education should be familiar with. Chapter 1 considers the nature of teachers *as professionals*, and why learning from published research, and even carrying out their own classroom research, is nowadays often considered an integral part of both being a professional teacher, and of postgraduate teacher education. Then, Chapter 2 offers a taste of what educational research is about, by offering examples of the kinds of claims about classroom teaching and learning found in published research. As well as providing an overview of the scope of research, this chapter introduces some studies that will be used as examples later in the book, and gives the reader an opportunity to ask themselves about the kind of processes and evidence that would enable researchers to make the knowledge claims they do.

To those coming to study education from some academic fields – those where particular ways of working are well established and applied by all those working in the field – it may seem that educational research is an immature field. Certainly the widely-different approaches taken may seem catholic and eclectic, if not anarchic. However, the initially confusing range of research strategies is not an indication that 'anything goes' in education research. Different approaches to research are based on different sets of fundamental assumptions and beliefs about what research is capable of finding out. Any particular study needs to use an approach consistent with the underpinning assumptions the researchers make – and the reader needs to recognise (but not necessarily share) those assumptions to appreciate the status of the claims being made.

Chapter 3 explores this issue and offers a simple model to help readers new to educational research. Approaches to research in education can generally be seen as part of two clusters that reflect two distinct traditions. It is important to appreciate this distinction, as researchers in these two different traditions are usually trying to develop very different forms of knowledge, and use different ways of going about this. These research traditions offer different types of findings that are to be understood and applied in different ways.

It is suggested in the book that thinking about and undertaking research takes place at three levels: the 'executive' level where the basic assumptions underpinning research are established; the 'managerial' level where a strategy is adopted and research is designed; and the 'technical' level where data is collected and analysed. In much classroom research the same person acts as the executive, the manager and the technician (often whilst being in the same class as the teacher at the same time!), but it is important to recognise the different roles. Chapter 3 considers the highest level where the most basic assumptions are set out, and introduces the two main clusters of approaches ('paradigms') for undertaking educational research. Chapter 4 then moves to the next level, where some key strategies ('methodologies') used in educational research are introduced.

The second section of the book, learning *from* educational research, builds upon this introduction by exploring how teachers can critically read and evaluate research studies. The final section, learning *through* educational research, provides a guide for teachers or students setting out on their own classroom research projects. Here the 'technical' level of actually doing the research is discussed. This section looks at how to operationalise the basic ideas about research from Section 1, through the collection and analysis of data, and how to report research (drawing upon the criteria used to evaluate accounts of research in Section 2). Throughout the book I discuss examples from published studies to demonstrate key points.

Before looking at how we can effectively critique and carry out research, though, we need to get a basic understanding of the role and nature of educational research in teaching.

1

The Professional Teacher and Educational Research

This book provides an introduction to research into classroom teaching and learning. It is *not* a textbook on teaching and learning that draws upon classroom research, providing teachers with lessons from research that they should consider adopting in their own teaching. Such books exist (see Box 1.1), and are useful, but this book is as much about the nature and processes of classroom research as it is about the outcomes. The reader *will* find many examples of research findings considered in the following chapters, and a careful reader will learn a good deal about teaching and learning by reflecting upon these findings.

Box 1.1   Suggested reading on teaching and learning

Some useful books about classroom teaching and learning

Joyce, B., Calhoun, E. and Hopkins, D. (2002) *Models of Learning – Tools for Teaching* (2nd Edn). Buckingham: Open University Press.
Moore, A. (2000) *Teaching and Learning: Pedagogy, Curriculum and Culture.* London: RoutledgeFalmer.
Muijs, D. and Reynolds, D. (2001) *Effective Teaching: Evidence and Practice.* London: Paul Chapman Publishing.
Sotto, E. (1994) *When Teaching Becomes Learning: A Theory and Practice of Teaching,* London: Continuum.

However, the book is as much about *how* teaching and learning can be explored through research as it is about what research has found. There are a number of linked, but distinct, reasons why a book for teachers, and those starting out on a teaching career, should have such a focus. These reasons are both principled, and pragmatic.

On the pragmatic side, teachers, and especially students on courses of initial teacher education ('teacher training'), are increasingly being expected to demonstrate 'evidence-based' practice, or 'research-informed' practice. Indeed practitioner (teacher) research has become very common in recent years, so that in many schools it may be normal, or even expected, that teachers engage in research as part of their work (McLaughlin et al., 2006). This book is designed to help teachers develop the skills for making sense of, and to plan, classroom research.

On the more principled side, this move to require teachers to be research-savvy, or even research-active, may be seen as part of the development of teaching as a profession. Teaching has been *referred to* as a profession for a very long time, and has been (in general) a graduate-entry career for some years. However, professionalism is more than earning a living – the key feature of *the professions* is that they are self-regulating groups of professionals. In the English context, for example, the government has only relatively recently handed over responsibility for registration of teachers to the General Teaching Council for England – a body representing teachers, and having the power to debar them by suspending registration. (Even now, registration depends upon being awarded 'Qualified Teacher Status' through the government's criteria.)

We would expect any professional to be well informed about developments in their area of work, and to follow guidelines for best practice. This is of course the case in teaching, but it is not straightforward for a teacher to meet this professional requirement. For many years we have seen what I would characterise as the 'weak' model of professionalism in teaching in this regard.

The weak model of teacher professionalism

In this weak model, the teacher fulfils the requirement to follow 'best practice' without taking a major responsibility for exploring what that might mean. In this model (which, of course, is a caricature – but nonetheless represents the general pattern followed in the past by many teachers), teachers are told what research has found out during their initial 'training', and are updated from time to time – perhaps through courses or staff development days, but largely through centralised official 'guidance'. In other words the government commissions research, interprets it, forms policy, and issues 'advice'. (In at least one instance, the case of the Key Stage 3 National Strategy in England, one can be forgiven for thinking that the government issues enough guidance to allow teachers *never* to have to think for themselves again. That is, if they can find the time to study all the files, and booklets, and videos, and charts and sundry other material that are produced and distributed at great expense). So in this model, the teacher teaches, and others (with more time and other skills perhaps), are given the responsibility to find out *how* they should teach.

There are two serious problems with such an approach. The first is in terms of that notion of professionalism. No matter how well meaning a government, and no matter how skilled its advisors, it is not the profession. If teaching is the concern of the teaching profession, then the profession should be taking the lead, not being told what to do. The government is of course a major stakeholder in education – it pays for most of it – but its agenda is inevitably political. Governments should act politically, but professions are meant to be independent and self-regulating. There is of course a distinction between what governments require teachers to do, based on education policy, and the guidance that is meant to suggest how they may best go about it. In practice, much of the guidance issued by government translates into *expectations* on teachers: for example what school Inspectors expect to observe during inspections!

If teachers are to be professional, then they need to question such expectations – not for the sake of being difficult, but to ensure that they are confident that the guidance is appropriate in their professional context. A teacher must be free *not* to follow inappropriate guidance. To do this, without penalty, they need to be able to argue a case for their actions (to colleagues, to school managers, to parents and governors, to school inspectors, and to those most intimately involved, the pupils), *based on evidence*.

Before the reader starts to suspect that they are being asked to be some kind of subversive element – disrupting the carefully researched and disseminated approaches recommended by government agencies – it is important to point out that the government itself explicitly recognises that this weak model of professionalism is not appropriate (even if the sheer quantity of guidance documents seems to suggest there is often an *implicit* mistrust of teachers acting on their professional judgement).

There is a very good reason why government and the profession accept the need for teachers who are critical and reflective in considering advice. This is that educational research seldom offers clear unambiguous guidance about the best way to teach. This will be no surprise to teachers with backgrounds in social science or the humanities. It is not difficult to find different research studies that at first glance offer opposite conclusions. (The reader will meet some examples later in the book.)

Such contradictory research findings may sometimes indicate shoddy work (and this book will provide skills in making judgements about the quality of research), but it is often the case that such apparent contradictions may derive from well-executed studies. This leads us to ask how it can be possible that two carefully undertaken studies can lead to different conclusions.

Schools, children, classrooms, etc., are very complex entities, and it is seldom possible to make statements about, teaching history say, which are as definitive as the statements we can make about the melting point of lead, or the type of landscape produced when glaciers retreat.

General statements about teaching and learning are often *too general* to inform teacher decision-making for specific classes. Whilst there are some important general principles that are always useful, it is not possible to assume that research that showed X worked in classroom Y will *necessarily* tell you anything about your class Z.

Because of the complexity of the individual classroom context, most detailed ideas from educational research need to be tested-out to see if they *transfer* to our own context and apply in our classes. Moreover, we can save ourselves a lot of work and anguish if we are able to read research in ways that help us filter out ideas that are unlikely to 'work here'. Again, that is something that this book sets out to provide.

The strong model of teacher professionalism

Although the widespread incidence of teacher-research is a relatively new phenomena, in practice teachers have always had to find out 'what works here'. However, this is now formally recognised. So one of the 'standards' against which new entrants to teaching are judged for qualified teacher status (QTS) is:

> Those awarded Qualified Teacher Status must [demonstrate that] they are able to improve their own teaching, by evaluating it, learning from the effective practice of others and from evidence. They are motivated and able to take increasing responsibility for their own professional development.
>
> (TTA, 2003)

This is part of what might be characterised as a *strong* model of teacher professionalism: each classroom teacher is expected to actively evaluate his or her own work, and to seek to improve it – using evidence. To some extent, researching one's own professional work is 'part of the job' for today's teacher.

This certainly does not mean that teachers are expected to 'reinvent the wheel'. As the professional standards suggest, the starting points for improving teaching are a reliable evaluation of current strengths and weaknesses, and having access to ideas about what 'effective practice' might be. So teachers need to know both:

- what might be considered 'effective practice' in other classrooms (and be worth testing out in the present context); and
- how to collect suitable evidence to inform evaluations of (a) existing practice, and (b) the effect of any innovations introduced.

This clearly requires the teacher to have both the procedural knowledge to undertake small-scale classroom enquiry, and 'conceptual frameworks' for thinking about teaching and learning that can provide the basis for evaluating their teaching. In other words, the professional teacher needs both the ability to do her own research, and knowledge of what existing research suggests.

So, do teachers need to be educational researchers?

The strong model of teacher professionalism puts more responsibility and autonomy in the hands of the individual teacher. It is primarily the teacher's role to make decisions about how to teach, but – being a professional – these decisions must be justifiable. Teaching decisions can be justified in terms of theory and practice: research-based knowledge and the analysis of evidence collected in the classroom.

So *in a sense*, the teacher is an educational researcher. But there are also other individuals who have the specific job description 'educational researcher'. It is important to realise that there is in principle a substantial difference between the 'research' that teachers are being asked to undertake as a matter of course, and the academic research being undertaken by professional educational researchers. The latter have an in-depth training in research methodology, substantial time (and institutional resources) for research, and an obligation to produce 'public knowledge' (Ziman, 1991). The expectations on academic researchers, in terms of the level of scholarship, the rigour of research and the robustness of findings, do not apply to teachers. Teachers may often be *capable* of this type of work. Indeed, sometimes teachers are able to demonstrate that their research does meet these standards, and publish their findings in research journals. However, in general, it would be totally unreasonable to expect this of busy classroom teachers.

So there is a spectrum here, rather than a dichotomy, with published professional academic research at one pole, and small-scale practitioner enquiry undertaken to improve one's own teaching at the other pole. There is a minimum expectation for teachers to be active at one pole, and nowadays in many schools teachers are encouraged to go further and undertake enquiry that is 'published' internally through departmental meetings, school intranets, at meetings of schools working as 'learning networks' or 'learning communities' (see the examples in McLaughlin et al., 2006).

Many teachers undertake research projects for masters or doctoral degrees, where basic training in research methods is provided, and increasing levels of academic rigour are applied. Teacher research scholarships are available to fund teacher research that provides some release from classroom teaching, and access to research mentoring, but requires a short report of the work. The government funded 'Best Practice Research Scholarships' worked on this model, and although they have now ceased, a similar model has been adopted by the National Academy for Gifted and Talented Youth.

The message is that all teachers are now required to be able to demonstrate research-informed and evidence-based practice, and many are going much further than this.

Support for the teacher as researcher in initial teacher education

So there is now a minimal expectation on all teachers to be able to show that their work is informed by published research and the analysis of evidence collected in their own classrooms. As with any other aspect of the teacher's work, it is important that teachers are supported in meeting these requirements. This is especially important during initial teacher education, if only because for many teachers this may be the only stage of their career when they have:

- ready access to academic advisors;
- ready access to a research library;
- on-going mentoring from experienced practitioners;
- a teaching programme and timetable designed to allow sufficient time for thorough planning, reflection and lesson evaluation;

- a substantial peer group at a similar stage of development, struggling with the same issues and skills;
- regular observation and feedback on their teaching;
- regular opportunities to visit other classrooms and see teaching and learning with different teachers and groups of learners.

Few 'trainee' teachers probably appreciate just what luxury they have in this regard – at least until they move into their first teaching appointment!

PGCE, Postgraduate Certificate in Education, courses traditionally require students to submit a variety of assignments, usually incorporating evidence of both understanding of 'theory', and the application of such ideas to classroom practice. Passing the course normally means satisfying the examiners in these assignments, as well as demonstrating all the competencies outlined in the QTS standards.

In many of the universities, the PGCE includes at least one assignment that is based on a fairly substantive project, where the student is expected to demonstrate familiarity with some area of research literature, and to undertake some type of empirical study. For example, this may be based around the development of teaching resources, with a critical evaluative commentary based on evidence of learning outcomes.

The assignments on a PGCE are an academic requirement of the course, but have in the past sometimes been designed and judged from the perspective that the students are *primarily* engaged in a professional training course, and academic demands should not be too burdensome. Such a view is changing.

'Mastering' the PGCE

In effect, the Postgraduate Certificate in Education has recently become an academically more rigorous qualification. There are two reasons for this. One concerns routes into teaching. Since teaching has been considered a graduate profession, the two main routes into teaching have been by studying for an education degree, or for those already holding a degree, taking a PGCE course. The curriculum for the PGCE was largely at the discretion of the awarding university.

In recent years the government has introduced centrally-determined teaching standards (QTS), which are seen as the means to qualify as a teacher. PGCE courses must incorporate these standards, but in addition there has been the development of a range of alternative routes to QTS for graduates. PGCE is no longer the only way for a graduate to become a teacher.

It therefore becomes pertinent to ask why a student should enrol for a year at a university, when they could train whilst employed in a school. This is not the place to debate the relative merits of PGCE, but clearly one of its characteristics is that it is an *academic* university qualification.

In parallel with these developments in preparing teachers, there has been a move to rationalise the qualifications framework at all levels of the education system.

Under these developments, universities have agreed to a common understanding of the level of their awards, and the terminology used. As part of this understanding, the expression 'postgraduate' is taken to mean a qualification at a *higher level* than a first degree (not just something taken afterwards). In many universities, therefore, the PGCE qualification is being developed in response to the requirement that any qualification labelled *Postgraduate* (rather, than say, a *'professional* graduate qualification') should be substantially at M (masters level), so that:

> Much of the study undertaken at masters level will have been at, or informed by, the forefront of an academic or professional discipline. Students will have shown originality in the application of knowledge, and they will understand how the boundaries of knowledge are advanced through research. They will be able to deal with complex issues both systematically and creatively, and they will show originality in tackling and solving problems.

> (QAA, 2001)

One of the consequences is that many students applying for a PGCE will find that universities increasingly see the PGCE as (potentially at least) the first part of a masters programme that will be taught over the training year and the first few years in post. Applications will be considered accordingly, and applicants may be expected to demonstrate masters level aptitude if they wish to take this route.

To meet the expectations of the PGCE being a postgraduate course, universities are scrutinising their assignments, and the assessment criteria by which they are marked, to ensure that they enable the university to judge that the students meet the expectations of postgraduate study (see Box 1.2). Such an agenda fits well with the expectations outlined above for the teaching profession.

Box 1.2   The expectations on masters level courses such as PGCE

Students following postgraduate courses in education should be able to demonstrate that they:

- are informed by the forefront of education as a discipline;
- have shown originality in the application of knowledge;
- understand how the boundaries of knowledge are advanced through research;
- are able to deal with complex issues both systematically and creatively; and
- show originality in tackling and solving problems.

Those students who use their PGCE as the first stage of a full masters programme will go on to write a substantial thesis – some type of synthesis of research literature, or more often an empirical enquiry informed by existing research – and so the

PGCE assignments will also become the first part of a programme of preparing students for planning their masters project and writing their thesis.

In summary:

- in the 21st century context of *being* a teacher, there is an expectation of engaging with, and to some extent in, educational research;
- in the 21st century context of *becoming* a teacher, there is an expectation of being prepared to engage with, and to some extent in, educational research;
- in the 21st century context of becoming a teacher through a *post*graduate route, there is an expectation of engaging with educational research at a high academic level.

It is in this context that the present book sets out to offer support to teachers and students by providing an introduction to educational research into teaching and learning.

Getting the most out of this book

The book has been planned to support your reading. Different readers will have different needs, and different learning styles. Not everyone will wish to work through the book from start to finish. However, in writing a book the best assumption is that material should be presented in the book in the order that the author wants readers to meet it!

Writing a book for learners is a pedagogic task, and needs to be planned in a similar way to a lesson or course of instruction. As in classroom teaching and learning, it can be helpful for the author (as a teacher) to be explicit to readers (as learners) about how material is structured: thus a textbook has a contents list, headings, an index, etc.

In planning this book the major considerations were:

- to break down a complex topic into more manageable 'chunks'. In particular, consideration of methodology is presented separately in the book from a discussion of common data collection techniques, to emphasise the importance of thinking about these issues separately;
- to present these 'learning quanta' in a sensible sequence. In planning that 'sensible sequence' I have largely used the principles of going from the general to the more specific, and of following the sequence in which themes are usually tackled when planning a research project;
- to discuss real examples (of published research studies) to give readers an idea of *the variety* of educational research, and *to illustrate* the abstract ideas raised in the book. There is a vast literature on teaching and learning, so I have selected examples of studies that offer a range of approaches, and which provide useful contexts for discussing key points made in the text.

Inevitably, this approach is imperfect. Key points from different chapters are strongly linked, and so I have included cross-referencing forward and backwards in the text. Some 'jumping around' when reading the text not only reflects the inter-linked nature of the subject matter, but is also likely to be a more effective way of learning about the topic (both requiring greater engagement in reading, and giving opportunities to review and consolidate ideas already met, and to preview those to come).

In a similar way, understanding the strengths and limitations of research studies requires a consideration of all aspects of how those studies are planned, executed and reported. I have had to bear this point in mind when making decisions about where to locate examples in the text for them to be most effective. Such decisions are inevitably compromises, and to make best use of the examples the reader will need to use the book in a somewhat iterative way – returning to re-examine examples in the light of further reading.

Question for reflection

If the purpose of the book is to inform readers, why does the author keep posing questions for readers to answer?

I have also included a good many 'reflective questions' in the text. The suggestion is that at these points the reader stops and considers their answer to the question before reading on. In classroom teaching we often attempt to make learners' current thinking explicit, to help them see how new ideas might fit into, or extend, that thinking. The same principles can help when learning from a book – although readers are of course at liberty to ignore this device and just read on. (You might, however, first want to think about how you view those learners you teach who habitually want to be told the 'right' answers before they have intellectually engaged with the question!)

Finally, the discussion of examples in this book *inevitably* distorts and simplifies the original authors' own accounts. In attempting to draw on these studies as teaching examples, I have simplified them and been selective in which points I've considered. (This is what teachers do, to work at the level of their students.) Readers should remember that papers published in research journals have passed through a strict editorial process, involving peer-review by other educational researchers (see Chapter 5). Despite any flaws, these studies have all been judged to make original contributions to our knowledge of teaching and learning.

Readers of the book will identify the literature that is potentially most relevant to their own projects, and will need to read identified studies critically to appreciate both the strengths and limitations of the research. To prepare the reader for this work, studies with a range of research foci, and differing methodology have been selected to demonstrate the variety of educational research.

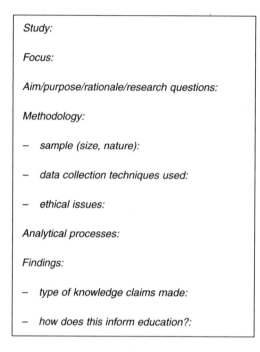

Study:

Focus:

Aim/purpose/rationale/research questions:

Methodology:

  – *sample (size, nature):*

  – *data collection techniques used:*

  – *ethical issues:*

Analytical processes:

Findings:

  – *type of knowledge claims made:*

  – *how does this inform education?:*

Figure 1.1   An outline for summarising the key points in research papers

I would suggest that readers might find it useful to use a simple summary sheet to outline any paper they wish to critique, with a set of headings relating to the typical structure of research reports (such as those in Figure 1.1). Then the paper should be interrogated in terms of the key questions and issues that will be introduced in the book.

Such a summary cannot provide full details of studies, but can be a useful framework for getting an overview of what a study is about. Boxes 1.3 and 1.4 provide two examples, giving overviews of two very different educational studies. Reading these brief outlines provides a concise précis of the two studies.

The importance of criticising (and 'forgiving') research

It is important to read research *critically*, carefully examining arguments, and the evidence put forward, to see *if the claims made are supported by the analysis of data presented.* This book exemplifies this by exploring weaknesses and limitations, as well as strengths, in published studies. For the reader who is not familiar with the educational research literature it could seem that some of the criticism of studies suggest that these papers have little value.

Box 1.3   Outline of a research study from *The Modern Language Journal*

Study: Sagarra and Alba, 2006.

Focus: learning vocabulary of a second language.

Aim/purpose/rationale/research questions: to compare three methods of learning vocabulary (rote memorisation; the keyword method; semantic mapping).

Methodology: experimental – learning of 24 new Spanish words, eight by each of three different techniques. (Order of technique was varied for participants.)

– sample (size, nature): 916 undergraduates in a large US university, of whom 778 provided data used in the analysis.

– data collection techniques used: immediate and delayed post-tests involving matching vocabulary to diagrams.

– ethical issues: all participants were adult volunteers, who were told the purpose of the research.

Analytical processes: statistical – results given as means and standard deviations; comparisons made using analyses of variance.

Findings:

– type of knowledge claims made: effectiveness of learning technique – the keyword method facilitated retention more than rote memorisation which gave better retention than semantic mapping.

– how does this inform education?: could inform second language teaching – 'when presenting new vocabulary, language teachers can provide learners with a keyword or suggest that they create a keyword to help them remember the new L2 [second language] word' (p. 239).

It is easy to find fault in studies, and we can find ready reasons for this:

- educational research is difficult to do well;
- many studies are severely limited by the available access to classrooms and learners;
- many studies are severely limited by the available resources;
- most research journals have severe word limits on papers, which can prevent authors from offering the level of detail they might wish.

Box 1.4   Outline of a research study from *Research in Education*

Study: Biddulph and Adey, 2004.

Focus: 12–13 year-old pupils' perceptions of history and geography lessons.

Aim/purpose/rationale/research questions: to find out what pupils enjoyed in history and geography lessons in terms of topics and teaching and learning strategies.

Methodology: semi-structured group interviews.

– sample (size, nature): 12 groups of Year 8 pupils from 'a variety' of different types of schools; each group of six pupls of the same gender, but including a range of abilities and levels of interest in the subject. (Three groups for each gender in each of history and geography.)

– data collection techniques used: pupils were asked to complete a prompt sheet to focus their thinking, before the group interviews, which were 'recorded'.

– ethical issues: all pupils were volunteers, interviewing was in same gender groups.

Analytical processes: not reported in the paper.

Findings

– type of knowledge claims made: pupils reported enjoying research/authentic problem tasks, group work, field work, etc., but found making notes and answering questions tedious. Pupils tended not to see any relevance in the subjects to their future.

– how does this inform education?: Teachers are encouraged to be explicit about the relevance of the skills used in history and geography, and the importance of developing geographic understanding to issues that pupils would recognise as significant.

The Biddulph and Adey, 2004 study outlined in Box 1.4 does not, for example, explain how transcribed interview data was analysed to derive the findings. However, it is published in a journal that normally published papers of less than 4000 words (shorter than many PGCE assignments), which is restricting to authors. This allows the journal to report more studies, but limits the information available to the reader.

Often an individual study can only contribute in a small way to the development of knowledge: however, that does not mean that it has no value. Although it is important not to accept findings, and (especially) authors' suggested implications of their research, without examining them critically, it is also important not to completely dismiss a study because it has limitations.

Research studies and research programmes

The research literature is cumulative, with each new study adding a little more evidence. Research is always based upon a wide range of assumptions (it has to be) and so each study will involve many choices (where different underlying assumptions and values might lead to different preferred options). The resources available then constrain what may *actually* be done.

So although individual studies may be limited, and even flawed, they may still offer useful insights and relevant evidence that may be 'suggestive' and 'indicative', if hardly conclusive. Many researchers see their work in terms of research programmes: that is, they have a long-term interest in exploring issues and questions that they see as significant, but which are not capable of being 'settled' by a single enquiry. Successive studies are intended to help move understanding forward. Early studies may do little more than help establish the nature of the issue, the most useful definitions, the boundaries of the matters to be studied, and test out the suitability of appropriate approaches to research.

Research writing as rhetoric

A second very important consideration is that research in the social sciences (such as education) does not always match the image of 'disinterested' enquiry that is sometimes offered as a stereotype of the natural sciences.

Educational researchers may be inspired by issues that link to their personal values. Educational researchers may, for example, be strongly motivated by issues of social justice, equality of opportunity, or (say) the importance for society of supporting an intellectual élite. When researchers have strong commitments to such principles, their writing may be intended to be largely rhetorical, to argue the case for the educational policies that best reflect values they feel are important. Such writing will clearly marshal a case to support their arguments.

Perhaps in an ideal world such rhetorical writing will be clearly distinct from research reports that should document empirical studies in an objective fashion, without being reported with any 'gloss' or 'spin'. Even if such an ideal were feasible (if it were possible to be 'objective' in making all the myriad decisions that lead to a particular study having the final form it does), that is not the current state of affairs. Many papers published in respectable research journals offer 'empirical studies' that are clearly biased by such concerns.

The use of the term 'bias' may suggest something necessarily negative, but perhaps we should make a distinction between bias as preference, and bias as prejudice. Researchers are allowed their preferences, but should not prejudge empirical questions before they have undertaken careful and thorough empirical studies. Phillips and Burbules point out that although we may not consider subjective writing as appropriate in research, it is not sensible to expect research to be value-neutral:

Every enquirer *must* adopt a framework or perspective or point of view. It is a truism that, given this framework or perspective, he or she may see phenomena differently from the way other investigators see them.

(Phillips and Burbules, 2000: 46)

The responsibilities of writers and readers

The reader of educational research is invited to 'buy into' the account being provided by the author of a research paper. It is the author's responsibility to make the case for any conclusions offered. However, it is the reader's responsibility to check the argument proposed. An argument's worth depends upon both its logical structure, and the strength of the evidence offered. Inevitably, any argument presented in an educational research study will in part depend upon data, and in part upon the interpretation of that data – an interpretation that draws upon the author's own theoretical perspectives. A reader's evaluation of the argument will similarly depend upon the theoretical perspectives that they have developed about the topic.

By the time you have read the book you should have developed a good basic framework for interrogating studies in order to evaluate them to inform both your own teaching, and your own classroom enquiry. You should also be able to apply this framework to recognise the strengths and weaknesses of your own work, and so be able to plan and report work that you yourself would consider competent and informative. At that point you can feel you are ready to be a professional teacher in terms of the 'strong' model of teacher professionalism.

2

What is this Thing Called Educational Research?

> Central to educational research … is the attempt to make sense of the activities, policies and institutions which, through the organisation of learning, help to transform the capacities of people to live a fuller and more distinctly human life.
>
> (Pring, 2000: 17)

This chapter gives some examples of the outcomes of educational research – the findings and conclusions about aspects of teaching and learning that researchers claim to show in their published accounts of research. Taken together, these studies give an indication of the *range* of foci that such research projects can have. More importantly, this chapter should get you thinking about how such findings are derived.

What does educational research find?

This chapter, then, gives a taste of the kind of things that educational research investigates, and the types of suggestions and recommendations that may arise from research. Often these suggestions and recommendations are potentially significant for teachers, in that they may indicate that changes of teaching behaviour would lead to more desirable classroom outcomes. As professionals, teachers want their work to be informed by research. However, changing familiar ways of doing things may be difficult, uncomfortable, and indeed risky (as it may well take time to become as effective in applying new skills and approaches). It is therefore important that teachers do not simply take up every potentially relevant recommendation that they find proposed in a research report. Rather, *teachers must be confident that change is likely to be worthwhile.*

So, changing teaching behaviour on the basis of research is only advisable when we are convinced that: (a) the research has been done well; and (b) is likely to apply in our own professional context – which may be quite different from the sites where a published study is carried out.

In this chapter the range of educational research into learning and teaching is illustrated in terms of reference to a small number of (mostly) recent studies. This chapter considers findings that should be of interest to all teachers, as it touches upon a range of topics that are central to classroom teaching and learning. It does, however, only describe a selection of the great number of studies about teaching and learning being published.

The reader is advised to look at these 'findings' with a curious eye, and to reflect on how the authors came to their conclusions.

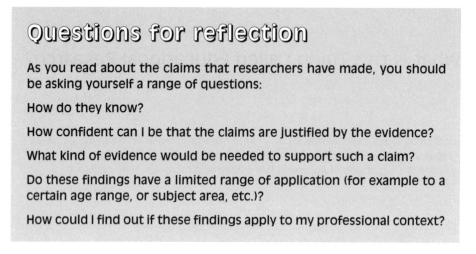

Questions for reflection

As you read about the claims that researchers have made, you should be asking yourself a range of questions:

How do they know?

How confident can I be that the claims are justified by the evidence?

What kind of evidence would be needed to support such a claim?

Do these findings have a limited range of application (for example to a certain age range, or subject area, etc.)?

How could I find out if these findings apply to my professional context?

Bibliographic details of all of the studies mentioned in this chapter are listed at the back of the book. This will enable you to locate the original accounts if you decide to read them to make *your own* judgements about the extent to which the authors have a convincing case for the claims they make. Some of the studies are also discussed in more detail later in the book, where they are used as examples to illustrate the nature, strengths and limitations of different kinds of educational research.

What kind of things does research tell us about student thinking?

One area of educational research explores student thinking about various topics – including their understanding of the subject content that makes up the curriculum of school, and their views about aspects of school life and classroom learning.

What do pupils think of school subjects?

It can obviously be useful for teachers to be aware of how students perceive their subject. In a paper in the journal *Music Education Research*, Button (2006) reports on a study exploring the perceptions of music held by Key Stage 3 (11–14 year-old) students. He reported that there were a number of gender differences in student responses to a questionnaire. Girls had more positive attitudes to the subject, being more enthusiastic for and interested in music, whereas boys reported being more anxious about taking part in musical activities. Three-quarters of the girls, but only about half the boys, reported having access to a musical instrument at home.

In a study of Year 8 (12–13 year-olds) students' perceptions of history and geography lessons, reported in the journal *Research in Education* (see Chapter 1, Box 1.4), Biddulph and Adey suggest that 'pupils were unable to distinguish between subject content and the learning process' (Biddulph and Adey, 2004: 2) when asked about their enjoyment of particular topics and teaching approaches. For example pupils had enjoyed learning about Mary Tudor by designing posters or learning about Antarctica by writing poems, but could not separate out the influence of the subject material from their experiences of the learning activity. This could be seen to suggest that for many pupils particular content is not intrinsically interesting or boring, but may be made the basis for enjoyable lessons as long as teaching and learning activities are chosen to engage the students.

How do students understand ideas they meet in lessons?

In terms of student thinking about curriculum topics, there is a vast amount of research. This is especially so in science, where research has revealed that students often hold 'alternative conceptions' or 'frameworks' that are inconsistent with the curriculum models that are presented as target knowledge in school (see, for example, Taber, 2006).

For example, Watts (1983) published a study in the *European Journal of Science Education* claiming that secondary age students understood the key physics concept of 'force' in ways that did not match scientific understanding. Furthermore, Watts claimed that he had discovered eight distinct 'alternative conceptual frameworks' that described the ways that students thought about forces. Watts argued that his findings would inform teachers trying to teach this concept in school science. However, such 'findings' are not always universally accepted. In 1994, Kuiper published a study in the *International Journal of Science Education* claiming that secondary students 'in general do not have a set of mutually consistent ideas about force, and that it is not therefore correct to describe such understanding as "alternative frameworks", which implies a coherence in student ideas' (Kuiper, 1994: 279).

Question for reflection

Why might two studies produce such contrary findings? What considerations might a teacher use to decide which (if either) study forms the better basis for informing their teaching?

Are pupils constructivist learners?

This area of research has been seen as significant as it is strongly linked to theories of learning, and models of good teaching. So-called 'constructivist' perspectives emphasise the importance of learning as being a process of building on existing knowledge and experience. There are many flavours of 'constructivism' but teaching approaches believed to be consistent with such beliefs about learning (sometimes identified as 'progressive', 'student-centred', 'active' learning, etc.) may be contrasted with so-called 'traditional' approaches, which are considered to be based around a model of learning as knowledge being transferred from the teacher to the students – usually largely by the giving of notes to the class, or directing students to read textbook passages.

In 2004, the journal *Educational Research* published a study by Kinchin which concluded that secondary school students had an 'overwhelming preference … for a constructivist learning environment', thinking this 'would be more interesting, more effective at developing students' understanding and would permit them to take greater ownership of their learning' (Kinchin, 2004: 301).

According to Kinchin, this work is significant, because 'not only [would] students be receptive to moves by teachers towards more constructivist principles in the classroom, but also that a failure to promote such a transition may contribute to an epistemological gap between teaching and learning styles that will be an impediment to meaningful learning' (Kinchin, 2004: 301).

Question for reflection

What do you feel Kinchin would need to do to make the case for there being 'an epistemological gap between teaching and learning styles'?

Asking students to provide their views about schooling and teaching (sometimes known as 'pupil voice' or 'student voice') has become more common in schools, and so has been the focus of research. In one recent paper in the journal *Research Papers in Education*, McIntyre et al. (2005) reported a study where Year 8 (12–13 year-old) students were invited to feedback on their English, maths and science lessons, and this feedback was shared with the teachers. Among the findings reported, McIntyre and colleagues claim that the student feedback had a constructive focus on learning and that students had common ideas about what helped their learning. Students believed that the following were all helpful:

• interactive teaching focused on achieving understanding;
• teaching that enables collaborative learning;
• having the ideas to be learnt suitably contextualised; and
• being given more feeling of ownership of their learning.

What kind of things does research tell us about learning?

Learning is the central purpose of education, and so it is not surprising that educational researchers have explored many aspects of learning.

Do pupils have learning styles?

One notion that teachers often come across is that of 'learning style' (preferred ways of learning), although a major review conducted on behalf of the Learning and Skills Research Centre reported that the research base for many of the popular models of learning styles was inadequate:

> Research into learning styles can, in the main, be characterised as small-scale, non-cumulative, uncritical and inward-looking.
>
> (Coffield et al., 2004: 54)

However, in a paper published in the journal *Music Education Research*, Calissendorff (2006) argues that the ways that 5 year-olds learn to play the violin can best be described in terms of their learning styles. Calissendorff offers a nuanced model of what this notion of learning style means in the particular context she researched.

Question for reflection

How might one collect data that allows us to conclude that 5 year-olds have preferred ways of learning?

Exploring the processes of learning

In a paper in the *The Modern Language Journal*, Sagarra and Alba (2006) reported a study showing the relative effectiveness of the 'keyword' approach to learning foreign language vocabulary (see Chapter 1, Box 1.3). In this technique the new second language word is linked to a familiar first language word that looks or sounds similar, and students learn a sentence or mental image connecting the keyword with the first language translation of the target second language word. They give the example of 'a messy table' to connect the Spanish word *mesa* with its English equivalent, table.

Learning can be a very complex set of processes. In a paper published in 1998, Petri and Niedderer explored how a student's understanding of a key science concept, the atom, developed over time. They reported that the student's conceptualisation passed through a number of stages, but that the student actually operated with a mixture of the different versions of the concept, rather than cleanly moving from one to the next. In their paper 'the student's learning pathway is described as a sequence of several meta-stable conceptions', and they found that after teaching the students' notion of the atom seemed to be a complex entity – 'an association of three parallel conceptions' (Petri and Niedderer, 1998: 1075).

Question for reflection

What kind of evidence do you think researchers would need to collect to explore an individual's learning in such depth?

Can learners regulate their own learning?

Self-regulated learning (SRL) is often seen as an important goal of education, where the learner has enough metacognitive awareness and sufficiently well-developed 'study skills' to operate as an independent learner – rather than being dependent upon a teacher to offer direction whenever a decision needs to be made (Have I done enough?, Is this good enough?, What should I do next?, etc).

It is obviously unrealistic to expect young children to be fully-independent learners, but an effective school system should encourage learners to take on increasing levels of responsibility for monitoring and directing their own learning, to equip them for further education and life-long learning. Rogers and Hallam (2006) published a study in the journal *Educational Studies* considering the study habits of high-achieving students in Year 10 and Year 11 (14–16 year-olds). In their sample they found that, typically, high-achieving boys had better studying strategies than high-achieving girls, as they managed to achieve high standards while doing less homework.

In a 2004 study, published in the *International Journal of Science and Mathematics Education*, Corrigan and Taylor (2004) suggest that the requirements for promoting SRL may include:

- offering students choice;
- setting learning goals and timeframes (within parameters);
- opportunities to reflect;
- a relaxed and supportive environment;
- a hands-on, activity-based, fun learning environment;
- access to a wide range of resources.

Question for reflection

How might researchers go about identifying factors that help develop self-regulated learning?

Exploring the significance of language skills in school learning

One area of concern in many schools is the learning of students for whom English is an additional language (EAL), i.e. not their first language. This is considered an important enough issue to specifically require trainee teachers to demonstrate their ability to support 'EAL students' as part of achieving the QTS standards. When English language is the medium of instruction in schools, it is clear that students lacking basic language skills could struggle to learn from teaching. In a paper published in the journal *Educational Studies*, Strand and Demie (2005) report a study analysing results on National KS2 tests (taken at age 10–11) in a local education authority. Strand and Demie reported that EAL students at the early stages of developing fluency in English had significantly lower KS2 ('SAT') test scores in *all* the test subjects than their monolingual peers, and this seemed to be linked to the low fluency in the language. They also found that EAL pupils who were fully fluent in English achieved significantly *higher* scores in the SATs than their monolingual peers (although they recognised that this finding could be associated with factors other than language fluency).

What kind of things does research tell us about teaching?

If learning is the central purpose of education, then teaching is the means by which that aim is achieved. Whereas learning often needs to be studied through indirect measures, some aspects of teaching are more readily investigated. Many aspects of what teachers do in the classroom, and how they plan for lessons and organise their classes, have been studied.

What kinds of classroom discourse do teachers encourage?

In the current political climate in the UK, many aspects of classroom practice are subject to significant levels of 'guidance' that have official approval, and may act as the source of criteria used to evaluate teaching. Understandably, many aspects of official policy and guidance (especially where not considered to be based upon a strong research-base) are subject to close research attention.

Hardman et al. (2005) report a study in the journal *Educational Review* that investigated the nature of classroom interaction and discourse in primary schools during the 'literacy hour' required in the National Literacy Strategy (NLS) – with a particular focus on students with special educational needs (SEN). They reported that although the NLS was encouraging teachers to involve pupils with SEN in the literacy hour, the classroom discourse was dominated by teacher explanations and sequences of questions and answers that did not provide sufficient opportunities for *all pupils* to offer and develop their own ideas.

Questioning is a major technique used by teachers, and types and purposes of teacher questions have been widely studied (e.g. Edwards and Mercer, 1987). It has been argued that teachers should use a high proportion of 'open' questions that give students scope for a potentially wide range of responses. Research also suggests this is *not* what teachers actually do.

In a paper in the journal *Educational Studies*, Harrop and Swinson (2003) reported that teachers in infant, junior and secondary schools used about five times as many closed questions (where only one answer would be considered correct) as open questions (that invite more creative thinking and several or many potentially acceptable answers).

Question for reflection

What kind of data would researchers need to collect to be able to draw such a conclusion?

How are teachers using ICT in their classrooms?

One feature of modern classrooms is the increasing availability of computers and other Information and Communications Technology (ICT), and the incorporation of such resources into teaching. Hennessy, Ruthven & Brindley (2005) report a study in the *Journal of Curriculum Studies* of how secondary teachers of the core subjects of English, mathematics, and science are integrating ICT into their classroom practice. They suggest that changes in this aspect of teaching behaviour are gradual and evolutionary: that teachers reported using ICT to enhance and develop their existing classroom practice, and adopting new ICT supported activities that modified or complemented their current practice.

In a study reported in *Educational Review*, John (2005) explored how teachers across a range of curriculum subjects (maths, science, English, music, modern foreign languages and geography) used ICT in teaching. John also found that adoption of ICT by classroom teachers seemed to be evolutionary, with changes in teaching practice being considered as 'adoption'. John also found that there were subject-based differences in the ways that teachers perceived the strengths and limitations of ICT use in lessons.

Macaruso et al. (2006) report a study in the *Journal of Research in Reading* that reports that when 6–7 year-old students initially considered to be 'low-performing' were given access to supplementary computer aided instruction in phonics over a school year, they made sufficient progress in reading skills to demonstrate comparable performance with peers who had not been considered 'low performing'.

Teaching and learning are closely linked, and often studies that focus on teaching are concerned (quite naturally) with its effect on learning. In a paper published in the journal *Educational Review,* Taylor et al. (2005) report a study of 14–15 year-old students using an 'electronic learning tool' to develop their writing in German as a foreign language. The writing tool, developed by teachers, enabled students to write in ways judged as more complex, accurate and imaginative.

Can textbooks impoverish teaching?

Teaching resources are suitable foci for educational enquiry. In some subjects, and certainly in some educational systems, teaching is often closely linked to adopted textbooks. In a paper in the journal *Teachers College Record,* Aldridge argues that this is the case for history teaching in the USA where 'teachers relied on these textbooks, consequently denying students an accurate picture of the complexity and richness of American history' (Aldridge, 2006: 662). He suggests that American history texts oversimplify material in ways that distort the topics being studied. He argues that when teachers rely heavily on the class text as a basis for classroom teaching, the students are 'deprived of a conceptual lens that would help them better comprehend the world around them' (Aldridge, 2006: 680).

Meeting the needs of learners of different 'abilities'

One major ongoing concern of those working in education concerns how teaching is organised to meet the needs of students who are considered to be of different 'abilities'. There has been discussion over whether students in a year group should be taught in 'mixed-ability' groups, in sets (i.e. for different subjects), in ability bands (for all subjects), or even in different schools.

In many parts of the UK, state schools are largely non-selective ('comprehensive') but selection on assessments of 'ability' is still carried out in some places. In a study reported in the journal *Assessment in Education: Principles, Policy & Practice*, Gardner and Cowan (2005) report that the methodology used to assess ability (and so select students for grammar schools) in Northern Ireland is flawed, as the system used for ranking candidates has the potential to misclassify up to two-thirds of a cohort taking the selection tests by as many as three grades.

There are, of course, many variations in practice. In many secondary schools some subjects are 'set', with setting in different subjects starting in different year groups. In a study reported in *Research Papers in Education*, Hallam and Ireson (2005) set out to compare the pedagogical practices of secondary school teachers from across the curriculum, when they taught mixed and ability grouped classes. They found that the curriculum was differentiated more in ability-grouped classes than in lessons taught to 'sets' – in terms of content, depth of treatment, the activities undertaken and the teaching and learning resources used.

Question for reflection

Hallam and Ireson (2005) report that teachers of set classes differentiate work for students less than teachers of mixed-ability class. What potential factors can you identify that could be investigated as possible causes of this effect?

Hallam and Ireson report that this did not seem to be due to the styles or skills of teachers, as differences in pedagogy were found when the same teachers taught both mixed ability and set classes.

In a paper in the journal *Educational Studies*, Lyle claims that teachers with mixed-ability classes can help their pupils develop their literacy by forming mixed–ability groups (rather than similar ability groups):

> Mixed-ability teaching provides a setting in which both low- and high-achieving students value the opportunity to work together where both groups believed they benefited ... the children themselves value this way of working and ... the social experience of collaboration affects the course of individual development regardless of ability.

> (Lyle, 1999: 293–4)

Question for reflection

What type of evidence would be needed to convince you that Lyle's (1999) findings are sound?

Teaching to the test?

Another concern for many teachers is how assessment is often thought to channel and constrain teachers' decisions about how best to teach their subjects. This is an important topic, as over a period of decades public examinations in the UK have shifted from being based almost exclusively on examinations taken at the end of courses, at age 16 and age 18, to modular courses, where examinations may be taken at different stages in the course.

In a paper in the journal *Educational Research*, McClune (2001) argues that students following modular courses, where some of the credit for final grades is awarded for examination papers taken early in the course, may be disadvantaged compared with students taking linear courses for the same award, and being examined on all aspects of the course in terminal examinations:

> In this study, upper-sixth pupils performed better than an equivalent group of pupils in the lower-sixth year when tested with the same examination questions in physics.

> (McClune, 2001: 87)

Question for reflection

What are the potential difficulties of undertaking a study that tries to make a fair comparison between examination performances of students taking examinations at different points in a course?

The A level course was traditionally a two-year course, most commonly studied in the first two years of post-compulsory education (ages 16–18) with terminal examinations at the end of the second year. In recent years there have been a number of changes to the A level examination, including the possibility of modular examinations which could (but did not need to) be taken at earlier points in the course. The modular courses offered four assessment points during the two years. Students could enter for examination in all modules at the end of the course, or be entered for examination in some modules earlier (with the opportunity of retaking modules as well as spreading out the examinations).

More recently, A level has been divided into two somewhat distinct qualifications, with AS level seen as the usual target for the first year of the course, and often as an indicator for deciding whether progression to the 'A2' year should be permitted. This new structuring of the A level examination means it became the norm for students to be formally examined in all their subjects at the end of their first year of post-compulsory study – something that had previously been possible but optional (for the school if not the individual student).

A key issue is raised here about the nature of learning. Can learning a subject at A level be seen as the accumulation of relatively discrete knowledge, or does effective learning require consolidation and integration through teaching in one topic supporting, reinforcing and providing context for learning in other topics?

What kind of things does research tells us about teacher thinking?

Research into learning and teaching is building-up detailed knowledge about how students learn, and what teachers do, and how different teaching behaviours can support (or impede) student learning. However, it is only likely that such research-based knowledge will influence teacher behaviour in fundamental ways to the extent that teachers are aware of, and trust, research findings.

Earlier in this chapter, research into student thinking was discussed. Understanding student ideas about school and learning can help us understand (and perhaps change) their learning behaviours. Understanding students' existing beliefs about topics that appear in the school curriculum helps teachers recognise misconceptions, and also helps them plan teaching that builds upon existing knowledge and experience.

In a similar way, educational researchers explore teacher thinking and beliefs. Teachers' beliefs about teaching and learning (including beliefs that may be tacit, i.e. significant even though the teacher is not consciously aware of them) influence teaching behaviour – especially the myriad decisions that a teacher makes in the classroom every day, responding in real-time to the developing milieu. Exploring teacher thinking provides insights into teaching behaviour, and informs those charged with developing those beliefs through teacher education and continuing professional development.

Do teachers understand the intended curriculum?

Sade and Coll (2003) undertook a study to explore the perceptions of technology and technological education among primary teachers and curriculum development officers in the Solomon Islands. Clearly, technology education is an important part of education, but Sade and Coll found that the teachers in their sample had a particular (arguably distorted) view of what technology education should be about. The sample did not seem to consider *traditional* technologies as being part of the remit of technological education, rather '…the most widely held view of technology education was that it consists of learning about, and how to use, modern artefacts' (Sade and Coll, 2003: 102) such as (as one of their informants volunteered) 'computers, televisions, telephones, emails, photocopiers, and fax machines'.

What do teachers believe about how their students learn?

One important focus of research has been what teachers believe about pedagogy – how to teach. In a paper in the journal *Teacher Development*, Avis and colleagues report their study of 'the experiences and understandings of a group of full-time further education trainee teachers…' (Avis et al., 2003: 191). These were teachers in training who through their course had been introduced to ways of thinking about teaching and learning that might be labelled 'constructivist', 'student-centred' or 'progressive'. Yet they found that students' own accounts of their classroom work were 'very far from our construction of a dialogic practice' instead focusing on 'skill acquisition' by students, and seeing the ideal teaching context in more traditional ways (Avis et al., 2003: 203).

Ravitz et al. (2000) report a study exploring teacher views about pedagogy, and teacher beliefs about student views about pedagogy. They found that teachers thought that students could learn as well from traditional approaches (being given notes to learn from) as from more progressive 'constructivist' ('student-centred', active learning) approaches. However, the teachers felt more comfortable using traditional approaches, and believed that their students would also be more comfortable learning in traditionally organised classrooms.

Question for reflection

How do the findings of Ravitz and colleagues (2000) of teacher beliefs about students' preferences compare with those of Kinchin (2004) of students' reported preferences that were discussed earlier in the chapter?

Strictly the findings of Ravitz et al. are *not contradicted* by Kinchin's work, as the informants in the Ravitz study were teachers and not the students themselves. The teachers may have *false* beliefs about their students' preferences, or their students in the United States may have *different* views to the English students in Kinchin's sample.

In a paper published in the journal *Teachers and Teaching: Theory and Practice*, Wong (2005) reports a study comparing the beliefs of music teachers in two different cultures (Vancouver, Canada and Hong Kong, China). She found that both sets of music teachers in her sample held similar beliefs about the conceptual aspects of music education, but they had different beliefs about the value of music education for their students' psychological or character development. Wong reported that in Canada more classroom activities were often student-centred, based around the students' enjoyment and interest, whereas music teaching in Hong Kong, where music education is viewed as a means of nurturing the student's temperamental development, the lesson activities were more tightly prescribed.

Tobin and his colleagues (Tobin et al., 1990) have explored how teacher behaviour is linked to the way that teachers conceptualise the role of the teacher. He reported a study of two science teachers, claiming that their different metaphors for the job of teaching influenced their classroom behaviour. The teacher who saw the role of the teacher as being a resource for learners taught very differently to the teacher who saw his job as being an entertainer or the 'captain' of the ship (i.e. class).

What do teachers believe about how they learn?

As readers of this book will appreciate, teachers are expected to undertake professional development throughout their careers to update and develop their knowledge and skills. As with any 'learning activities', such courses will only be effective if teachers engage, and so it is important to understand their experiences of such 'training'. Garet and colleagues (Garet et al., 2001) report an American study, published in the *American Educational Research Journal*, which explored teachers' perceptions of the type of professional development courses that were effective. They claimed that certain 'structural features' of the courses were important, including the form of the activity, the collective participation of teachers who shared professional concerns (e.g. teachers of the same subject, or grade level, or from the same school), and the duration of the activity (Garet et al., 2001: 916).

Finding and evaluating studies

The (mostly recent) studies referred to above provide just a taste of those continuously being undertaken and put into the public domain to inform teachers, policymakers and other researchers. Luckily there are abstracting services and electronic searching tools to help identify relevant studies in different topics (gender issues, ICT, gifted education, etc), which are related to different age groups or curriculum subjects. Most libraries have access to these tools, and staff to help you use them.

However, with so many studies, undertaken in many different ways, and sometimes offering contrary findings – for example, the studies of Watts (1983) and Kuiper

(1994) mentioned above – the task of deciding which research might be significant for our own classroom work is more challenging. We might be tempted to assume a study with a large sample size offering 'statistically significant' results should always be taken more seriously than an in-depth account of a case-study of a single teacher working with one class. However, before we make such judgements, it is important to understand what researchers are doing in different types of studies, and – just as important – why some researchers deliberately choose to avoid large samples and the apparently definitive results that statistical studies seem to offer.

3

How do Educational Researchers Think about their Research?

Having considered some examples of the kind of findings offered by educational research, we now turn to considering *how* such findings are acquired. To evaluate research we need to appreciate what educational researchers do in order to 'find' their findings.

As the reader will discover, there is actually quite a range of different activities that are sometimes considered as appropriate in educational enquiries – so that educational research may seem quite an eclectic activity. The educational professional who wants to learn from published research, and perhaps even undertake educational enquiry, needs to appreciate a little about:

- *the range* of activities that can form part of educational research;
- *why* such a range of activities are used;
- *when* different approaches may be appropriate;
- *the distinct ways* that different types of studies can inform educational practice.

The research executive, the research manager and the research technician

'Doing' research may be divided into activities at several levels: we might think of these levels as *executive*, *managerial* and *technical*. In some studies, much of the work of collecting and analysing data is carried out by research assistants, whilst the major decisions are made by a principal investigator. Of course, in many studies (and nearly always in teacher practitioner-research), the executive, the manager and the technician are the same person: but it is still very important to appreciate how these *different roles* contribute to the overall process.

The extent to which the principal researcher on a project feels the need to be involved in working with the data does not only depend upon the availability of technical support: it also depends upon the type of data collected, and the nature of the analysis to be undertaken.

Question for reflection

What type of data collection and analysis would make it more appropriate for a researcher to author a research report when all the work of collecting and analysing the data has been carried out by research assistants?

The 'nitty-gritty' of 'doing' is using the techniques for collecting and analysing research data. At this level, the research plan is executed by the research technician (or the *researcher-as*-technician in a single-handed project). Common techniques, the *tactics* of educational research, will be met later in the book.

Carrying out research techniques will only comprise research when they are part of a coherent research plan, and this needs a research *strategy*. This is what is described as methodology: an *educational research methodology* guides the selection and sequencing of appropriate techniques in a study. The main types of methodology will be considered in the next chapter.

The present chapter considers the role of the executive, where decisions are made at the highest level. Whereas the manager sets the strategy for a particular research project, the executive may be thinking in terms of how that study fits into a coherent *programme* of research. In business (which is often considered to include schools these days) we might think of this level in terms of providing the 'vision'. However, here I will risk considering the executive level as providing the *philosophy* of the enterprise.

Clearly the philosophy (or vision) needs to be established first, as this will give direction to the research to be carried out. Once this is in place, a strategy may be chosen, which will in turn guide the choice of tactics. In educational research, the 'philosophy' is usually described in terms of something called a *paradigm*. This metaphor is represented in Table 3.1.

Question for reflection

Why do you think it might be important to consider questions of philosophy for someone (a) reading educational research; (b) planning enquiry into their own teaching?

(It may be useful to revisit this question after reading the chapter, and again after completing the book.)

Research paradigms

Often educational research is labelled as being 'qualitative *or* quantitative', and certainly many researchers favour either approaches that rely heavily on numerical

TABLE 3.1   The relationships of paradigm, methodology and techniques

Role metaphor	Level	Responsible for	See
Executive	Philosophy	Paradigm	This chapter
Manager	Strategy	Methodology	Next chapter
Technician	Tactics	Techniques	Chapters 8 & 9

analysis, or those that avoid this. The qualitative/quantitative distinction is actually something of a caricature as it does not really reflect a fundamental distinction between studies (and there are many studies which draw heavily on both types of data). However, it is useful to identify two main types of approach to educational research that do have rather different purposes, methods and outcomes. This distinction has been described and characterised in various ways, but is usually framed in terms of what are known as 'research paradigms'.

Some academic fields have well-accepted ways of working that are understood and followed by all those in that field. Thomas Kuhn (1996) studied the history of science and described scientists as working within 'a paradigm' (or a 'disciplinary matrix'). The term paradigm meant an example that provides a pattern, such as the examples used in language teaching to illustrate patterns in languages for learners. Kuhn believed that the researcher does not learn about his or her field primarily by being taught formal definitions, but more by working through examples. Kuhn was describing what he thought happens in the natural sciences, but the term 'paradigm' has become widely used in social sciences, such as education.

Question for reflection

Do you think the natural sciences should be used as a model for research in education?
What might be the arguments for and against using research in the natural sciences as a referent for educational research?

In experimental psychology the term 'paradigm' is often used in a slightly more restricted sense to mean a specific outline research design that can be adopted in similar studies. In education (and most social sciences) paradigm has a more general meaning: studies in the same paradigm may have quite different designs, but share basic assumptions about the nature of research.

Paradigms in educational research

In education, and other social sciences, the notion of different research paradigms has been seen as important for those who want to make sense of what researchers are

Educational research paradigm **ERP1**	Educational research paradigm **ERP2**
positivistic	interpretivist
nomothetic	idiographic
confirmatory	discovery

FIGURE 3.1   **Distinguishing two approaches to educational research**

trying to do, and how they are setting out to do it. Perhaps unsurprisingly (in view of the complexity of social sciences), research paradigms have been characterised in many ways, with different labels used, and a number of 'candidates' for educational research paradigms may be found in the literature.

Despite this, it is commonly accepted that much educational research seems to fall into two main clusters of approach, informed by distinct perspectives on the research process. Appreciating the distinction between these two 'paradigms' offers a good deal of insight into why many studies are carried out and reported in the way they are, and what kind of lessons the reader should expect to draw from the reports.

The model of these two research paradigms presented here is necessarily a simple one, but at an appropriate level for those who are new to reading educational research. I will signify these two clusters as being educational research paradigms 1 and 2, which can be denoted as ERP1 and ERP2 for brevity (see Figure 3.1).

Additional candidates for educational research paradigms have been suggested (e.g. Carr and Kemmis, 1986; Biddle and Anderson, 1986). Whilst recognising the value of some of these alternative suggestions, this model of educational research (as usually being developed within either ERP1 or ERP2) seems to offer a good starting point for thinking about the different types of studies that may inform teaching, and will be adopted in this book.

Question for reflection

To what extent do you expect that individual educational research studies can readily be assigned to one of the two paradigms discussed here? (And can you suggest what your response to that question suggests about your assumptions about educational research as an activity, and the type of categories that ERP1 and ERP2 are?)

Are there really two paradigms in educational research?

Any reader asking himself or herself 'Are there really two educational research paradigms, or actually more?' has the author's sympathy. Educational research, like education, is socially constructed. The notion of an educational research paradigm is a way of thinking about, and making sense of, educational research approaches. What is presented here is a way of modelling a very complex, and ill-defined, phenomenon. This model is neither right nor wrong. It is a representation that is designed to reflect some key features of the complex phenomenon that is educational research.

However, to the extent that such a model is seen as a *prescription* of what should be done (what educational research *should* be like), it can become a 'self-fulfilling prophecy'. If research students are expected to think in terms of ERP1 or ERP2 when planning their enquiries, and write according to such a model in their theses, then such a model could increasingly match actual practice. Luckily this pressure may be balanced by those academics – having already had their theses safely examined – who claim originality in their work by seeking to extend, develop, or even overturn such models!

So the model is a simplification of a more nuanced situation, used as a pedagogic device. In teaching complex ideas from history, geography, literature, physics, etc., the educational community develops models for use in teaching. Current scholarship is simplified to form curricular models to act as target knowledge for teaching. When these models have 'the optimum level of simplification' (Taber, 2000a) they reflect the original ideas in 'intellectually honest' (Bruner, 1960) ways, whilst being simple enough to make sense to the learner. The notion of a spiral curriculum (Bruner, again) means that we look to use these models as the foundations for building more sophisticated understanding as learners progress through their schooling.

This same principle should apply at *all* levels of teaching – even postgraduate level. For those just setting out to find out about educational research, then the 'two-paradigms' model offers a good starting point, as much educational research can be understood in relation to these two clusters of approaches. For those who wish to have a basic understanding of educational research to inform classroom practice, it is largely a sufficient model.

Those readers who anticipate undertaking educational research at a higher level (perhaps reading for a PhD in due course), then it will become important to move beyond this model, to appreciate the finer distinctions within, and the approaches that do not quite fit, either paradigm. However, in learning (at postgraduate or any other level) it is important to build up understanding. This book will provide opportunities to apply the basic model presented here.

A good curricular model provides the basis for later developing more advanced understandings. Readers are advised to make sure they are able to think with, and use, this introductory model, before looking to move beyond it. As with the students we teach, it takes time to fully consolidate new learning before it is suitable to act as a foundation for progression.

As a final point, before proceeding to the model, do not be concerned that this chapter 'only' presents a model of the nature of educational research. There is a real sense that all that research or scholarship can ever do is lead to models, even if sometimes they become so familiar and taken-for-granted that we act as though they are true representations of the world. Beliefs such as that the sun will rise tomorrow, or that food will continue to offer nutritional value, are in effect predictions made from models that we are very confident about. We more readily recognise that other beliefs (that Year 9 will continue to hand in their homework; that the AS group will get good grades; that the threat of detention is a useful deterrent) are based on models that may be incomplete and need revising as new evidence becomes available.

The philosophy underpinning the paradigms

The two aspects of 'philosophy' considered to underpin research paradigms are beliefs (or 'commitments') about the nature of the world (what kind of things exist in the world, and what is their nature?), and so the nature of the phenomena studied in research; and beliefs about the nature and status of human knowledge, and so how we might come to hold knowledge. These concerns are known technically as 'ontology' and 'epistemology' respectively.

Some students who are new to educational research may feel that they do not need to be concerned with philosophical issues such as ontology and epistemology, but if so they are very wrong.

Although it may be possible to do effective research that avoids using *the terminology*, it is certainly not possible to plan coherent research without taking the issues seriously.

What do we mean by a student's ability?

For example, several of the studies surveyed in Chapter 2 referred to 'ability'. This is an everyday word, which teachers commonly use as if it has an agreed and obvious meaning. In fact, this is far from the case. Anyone wanting to undertake research relating to student ability would need to seriously consider both ontological and epistemological questions before setting out on the research (see Figure 3.2).

The researcher's assumptions (either explicit or tacit) in relation to these sorts of questions will determine their research plans, as they inform all aspects of the research process. A failure to make such assumptions explicit at the start of the research process is quite likely to lead to the researcher making poorly considered decisions and failing to collect the type of evidence needed to illuminate his/her research questions. If this is only recognised when this is pointed out by someone else (a tutor or examiner for example), who does examine the assumptions carefully, it may also lead to embarrassment, or worse.

Question for reflection

As you read through the descriptions of the two main educational research paradigms, can you identify the ontological and epistemological commitments that are associated with each?

Ontological concerns	Epistemological concerns
What kind of 'thing' is ability? Does it have different dimensions? Is it fixed, or does it change? Is it the type of thing that can be measured, or is it better described?	How can I find out about student ability? What type of evidence will inform me about ability? How will I know if my analysis of that evidence is reliable? How can I tell I have developed an authentic account?

FIGURE 3.2　**How our assumptions influence our approach to research**

ERP1 – finding the laws explaining educational reality

The first paradigm may be considered to be 'positivistic'. Positivism is based on an assumption that it is possible to report unambiguous truth, in terms of observable phenomena and verified facts. The term positivism may be used as a label for 'any approach that applies scientific method to the study of human action' (Schwandt, 2001: 199). A positivist approach assumes that the aims, concept, methods and model of explanation employed in the natural sciences may be applied non-problematically (Carr and Kemmis, 1986: 62; Walford, 1991: 2).

> When this view [positivism] is applied to educational research … . All things are seen as predictable, regular, and capable of being fitted into the pre-determined structure.
>
> (McNiff, 1992: 12)

Gilbert and Watts (1983: 64) refer to this paradigm, as a tradition 'in which explanation is the goal', and associate it with such descriptors as 'scientific', 'experimental', and 'traditional'. ERP1 research is 'nomothetic' – that is concerned with finding general laws – and it is commonly associated with quantitative research methodology.

Biddle and Anderson characterise research that 'presumes to establish objective information about social behaviour that can be generalized' (Biddle and Anderson, 1986: 231) as a *confirmatory* perspective, where:

> Two methods have dominated … the cross-sectional survey in which data are gathered, on one occasion, often from a sample of persons taken to represent some universe of human beings in whom we are interested [or an alternative approach of] manipulative experiments … in which the investigator controls irrelevant sources of variation, manipulates an independent variable, and then observes effects in a dependent variable.
>
> (Biddle and Anderson, 1986: 234)

The positivist viewpoint underpinning research in this tradition is based on the belief in 'a single independently existing reality that can be accessed by researchers' (Greenbank, 2003: 792). It is likely that many researchers in the physical sciences would see such an assumption as reasonable, and certainly, in practice, many scientists behave as though they are revealing pre-existing truths about nature.

However, it is important to realise that few researchers, no matter what their strength of belief in an objective reality, would consider that there are *simple* ways to find certain knowledge about that reality. Perspectives that acknowledge that 'scientific research' can only provide provisional, tentative 'truths' are often labelled 'postpositivist' (Phillips and Burbules, 2000).

Although concepts such as energy, element, force or metal are human inventions, they are useful because they seem to map onto regularities in nature that are totally independent of the human observer. The role of science could be seen as developing and refining models to give ever-improving fit to what is observed in the natural world.

Question for reflection

To what extent do you think that educational research can be seen as uncovering the general laws that reveal the truth about educational reality: when might this be a suitable mind-set for exploring learning and teaching, and when might such assumptions prove problematic?

Testing hypotheses about an objective reality?

ERP1 is based upon 'the view which treats the social world like the natural world – as if it were a hard, external and objective reality' leading to 'scientific investigations' which 'will be directed at analysing the relationships and regularities between selected factors in that world. It will be predominantly [sic – not exclusively] quantitative' (Cohen et al., 2000: 7).

> Studies … give stress to careful research design, to reliable measurement of variables, to statistical manipulation of data, and to the detailed examination of evidence. Hypotheses are stated to indicate knowledge claims, and these are judged to be confirmed if they are supported by inferential statistics that reach arbitrary levels of significance. Confirmed hypotheses ('findings') are presumed to generalise to populations or contexts similar to the one studied.
>
> (Biddle and Anderson, 1986: 231)

However, the subject matter of the social sciences, such as education, are often phenomena – institutions, processes, events, etc. – that have been set up by people with particular purposes in mind, and with various participants (teachers, students, parents, etc.) who are seen as having varying roles (swot, bully, trouble-maker, etc.) and who may have different motivations for their involvement (vocation, paid employment, desire to learn, fear of punishment, etc.). Concepts such as 'lesson', 'class', 'student', 'effective teacher', 'assessment activity', 'homework', 'detention', etc. do not relate to patterns that are found in nature outside the world of human activity and interactions. There is a very big doubt about the extent that it is reasonable to expect human activity, such as education, to be suitable for describing through one particular 'best-fit model'.

> Researchers working within the positivist paradigm see reality as separate from themselves and expect investigators to have the same perceptions of shared phenomena and thus common understandings. Researchers working within the interpretive paradigm see reality as a social construct and so do not necessarily expect other investigators to have the same perceptions or understandings of shared phenomena.
>
> (Bassey, 1992: 6–7)

Confirmatory research?

One of the studies referred to in Chapter 2 was Harrop and Swinson's (2003) study of the nature of questions used by teachers, published in the journal *Educational Studies*. A key referent that Harrop and Swinson cite is previous research in junior schools undertaken by Maurice Galton and colleagues (1999), which had reported on the proportion of teacher questions in a number of categories. This work, which is well known, is significant to Harrop and Swinson's study for a number of reasons, which include:

- Galton's research took the form of large scale surveys;
- Galton's studies had focused on junior schools, and had not included infant or secondary classes.

Harrop and Swinson's study (2003: 52) used the re-examination of a relatively modest amount of classroom recording (five hours at each of infant, junior and secondary level) – a series of snapshots from a small sample of classrooms. They explain that their research had two purposes:

- to see the extent to which the different methodology employed would produce results similar to those obtained by Galton and his colleagues;
- to examine *differences* in patterns of questioning between the three levels of schooling. [my emphasis]

Question for reflection

In terms of Harrop and Swinson's (2003) second aim ('to examine differences in patterns of questioning between the three levels of schooling'), can you formulate a hypothesis that the research could be testing?

Harrop and Swinson (2003) report that their findings in junior schools closely reflect those from the much larger survey undertaken by Galton's team at about the same time. This suggested that their approach is able to produce valid and reliable results, and gave them confidence that their comparison across levels would be meaningful.

Harrop and Swinson's 2003 study can be seen as being located in a confirmatory research paradigm (ERP1), where a specific prediction or research hypothesis is tested by collecting data suitable for statistical analysis. Their *expectation* was that the profile of teacher questions would *vary* across infant, junior and secondary levels.

What Harrop and Swinson (2003: 49) actually found was that the profile of questions across categories '*differed very little*' in infant schools, junior schools and secondary schools.

Question for reflection

In terms of the usefulness of the research study, does it matter that Harrop and Swinson (2003) were wrong?

It would have been possible for the authors to have explored their research focus from an assumption that they would find no significant differences in the profiles of question types used in the different levels of schools (i.e. a so-called 'null hypothesis'). Had that been the case, they would have found the same results, but would have been 'right' rather than 'wrong'. The validity and reliability of a study should be judged in terms of technical competence (in building a sample, carrying out observations and analysis, etc.), without consideration of whether a hypothesis is found to be supported or not. So, in that sense, the 'negative' result found by Harrop and Swinson does not in any way undermine the study.

Question for reflection

If 'the "negative" result found by Harrop and Swinson (2003) does not in any way undermine the study', does this imply that the choice of a hypothesis is arbitrary?

To appreciate why Harrop and Swinson predicted differences across the phases of education, we have to appreciate the conceptual framework that informed their study. We consider the process of conceptualising a field of research later in the chapter.

ERP2 – constructing understandings of education

Not all researchers are happy with the notion of there being 'a' truth that researchers are meant to discover:

We do not *believe* that there is such a thing as objective (absolute and uncondi-
tional) truth... . We do believe that there are truths but think that the idea of truth
need not be tied to the objectivist view ... truth is always *relative to* a conceptual
system that is defined in large part by metaphor.

(Lakoff and Johnson, 1980: 159) [*present author's emphasis*]

The second common approach to educational research avoids the problems of trying to find universal laws or definitive accounts that tell '*the* way' things are, by dealing with the particular, and by focusing on understanding the meanings that those
participating in educational situations give to what they experience.

Research as developing interpretations?

Gilbert and Watts (1983: 64) refer to ERP2 as being in the *verstehen* tradition ('in which
understanding is the goal') and they describe it in such terms as 'holistic' and 'naturalis-
tic'. ERP2 research is *idiographic* – concerned with the individual case – and is often associated with qualitative methods. This paradigm may be considered as interpretivist, based
upon 'the belief that all knowledge claims are interpretations, and that there is nothing to
appeal to in judging an interpretation but other interpretations' (Schwandt, 2001: 68–69).

This interpretivist perspective may seem rather defeatist to those who assume that
we can always decide between different interpretations by collecting sufficient evidence. That would be the assumption within ERP1: a hypothesis is formed, and then
a study designed to collect the data needed as evidence to decide whether the
hypothesis is correct. This is the basis of the experimental methods used in the natural sciences (on which ERP1 approaches are modelled). However, the interpretivist
view is that such data 'cannot provide any special basis or foundation for knowledge
claims that is somehow free of interpretation' (Schwandt, 2001: 68–69).

This is not to suggest that data cannot help decide the worth of a hypothesis – but
that it can only do so provided that a great deal is taken for granted. This is a theme
that will be illustrated in the studies considered later in the book.

Biddle and Anderson (1986) contrast their 'confirmatory position' with what they
label the '*discovery* perspective'. This term is used for approaches that:

Have in common the belief that social concepts and explanations are socially
constructed by both citizens and social scientists. Social knowledge and its use
are both assumed to be based on values ... and social facts are uninterpretable
outside of a theoretical, hence historical, context.

(Biddle and Anderson, 1986: 237)

Question for reflection

If the results of social (including educational) research only have meaning within the specific research context, then how can we know that
findings have any significance elsewhere?

Research undertaken in the discovery perspective could be said to only apply *strictly* to the particular time and place (and people) where it was undertaken. Biddle and Anderson recognise the potential implication of this, that 'taken to its extreme, such a critical stance decries the usefulness of all social research and claims that each event in the human world is unique and is unlikely to be replicated by any other event, ever' (Biddle and Anderson, 1986: 237). It is common for studies within ERP2 to provide 'thick description' of the specific research context, to allow the reader to make a judgement about the relevance of the study for the context of concern to the reader (see Chapter 6).

Understanding educational issues

Sade and Coll (2003) undertook a study to explore the perceptions of technology and technological education among primary teachers and curriculum development officers in 'a small Island Nation in the South Pacific', the Solomon Islands. In this study it was important to find out what the informants (the teachers and curriculum development officers) understood technology education to be about.

> The methodological approach selected for this research inquiry is a qualitative approach within an interpretivist paradigm … . A qualitative approach, drawing on situated cognition and sociocultural views of learning … was deemed to be the most appropriate approach, as the researchers wished to gain understanding of the Solomon Islands curriculum development officers and primary teachers' perceptions … . An added benefit … is that such an approach allows participants to clarify ambiguity in questions. This latter issue is important in this work, since English is a third language for many Solomon Islanders.
>
> (Sade and Coll, 2003: 102)

In reporting their research, Sade and Coll quote examples of the comments made by some of their informants. So we are told that:

- Monica thought that technology meant things like 'computers, televisions, telephones, emails, photocopiers, and fax machines' (p. 98);
- Brody thought that technology was 'replacing our traditional materials and old ways of doing things' (p. 98);
- Jason believed that 'technology education is learning about new things because everyday things are changing' (p. 102).

The decision to quote individuals is consistent with research within ERP2 where researchers wish to gain understanding of how individuals make sense of their worlds.

Incommensurate approaches: researchers living in different worlds?

For Kuhn (1997), a paradigm:

- provides the theoretical basis of the field;
- is accepted by all the workers in the field;
- determines what is judged to be the subject of legitimate research in the field;
- determines the procedures, rules and standards that apply in the field.

According to Kuhn, this in effect means that those researchers who share a paradigm use a commonly understood language, work with essentially the same concepts, and assume much the same meanings for technical terms. Kuhn argued that researchers working in different paradigms would in effect talk across each other and so they would have a limited basis for effective communication:

> The result was an incommensurability of viewpoints and a partial breakdown of communication between the proponents of different theories … . Proponents of … different paradigms … speak different languages – languages expressing different cognitive commitments, suitable for different worlds. Their abilities to grasp each other's viewpoints are therefore inevitably limited by the imperfections of the processes of translation and of reference determination.
>
> (Kuhn, 1977: xxii–xxiii)

Question for reflection

Given that ERP1 and ERP2 offer two very different sets of assumptions about what educational research can investigate, and how it should go about it, and what kind of outcomes can be found, do you think it will be just a matter of time before one approach becomes the accepted way for thinking about research in education?

Why does the reader of educational research need to be concerned with 'paradigms'?

ERP1 and ERP2 both have strengths, and can both help produce valuable knowledge that offers useful ways of thinking about educational contexts. The products of both are types of theory, or models – that is, useful thinking tools. The alert user of educational research can appreciate the strengths and limitations of each paradigm, and so can judge the likely value of the type of knowledge each offers.

Indeed, reading a study without appreciating the type of research approach being used can sometimes make it very difficult to draw-out anything of value. The critical reader needs to know how to interrogate a research paper (a skill that this book is designed to help develop), but the types of questions to ask in judging the quality and relevance of research can be very different in the two paradigms.

Why do educational researchers have to be concerned with paradigmatic issues?

Even though studies from both approaches to educational research can have an important part to play in informing educational practice, it is usually considered important that any specific study can be seen to be 'located' within a particular paradigm. This is because *it is important that any research study offers the reader a coherent and consistent argument about what is being claimed.* Indeed, at doctoral level this is the most significant criterion used to judge whether a student's thesis is satisfactory. (This theme will be revisited later in the book, when considering how to report your classroom research – see Chapter 10.)

The two different paradigms make different assumptions about the kind of knowledge that research can produce, and so lead to different sorts of knowledge claims. A study that was undertaken using an interpretivist approach (ERP2) cannot make justifiable claims in the form of generalisable laws, such as:

- mixed ability teaching *is* more effective;
- girls *are* less likely to offer answers in class;
- effective teachers *tend to* use longer wait times when asking questions in class.

Indeed, the paradigm in which a study is undertaken reflects fundamental assumptions about research that have consequences throughout a study. A choice of paradigm is based on assumptions about the world being studied and the nature of knowledge that can be obtained about that world. The terms ontology and epistemology were introduced earlier in the chapter: ontology being the study of the nature of things that exist in the world, and epistemology being the study of how we can come to know about those things.

For example, an (ontological) assumption that there is an observable objective world leads to different research choices than a belief that social worlds are created by participants, who each inhabit their own unique realities. It is sometimes suggested that we have to make a choice as researchers about where we stand on such issues.

Does a researcher have to make a binding commitment to a paradigm?

So in any particular study, we need to consider the nature of the 'reality' being investigated. However, it is possible to believe in an objective world independent of human thought (perhaps the moon would still be there, if not known as the moon, and not having the litter of human visits), and still consider some foci best understood in more 'subjective' terms. We can objectively study *the level* of school exclusions for offences classed as bullying: but any study of what counts as bullying, why it happens, and how it feels to be bullied, would need to consider the various perspectives of those who are involved as offender, victims, etc.

An (epistemological) assumption that it is possible to produce an objective account of the world that is independent of the observer leads to different research choices than a belief that the researcher inevitably becomes a significant part of the research context being studied. For example, a study that explored student learning through a survey of examination and test results could be objective (although it would only be considered meaningful to those who accepted such outcomes as valid measures of learning). However, a study that explored learning through in-depth interviewing of learners is likely to channel student thinking in ways that would not have happened in the absence of the interview (e.g. Taber and Student, 2003): and so may 'scaffold' responses that reflect learning during the interview itself. (Anyone who doubts this would happen, must surely also doubt the efficacy of much teacher–student dialogue carried out in classrooms to facilitate learning.)

It is important to recognise that sometimes these two different types of studies, although based on apparently inconsistent assumptions, and addressing different types of questions, may be complementary in developing our wider understanding of a research topic (National Research Council, 2002).

Paradigmatic differences between researchers

When learning about unfamiliar abstract ideas, it is helpful to have examples that provide a more 'concrete' context for making sense of those ideas. This is true of the many abstract ideas we teach in the school curriculum – and equally important when learning new concepts (such as 'educational research paradigms') at more advanced levels.

Here we briefly consider two educational research studies, which came to opposite conclusions when investigating whether secondary level students hold what are known as 'alternative conceptual frameworks' of the science concept of force. Considering the differences between the way the two researchers went about their studies illustrates the notion of research paradigms, and highlights why *readers* of educational research need to pay attention to such matters when drawing conclusions from published research studies.

The two studies referred to (Watts, 1983; Kuiper, 1994) will be available in most academic libraries. Readers will benefit more from the following discussion if they have already had a chance to read, and judge, these papers for themselves.

Question for reflection

If you have had the chance to read the original papers of Watts (1983) and Kuiper (1994), you should consider how you would explain how these two studies appear to come to contrary conclusions.

Why does it matter whether students hold common 'alternative conceptual frameworks'?

One reason to study learners' ideas is because much of the rationale of school teaching is concerned with helping learners to develop their knowledge and understanding in those areas of human activity considered important enough to be reflected in the curriculum, and in helping them develop thinking and problem-solving skills that will enable them to make decisions and explore their own values and beliefs. Evaluating this aspect of what education claims to be about requires the ability to 'measure' (or describe) student knowledge and understanding, and abilities related to rational thinking, developing argument, and so forth. Such 'measurements' (or descriptions) need to be made both before and after teaching, to inform judgements about the learning that may have taken place.

Furthermore, research suggests that learning of academic subjects does not simply involve acquiring knowledge in areas where a student was previously ignorant. It has been found that often learners already have ideas about a topic before meeting it in schools. These ideas may match the target knowledge in the curriculum to varying extents, and may be more or less strongly held. Tenacious alternative ideas have been found to interfere with intended learning. In science, in particular, there has been a vast research programme designed to explore aspects of learners' 'informal' ideas to inform teachers of the way that many students may think about topics (Taber, 2006).

Question for reflection

It is suggested that there are two main paradigms used in educational research. Which paradigm do you think is more likely to help researchers find out about learners' thinking about topics in the school curriculum? Why do you think this?

In the early 1980s there was a burst of interest in exploring learners' thinking about science topics – and in particular, finding out what ideas students brought to the class with them that might contradict or distort what they were to be taught (e.g. Driver et al., 1994). One classic study from this substantial literature is Watts' (1983) study of secondary students' thinking about the key concept of 'force' – now identified as one of the 'key ideas' in lower secondary science in the UK (DfES, 2002).

Identifying alternative conceptual frameworks of force

Watts (1983) claimed that students across the secondary age range held 'alternative frameworks' for thinking about key science topic of force. Indeed, Watts claimed that he had uncovered eight distinct alternative 'conceptual frameworks'.

The basis of this claim was research where Watts (1983) interviewed secondary school students of different ages, who were taking a range of courses. To collect data, Watts used an approach called interviews-about-instances, where simple diagrams (such as a 'stick diagram' of a person playing golf) were used as foci (Gilbert et al., 1985). In this approach, a dialogue is usually initiated with an open question (such as 'Is there an example of a force shown here?'), with the interviewer probing to follow-up initial responses. The order of presentation of foci was flexible, and Watts reported that he attempted to respond to his interviewees by reflecting back the language they used to talk about the diagrams (rather than using the formal language of the curriculum subject).

Question for reflection

Research that explores student thinking in its own terms, rather than simply judges student ideas against curriculum knowledge, has been described as 'ethnographic'. What do you understand by the term 'ethnographic', and do you think Watts' (1983) study has any features of ethnography?

Watts (1983) audiotaped his interviews, and later transcribed them to give a verbatim account of the dialogue. He then used a 'mosaic method' to piece together conceptual frameworks reflecting the ideas students presented. He reported the frameworks as pithy summaries or 'vignettes'.

Watts reports eight different alternative frameworks that described the thinking of his interviewees, each of which was distinct from the notion of force being presented in school science. If Watts is correct, and students do think about 'forces' in these various ways at odds with school science, then it is useful for science teachers to be aware of this, and to plan and teach accordingly.

According to Watts the frameworks he reported were:

- models of student understanding;
- powerful enough to capture individual differences;
- suitable for testing with large samples.

Question for reflection

Watts (1983) described his findings as 'models' of student understanding: what might this imply about his assumptions about the type of knowledge research into student thinking is capable of producing?

Do students really have alternative frameworks of force?

Kuiper (1994) decided to check Watts' claim that students used this set of alternative frameworks to think about 'forces'. Kuiper attempted to test Watts' model and concluded that students did not seem to use Watts' frameworks. Indeed, Kuiper found

Study	Watts (1983)	Kuiper (1994)
sample	secondary students	secondary students
sample location	London, UK	Zimbabwe
sample size	12	143
data collection	interviews	written tests
data analysis	mosaic – composite pictures pieced together	classification of responses as intuitive, intermediate, correct; factor analysis
finding	eight alternative frameworks for force	confused ideas without logical coherency

FIGURE 3.3   Comparing two studies into student thinking about forces

that 'students in general do not have an "alternative framework" for force' (1994: 279). We might wonder how these different researchers came to such different conclusions.

One obvious difference is that although both researchers used a sample of secondary age learners, these were rather different samples. Indeed, whereas Watts undertook his original interviews in the UK, Kuiper tested Watts' theory in Zimbabwe. (Kuiper reports that additional data for his research was collected in the Netherlands, Lesotho, Botswana, Swaziland and Mozambique, although the 1994 paper is primarily concerned with the data from Zimbabwe.) However, both researchers present their results *as if* they were discussing results that related to secondary age students *in general.* Neither paper title – 'A study of schoolchildren's alternative frameworks of the concept of force' or 'Student ideas of science concepts: alternative frameworks?' – imply that they are discussing findings that *only* apply to one location or a particular sample.

It is not unreasonable to expect that cultural differences between such contexts as UK and Zimbabwe could be a relevant factor, but here there may be other explanations for the different results. Kuiper's study took a very different form to Watts' study and some of the key differences are given in Figure 3.3.

Paradigmatic commitments are shown by Watts (1983) and Kuiper (1994)

Figure 3.3 shows that very different approaches were taken by the different researchers. Watts was working with a small number of individuals, but using an approach that enabled him to explore their thinking in depth, and interact with them in the research. This is typical of ERP2, and reflects the nature of Watt's study as 'exploratory' research.

Indeed Watts' study can be seen to have a strong ethnographic flavour (see Chapter 4 for a discussion of ethnographic methodology in educational research). As ethnography derives from attempts to understand 'alien' cultures, as when a Western ethnographer visits a tribal society, it may not be immediately obvious how this is appropriate in research of this type. However, research into students' informal ideas in science has revealed that learners and science teachers do have very different ways of thinking, and – for example – use many of the same words to have different meanings. In this situation an ethnographic approach has often been considered appropriate (Solomon, 1993).

Kuiper's study is more typical of ERP1, being a 'confirmatory study' looking to test a model, using statistical techniques. Kuiper uses written tests, and later uses a quantitative technique (cluster analysis) to look for common patterns. Written tests are more often associated with a normative and positivistic approach – a large sample of learners respond to a standardised task under set conditions. The researcher does not attempt to interact with the subjects during data collection.

Another major difference is in the way the two researchers go about initially sorting their data – the student responses to either interview questions or test items. Where Watts uses a 'mosaic' technique – decomposing individual responses, and constructing models ('frameworks') to reflect them, Kuiper initially categorises responses into three main groups ('intuitive', 'correct' and 'intermediate'). Watts tries to describe and characterise students' ideas *in their own terms*, whereas Kuiper initially sets out to evaluate understanding *in comparison with the target understanding set out in the curriculum*. These approaches are typical of ERP2 and ERP1 respectively.

Although it would be wrong to suggest that researchers only ever find what they are looking for, it is certainly true that the way data is analysed channels the type of findings that can feasibly arise. (This is one example of the point made earlier, that paradigmatic assumptions have consequences throughout the research process.) So Watts, who set out to look at individual thinking, uncovered sets of conceptual frameworks that reflect individual differences. Kuiper classified students according to the extent that their thinking matched the 'right' answers: and found proportions of students whose thinking matched the curriculum answers to different extents!

Only later, after using the statistical technique of cluster analysis to identify consistent patterns of responses on questions having similar [sic] physical contexts, does Kuiper look for alternative frameworks. At this point Kuiper accepts that the younger students commonly demonstrate a particular way of thinking, at odds with curriculum science. However, Kuiper characterises the thinking of other students as correct, transitional (between the 'intuitive' and correct responses), or too inconsistent to be considered as any kind of coherent framework. It is significant that:

- Watts, in the role of the ethnographer, attempts to understand students' viewpoints, and patterns of thinking, and does not make assumptions about which contexts learners should perceive as similar; whereas
- Kuiper, acting as a positivist, initially evaluates student responses in terms of their match to the 'right' scientific answers, and then undertakes the cluster analysis on the assumption that coherency in student thinking must be based around similar responses to questions *that would be considered* as similar contexts *from the viewpoint of curriculum science*.

An example of why we need to take ontological assumptions seriously

One major problem with Kuiper's research *as a replication study* for Watts' findings is that Kuiper's account makes it quite clear that he is *not* testing for what Watts claimed to have found! Both authors talk of 'alternative frameworks' (Watts reported eight alternative frameworks based on his data on students' thinking about forces, and Kuiper claimed to be looking for alternative frameworks), but they use this term to describe different types of entities.

Watts made it clear that the eight frameworks presented in his 1983 study were *models that Watts constructed* to reflect aspects of his informants' thinking. He did not claim that students used these ideas consistently, nor even that any student's thinking would exactly match any framework.

However, it is quite clear from the published accounts that Kuiper used the term framework to signify something quite different from Watts – for Kuiper a framework actually *exists in the head of a learner*. Moreover, for Kuiper, a learner is only considered to hold a framework if it is consistently applied in those situations where (from the researcher's perspective) the framework should apply:

> The use of the term framework in the description of student understanding implies an ordered and schematic understanding of a concept. This term can be understood to mean that a particular student has a set of student ideas concerning one and the same concept which appear logically coherent and ordered.
>
> (Kuiper, 1994: 280)

So where Watts presented a set of *generalised thematic descriptions* that were each compiled from aspects of the thinking of several students, Kuiper expected to find these 'frameworks' fixed in the minds of students.

Pope and Denicolo (1986) had discussed Watts' research in some detail, and described how the kind of frameworks presented in this type of research were necessarily simplifications abstracted from the more complex patterns of thinking exhibited by the informants. They explicitly discussed how the actual thinking of individuals would often reflect 'multiple frameworks' from Watts' schemes. They warned that:

> Although starting from a holistic approach one 'end product' of his work is a much reduced description of the construing of the individuals in his study which, if taken out of context, is also devoid of consideration of the particular choices made by the researcher in his conduct of data collection and analysis.

They also suggested that:

> The busy teacher or researcher with a predilection towards reductionism may well ignore the 'health warnings' conveyed in our research report [and] indulge in a 'framework spotting' exercise using reified descriptions of frameworks and ignoring the ontology of these frameworks.
>
> (Pope and Denicolo, 1986: 157)

ERP1 research tends to be reductionist, and is often based on assumptions that the objects of study exist 'out there' and can be readily identified, unambiguously classified, and counted. Such assumptions may reasonably be applied to some sorts of things – as for example when stocktaking in a supermarket – but Pope and Denicolo suggest that Watts' conceptual frameworks are not of that kind. They are ontologically rather different.

In setting out to test Watts' findings by a survey approach, Kuiper is treating Watts' frameworks as being something in learners' heads, rather than a theoretical model to organise thinking from different individuals.

Kuiper's study presents a *normative* model of how the consistency of student thinking, and the match to the taught curriculum knowledge, varies across the different grade levels in the Zimbabwean sample. However, Kuiper's study does *not* have an optimal design to provide a test of Watts' model.

Question for reflection

If you accept that Kuiper's normative survey approach (ERP1) cannot negate the conclusions Watts draw from his interpretative (ERP2) study, then should you accept Watts' findings as representing students' common alternative conceptions of force?

We can accept that Kuiper's work is based on an approach that can offer useful knowledge of the level of understanding of students within the test population, *but* uses methodology that is not appropriate to test Watts' model. If we take this position, then Kuiper's failure to replicate Watts' findings are not pertinent to judging that model (as he was not looking at the type of entities Watts reported). However, this is not in itself any reason to accept Watts' model either. We would still have to be convinced that Watts has 'made his case', a notion that we will return to later.

The insidious nature of our paradigmatic commitments

This example of two very different studies, which at first glance come to opposite conclusions about the 'same' issue, shows why we cannot ignore paradigmatic issues when we undertake or read research. Our basic assumptions about the nature of the phenomena we study, and the nature of the research process and the kind of knowledge it can lead to, continue to influence all stages of planning, executing and reporting research. Even if we do not make out assumptions explicit, they will be working insidiously as we make research decisions and write-up our accounts, and their consequences will be reflected in our work. This is represented in Figure 3.4, where we see how our fundamental beliefs influence the stages of research.

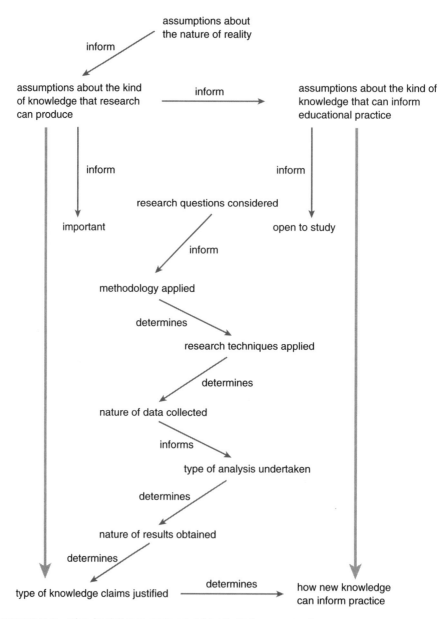

FIGURE 3.4   The insidious nature of beliefs in research

Complementary research approaches?

Both research paradigms would seem to be associated with rather substantial problems. ERP1 research uses a 'scientific' method to uncover general laws, but any findings can only be judged reliable if we accept the theoretical frameworks within which the research is undertaken. Critics of ERP1 approaches would argue that the complexity of social phenomena (such as learners, lessons, classrooms, schools) makes it inappropriate to look for general laws that will apply across very different contexts. Researchers who accept such an argument are more likely to undertake interpretivist enquiry, such as case study research, using approaches that explore individual cases in depth. These researchers have to accept that such ERP2 research can only strictly tell us about the particular focus chosen for research – and not about another time, another classroom, another class, another learner.

To caricature, ERP1 studies produce general decontextualised findings, that are usually bound to (and so are dependent upon) the theoretical assumptions the researcher(s) used to design their study; whilst ERP2 studies produce detailed studies of very specific educational contexts, that should not be assumed to apply to any other context. If developing our understanding of teaching and learning depended upon selecting one or other of these clearly limited approaches then the whole enterprise might seem somewhat futile.

These two research approaches have often been characterised as if *competing* paradigms, as 'an intellectual either/or situation' (Reynolds, 1991: 194), which can lead to 'clashes among researchers with different purposes who tend to see the others as engaged in the same enterprise as themselves, but simply doing it badly' (Hammersley, 1993: xix).

However, the assumption that 'scientific explanation and interpretative understanding are mutually exclusive categories' has been challenged (Carr and Kemmis, 1986: 105). Biddle and Anderson (1986: 239) have argued for an 'integrative approach', which makes it 'possible to assemble the visions of both confirmationism and the discovery perspective into a single, expanded view of the social sciences'.

The perspective suggested here is that although neither ERP1 nor ERP2 can offer us totally satisfactory ways of finding out about educational phenomena, both can still offer helpful insights, and provide valuable models of educational phenomena: models which are useful because they have explanatory and predictive power. Models often have limitations, such as restricted ranges of application, and sometimes (in social science, as in natural science) the best current understanding of a phenomenon involves several different partial models, each useful in some circumstances.

It is suggested here, then, that educational research from both traditions can be *useful*, and the types of knowledge produced in these different research traditions offer *complementary* insights to inform educational practice. Indeed, the Research Council of the US National Academy of Sciences offers a vision of 'scientific' research in education that encompasses a wide range of approaches. Research in areas where little is known indicate the need for 'descriptive studies [that] might be undertaken to help bring education problems or trends into sharper relief or to generate plausible theories' (National Research Council, 2002: 99). From this perspective, many ERP2 studies may be considered 'scientific'.

Illustrating the complementary nature of research paradigms

Earlier in this chapter, two studies were discussed which came to very different con-clusions about whether secondary age students hold 'alternative conceptual frame-works' for the physics concept of force. We also saw that Watts and Kuiper were working in different paradigms where they approached what would seem to be the same research focus from very different perspectives. At first sight this would seem to be an illustration of what Kuhn (1977, 1996) referred to as the 'incommensurability' of different paradigms.

However, it has also been suggested that research into learners' thinking about cur-riculum topics needs to be considered from both the interpretivist *and* the norma-tive standpoints, especially if research is going to be useful to teachers.

> The documentation of students' ... conceptions and the way these progress is a field of work that has its roots in the ethnographic tradition with its recognition of the centrality of personal meaning and of individual and cultural differences. Yet despite this orientation, there appear to be strong messages about apparent commonalities in students' conceptions that may have implications for future directions of work in this field.
>
> (Driver, 1989: 488)

Other studies have claimed to be able to move from in-depth studies of individual learners to normative models of common ways of thinking (e.g. Taber, 2000b). This approach requires the finding of common features in the accounts of individuals, and then discovering ways to test the frequency with which these students select items reflecting these commonalities in surveys. Part of this process involves ensuring that survey items are valid as ways of identifying the conceptions or frameworks proposed in the accounts of interpretivist studies.

So, for example, David Treagust (1995) describes a process for developing diag-nostic tests for teachers to identify student misconceptions. These tests consist of objective items – two-tier multiple choice questions, where students are asked to select which of several statements is correct (the first tier) and then which of several possible explanations explains why this answer is correct (the second tier):

> ... a teacher needs a starting place for addressing known students' conceptions and/or misconceptions, and a multiple choice diagnostic instrument, informed by research in students' learning problems in a particular content area, would appear to provide a relatively straightforward approach to student assessment.
>
> (Treagust, 1995: 329–330)

However, the process of developing the classroom tests involves three major stages. The first stage involves determining the curriculum understanding of the topic, in consulta-tion with subject matter and educational experts. The second stage involves identifying aspects of students' thinking about the topic, both from existing research and through open 'non-structured' interviews with learners (i.e. an ERP2 approach). Only then are the objective questions designed, piloted, and modified. This latter process also needs to involve interviewing students about their understanding of the questions, and their thinking in selecting answers to ensure that the closed response categories eventually represented in the final instrument are authentic reflections of common student ideas. A detailed description of the development of such an instrument, including accounts of the stages of testing and modifying test items, may be found in Tan et al., 2005.

The research process

We can appreciate the significance of a researcher's fundamental assumptions if we consider carrying out educational research as a process. The basic steps are normally:

- Selecting a focus – deciding what we want to study;
- Developing a conceptual framework – forming an understanding of what is already known relevant to our focus;
- Producing research questions – setting out the specific aims of our research;
- Selecting the most appropriate methodology;
- Designing the research (planning sample, schedule, forms of data collection and analysis);
- Data collection;
- Data analysis;
- Reporting.

This is, of course, a model of a complex process. In some forms of research, these are certainly not totally separate stages that have an invariant order. However, this type of sequence is the basis for most research studies.

Question for reflection

If paradigmatic concerns are so important in research, why is there not a step where a choice of paradigm is made?

To appreciate the 'logic' of this sequence, the reader is referred back to Figure 3.4, which reminds us how decisions made at one point during research have consequences for what becomes possible and sensible at later stages.

The research focus

The starting point is the choice of research focus – the area that the researcher wishes to explore and find out about. Academic researchers (i.e. university teachers employed to teach and undertake related research) usually follow their own 'interests' and often have ongoing research into particular issues, through which they may see individual studies as being part of a 'research programme'. Other professional researchers ('contract researchers') work on projects funded by funding bodies or research organisations, and are directed to particular studies according to the interests of their funding agency.

Practitioners are usually motivated to undertake research to investigate and improve some aspect of their own professional practice that has been identified as a concern (i.e. they undertake 'action research'; see Chapter 4). This is a simplified picture of course: academic researchers may be directed to study areas due to available funding or a recognition that the topic is currently seen as important; contract researchers can choose which contracts to seek; action-researchers may be influenced by wider institutional concerns or may have their concern for a particular topic initiated by colleagues in universities with particular research interests.

Selecting a focus for a course assignment

Students undertaking research as part of the requirements of an academic course are in something of an artificial situation, as the primary motivation for the research is usually a report that satisfies examiners. Two important features of the project are therefore that it will enable the writing of a report that meets specific assignment assessment criteria, and that it is feasible in the time-scale allowed. It is also important for the student to have a genuine interest in the topic, as a good deal of time will need to be invested to produce an acceptable report. This becomes more important as the level of the project increases: from an undergraduate or PGCE assignment undertaken over a few months, to a doctoral study that will be the main focus of work (and probably life) for 3–4 years.

A major consideration for students is their research context. For a full-time masters or doctoral student, the choice of research sites can be made later in the research process. However, for a PGCE student, and often for a teacher undertaking research part-time, the research site may be fixed and so the research has to relate to the placement or employing school. Academic supervisors will often be keen to suggest ideas for a research focus (as they will have to spend time discussing the student's work and reading drafts of the report). However, for a student teacher on placement the school mentor is the central person with whom to negotiate a research focus, as this will be the key person to advise what is feasible within the professional context, and to help facilitate the enquiry.

The selection of a focus for an enquiry involves the identification of the purposes of the study. There are many potential foci for educational research, such as:

- to find out if the establishment of schools with specialist status enables pupils to be better matched to their school;
- problems associated with colour-blindness in practical work in science;
- to find out if girls have greater listening skills than boys;
- students' metacognitive skills and study habits;

- increasing the use of formative assessment techniques in maths classes;
- to find a better way of teaching about elements, compounds and mixtures in the lower school;
- students' perceptions of humanities subjects in Year 9;
- teachers' attitudes to teaching citizenship within different curriculum subjects;
- a simple visual–auditory–kinaesthetic model of learning styles as a way of thinking about the way pupils in my Year 10 class learn.

Question for reflection

Which of the listed foci might be suitable for (a) a student teacher in a placement school; (b) a teacher undertaking part-time MEd study; (c) a full-time doctoral student in a university?

Some of the suggested foci above are presented as topic areas, some seem more like practical aims, and some are framed as questions. It is common to set out the aims of a research study in the form of one or more research questions, which need to be carefully formulated. (Selecting a focus and developing research questions in teacher-research are considered further later in the book, in Chapter 7). In a doctoral study, many months may be spent honing the question(s). Before this is possible, it is necessary to review what is already known and understood about the research focus.

Developing a conceptual framework for research

This stage of the research process is called 'conceptualisation': where the researcher writes an account of their way of thinking about the research focus. This conceptualisation will be informed by reading of relevant literature, and will clarify key terms (what is understood by 'specialist schools', 'humanities subjects', 'learning styles', etc).

Most accounts of research include a 'literature review'. When done well, this is not just a summary of the contents of relevant papers, but a synthesis of findings that sets out how the researcher understands the current state of the field.

At this point the researcher's ontological assumptions will play a part, as the conceptualisation will discuss the nature of the things that are considered to be important to the research focus.

> In pedagogic settings, [an empiricist] approach will help in questions such as: 'How many children have reached a certain level of achievement in the test?'; 'Have attendance figures improved over the last three years?'. A question of the type 'How can I explain and improve this situation?' [is] not accommodated.
>
> (McNiff, 1992: 12)

In other words, the type of things to be investigated, and the kind of knowledge sought about them, will normally determine the research paradigm that is appropriate – which in turn will inform a choice of suitable methodology, and so the selection of specific methods, a suitable sample, etc. The conceptualisation process is therefore an essential step in the logic of any research study, and being a step it needs to be correctly sequenced. It may be tempting for a student who is undertaking classroom research as an academic exercise (and requirement), and has limited interest in its outcomes, to leave the literature review until the writing-up stage. This is a very good way of inviting additional stress, and making the task of producing a coherent research report much more difficult than it needs to be!

Selecting a hypothesis

Earlier in this chapter, we considered research by Harrop and Swinson (2003) that found that the profile of question types used by teachers at infant, junior and secondary levels were not significantly different. This finding refuted their prediction that a difference would be found. It was suggested above that this 'negative' finding did not undermine the value of the study. Of course, this does *not* mean that the failure to confirm the hypothesis is not an important finding.

In research undertaken from a confirmatory perspective there is normally an expectation of what will be found based on the existing understanding of the research field. A hypothesis is formed, which derives from a conceptualisation of the existing research, and how this might apply in the context being explored. Harrop and Swinson introduce their paper by setting out their conceptual framework for the research: the importance of the topic of teacher questions, both in view of the role they take in teaching, and in terms of previous research showing that teacher questioning is a significant activity in terms of the sheer quantity of questions teachers use when teaching.

In setting out on their research, Harrop and Swinson were effectively testing a hypothesis about *differences* between teacher questions at different stages of education: 'to examine differences in patterns of questioning between the three levels of schooling' (Harrop and Swinson, 2003: 52). It would be possible to have set out a 'null' hypothesis, i.e. that the pattern of question types would not be significantly different at different levels. However, Harrop and Swinson had *theoretical* reasons for expecting more open questions to be used with the older children.

> We had thought that [Open Solution' category] questions would require more reflection on the part of the pupils than other questions so that teachers would be more liable to use them with older pupils, both because the older pupils would be more capable of handling such questions than the younger pupils and because such questions would be considered as helping the pupils to develop further their thinking processes. It seems we were wrong.
>
> (Harrop and Swinson, 2003: 55)

As the authors' prediction was based on their initial conceptualisation of the field, then if they believe their findings are trustworthy, they need to re-examine their conceptualisation of the topic to offer a new understanding consistent with their findings. This is not a failure. The whole point of research is to develop our knowledge. In confirmatory research we are often checking our understanding in new contexts, or in more complex situations. Research findings often raise questions for further research – something that may make this seem a frustrating enterprise to some outsiders, but is part of the fascination for most researchers.

Conceptualising ability

Lyle concluded from his study of how mixed-ability grouping facilitated literacy learning (see Chapter 2), that:

> … mixed-ability teaching provides a setting in which both low- and high-achieving students value the opportunity to work together where both groups believed they benefit.
>
> (Lyle, 1999: 283)

Question for reflection

Considering some of the learners you work with, how confidently would you be prepared to judge their intellectual ability?

Lyle reports that the study is about *mixed-ability* teaching, yet in order to identify pupils of different 'ability' (what they are *able* to do), judgements are made in terms of pupil *attainment* (what they have *demonstrated* they can do). This is an 'ontological' issue. Choosing to use 'ability' as a way of conceptualising the difference between learners shows that Lyle assumes that it is meaningful to label students in terms of ability, i.e. that a student will have a (singular) level of ability, and that this is a relatively stable (perhaps even fixed) characteristic. Ability could not be directly measured, so can only be inferred. By using an attainment measure to stand for 'ability', Lyle assumes (at least implicitly) that attainment is a reflection of ability, i.e. that all the pupils were working to their potential to a similar degree.

These assumptions may seem to be 'common sense', as in everyday conversation people are labelled as 'clever' or 'dull' as though intellectual ability lies on a single scale, and as if we can readily estimate where someone lies on this scale. However, these are assumptions, and assumptions that would be questioned by many working in education. Sometimes it is necessary to make simplifications and assumptions of this kind for pragmatic reasons – in order to produce a research design that is viable. However, pragmatics must be balanced against the extent to which such assumptions could undermine any findings that derive from our enquiry.

Conceptualising constructivist teaching

In 2004, Ian Kinchin published a study in the journal *Educational Research*, which claimed that students would prefer to learn in a 'constructivist' learning environment. The abstract of Kinchin's (2004: 301) paper claims:

- 'an overwhelming preference among students for a constructivist learning environment';
- 'Students anticipated constructivist learning environments would be more interesting, more effective at developing students' understanding and would permit them to take greater ownership of their learning'.

Constructivism (see Chapter 2) is a commonly used notion in education, especially in terms of approaches to educational research, and in terms of teaching strategies (particularly in maths and science). However, even within a particular field such as science education, the term constructivism is used in a number of ways (Taber, 2006).

So, a reader of Kinchin's paper needs a clearer understanding of what *this particular* author means by the term. Kinchin helps the reader here by offering an overview of how he is conceptualising this term early in the paper, both by providing a simple definition of a 'constructivist classroom', and by contrasting this with an alternative ('objectivist') perspective.

In doing this, Kinchin sets up a dichotomous classification (an 'either/or' situation), depending upon: 'whether a teacher expects students to act as passive receivers of information (= the objectivist classroom) or as active builders of understanding (= the constructivist classroom)' (2004: 301). In an accompanying figure these two classroom types are related to rote learning (i.e. learning 'by heart') and meaningful learning (i.e. learning for understanding).

Question for reflection

To what extent do you feel that the description of teaching styles as constructivist or objectivist is a valid reflection of the beliefs that inform teaching behaviours?

Kinchin describes his theoretical (conceptual) framework early in his paper to provide the background to his study. Pupils and teachers can have different, and changing, notions of learning. If teacher beliefs and student beliefs are mismatched (i.e. one objectivist, the other constructivist), then the classroom can become a very frustrating place. Experienced teachers will recognise the importance of this issue: most of us have come across complaints from learners at both ends of the spectrum – about the teacher who just gives notes and expects students to somehow learn from copying them; and from pupils who feel that they are being cheated by teachers who are 'not doing their job properly' because they set up interesting learning activities, but are reluctant to dictate definitive notes and provide 'the right answers'.

Defining terms

In a 1998 study published in the *International Journal of Science Education*, Petri and Niedderer reported their research into one 18 year-old High School student's learning about the atom.

Petri and Niedderer (1998) describe the focus of their study as a 'learning pathway'. This is because they are assuming that learning is not an 'all or nothing' phenomena, where the student non-problematically moves from ignorance to knowing as a result of instruction. The authors believe that learning is more nuanced than that, with students bringing existing ideas and beliefs to class (see the discussion of Watts' 1983 study), and that, in some subjects, progression involves learning about a succession of curriculum models of increasing sophistication.

When exploring complex phenomena, it is often necessary for a researcher to provide an operational definition, that characterises and delimits the phenomenon (and allows the reader to appreciate if the researcher is actually discussing what they understand by the term).

For the purposes of their paper, Petri and Niedderer (1998) define learning as 'a change in a cognitive system's stable elements' (Petri and Niedderer, 1998: 1075). They are also careful to explain that the 'cognitive system' 'is the model of a student's mind constructed by the researcher' (ibid). This is an important acknowledgement, as researchers have sometimes been considered to confuse knowledge represented in learners' minds with their own necessarily limited, and partial models (Phillips, 1987).

Petri and Niedderer (1998) develop their model for the reader. They consider the cognitive system to comprise of 'stable deep structure' and 'current constructions', that is, they make a distinction between 'stable cognitive elements' which are fairly permanent features of mind, and what the learner happens to be thinking right now. Petri and Niedderer explore the stable cognitive elements in the cognitive system they construct, to describe the learning processes of one German secondary school student who they call Carl.

As researchers we have to spend time clarifying our understanding of a field before we can set about planning our enquiries. We also have to remember to set out our conceptualisation for others when we later come to report and explain our work.

4

What Strategies do Educational Researchers Use?

The previous chapter looked at the type of 'executive level' thinking that provides a 'vision' (or philosophy) of research. The chapter considers some of the most common strategies, methodologies, adopted at the 'managerial level' of research planning. Selecting a methodology is very important, as it guides the research plan, which in turn determines what data is actually collected and how it is analysed.

What is methodology?

> Methodology: A way of thinking about and studying social reality.
> Methods: A set of procedures and techniques for gathering and analyzing data.
>
> (Strauss and Corbin, 1998: 3)

Methodology is more than the research *techniques* ('methods') someone uses, but also is more concrete than their paradigmatic (fundamental, philosophical) commitments. Methodology is the *strategy* used for answering research questions.

> This is a theory of how inquiry should proceed. It involves analysis of the assumptions, principles, and procedures in a particular approach to inquiry (that, in turn, governs the use of particular methods). ... Experience with data generates insights, hypotheses, and generative questions that are pursued through further data generation. As tentative answers to questions are developed and concepts are constructed, these constructions are verified through further data collection.
>
> (Schwandt, 2001: 110)

A simple way of thinking about methodology and techniques (sometimes confusingly called 'methods') is in terms of strategy and tactics. Effective research has an overall coherent strategy, which outlines the general way that the research aims will be achieved. This will translate into a set of specific tactics that will address sub-goals that collectively build towards the overall aim.

Can research designs be changed once research is underway?

This distinction is important for anyone planning research. Some methodologies are said to be *emergent*, meaning that it is not possible to plan the research in detail at the start, as the researcher has to be responsive to what is being learnt as the research proceeds. Indeed, in a 'grounded theory' approach (discussed below) it is totally inappropriate to set out a definite account of a research schedule and the data to be collected at the outset, and the flexibility within the design is seen as a strength as well as an essential part of the methodological approach. In such research, the techniques used (tactics) may be modified during the research. This is acceptable, but only within the overall coherent methodology (strategy).

However, anyone planning to use an 'experimental' design to test a hypothesis must plan the research in detail at the start, and so the techniques of data collection and analysis need to be firmly established before any data are collected. Research claiming to use this type of methodology, which involved substantive changes (in such matters as how 'subjects' are assigned to groups, or which statistical tests were to be applied) once the research was underway, is open to being challenged as failing to follow accepted procedures and so potentially invalid.

As with the identification of paradigms, the recognition of suitable methodologies in educational research (and how to label and characterise them) is a 'fuzzy' area. Different authors have different ways of defining, describing and labelling both paradigms and methodologies, and this can be an unhelpful source of confusion for those new (and sometimes those not-so-new) to the field.

An introductory way of thinking about research paradigms was introduced above, which is at the level of detail useful for those setting out on classroom research. In a similar way, the discussion of methodologies below is set at an introductory level, and readers are referred to more in-depth accounts if they wish to explore these issues in more detail. To reinforce the significant difference between methodology (research strategy) and techniques (tactics for collecting and analysing data), these topics have been deliberately separated in the book. Although techniques are mentioned here, a more detailed study of them is reserved for Chapter 8.

Common research methodologies include:

- experiments and quasi-experiments;
- surveys;
- case-study;
- ethnography;
- grounded theory;
- action research.

There are many books that describe research methodology, which can support the development of a detailed appreciation of the distinct features of these different methodologies. The following account is intended to give an outline of the nature of these approaches.

Sampling in educational research

One thing that virtually all educational research studies have in common is the discussion of findings from a relatively small proportion of the potential informants! Many studies explicitly discuss potentially vast 'populations' of learners, but then present research that has been undertaken with only a tiny proportion of that population.

Consider some titles of published research papers:

- An exploratory study of the effect a self-regulated learning environment has on pre-service primary teachers' perceptions of teaching science and technology;
- Secondary school teachers' pedagogic practices when teaching mixed and structured ability classes;
- Student ideas of science concepts: alternative frameworks?;
- An investigation of pupil perceptions of mixed-ability grouping to enhance literacy in children aged 9–10;
- A learning pathway in high-school level quantum atomic physics;
- Constructivist-compatible beliefs and practices among US teachers;
- A study of schoolchildren's alternative frameworks of the concept of force;
- A cross-cultural comparison of teachers' expressed beliefs about music education and their observed practices in classroom music teaching.

The titles of most of these papers suggest that the paper is about a group of people: 'pre-service primary teachers'; 'secondary school teachers'; 'children aged 9–10';' US teachers' or even 'students'; 'pupils'; 'school children' or 'teachers'. These are very large groups, and – of course – none of these papers present data from such large groups.

Question for reflection

One of the titles of published research papers listed does not seem to derive from a group of people: what does the title 'A learning pathway in high-school level quantum atomic physics' suggest about the nature of that particular study?

We would not suggest that these titles are deliberately misleading, because no one is going to read a paper expecting it to report results obtained from *all* children aged 9–10 or *all* US teachers! We clearly expect the authors to have collected data from *some* students, or *some* teachers. However, the more general references in the paper titles (and often in the way conclusions are phrased) suggest that it is assumed that the findings from the individuals studied tell us something about the wider group they are seen as being part of. There is no simple basis on which we can make such an assumption. This can be illustrated by some statements about 'school pupils' that could be made based on empirical investigations that collect data from some school children:

- School children are under 2.5 metres in height;
- School children eat food;
- School children drink milk;
- School children play football;
- School children support Manchester United Football Club;
- School children enjoy homework;
- School children are called Amanda;
- School children are better at maths than English;
- School children want to be educational researchers when they are older.

These statements might hypothetically reflect findings obtained from enquiry with *some* children – but some of them would be rather unsafe as *generalisations*. The question of how we can confidently make generalisations from specific research is not a trivial one, for in fact there is no logical basis that will ever allow us to generalise *with certainty* beyond the group of people we actually collect data from!

In looking at how researchers respond to this rather fundamental problem, we can again draw upon the distinction between ERP1 and ERP2 research (see Chapter 3).

Approaches to sampling in educational research

In ERP1 there are basically two approaches:

1: A sample may be constructed which is considered large enough, and representative enough, of a wider population to allow general findings from the research to be likely (in a statistical sense – using inferential statistics, tests designed to allow inferences to be drawn) to be reflections of the wider population. This approach is used in surveys (see below).

2: In experimental approaches there may be less control over the make-up of the sample of 'subjects'. However, by identifying the potential factors that may vary in a population and be relevant (think of the assumptions that need to be made here) it is possible to control for these factors.

In ERP2 there is an assumption that people are individuals who vary in so many, and such complex, ways that good research reports detailed case accounts (see below) with enough context to allow the reader to make a judgement of the extent to which findings might apply elsewhere (this process will be examined in more detail in Chapter 6). In the extreme, a study will offer an account of one case (e.g. 'a learning pathway …'). Other studies offer accounts of a range of contrasting cases to show what similarities and differences may be found across cases.

Neither paradigm solves 'the problem of induction' (how to draw general conclusions from specific examples), reminding us of the value of complementary approaches (see Chapter 3) or 'grounded theory' approaches (discussed below) which offer ways of building general models, starting from specific cases.

In reading about the examples of research discussed in this book, the reader should be alert to the size, and composition, of samples of informants providing the data upon which findings are based. Where studies attempt to offer general findings, the reader should ask whether the sample could be either diverse enough to be representative of classrooms generally, or large enough to buffer against the distorting effect of large variations between individual teachers, classes, and lessons.

Experiments and quasi-experiments

Experiments are set up to test specific hypotheses. In a 'true' experiment the researcher controls variables, so that only the factor which is hypothesised to have an effect differs between the experimental and control treatments. In reality, such control is rarely (if ever) possible in enquiries into teaching and learning – even if the range of potentially significant variables can be identified.

However, it is sometimes possible to make comparisons between situations that approximate to the conditions needed for an experiment. For example, an experimental procedure might require students to be assigned to one of two classes randomly – but the researcher may have to work with existing groups. However, if it can be shown that the two groups are sufficiently similar (on whatever measures are considered significant) if may be possible to continue as if there was an experimental set-up.

Experiments use statistical tests to check for 'statistically significant' results (i.e. those which have a low probability of occurring by chance) as well as for 'effect' sizes (as large samples may lead to *statistically* significant differences which may be of little practical importance). When quasi-experimental approaches are used, statistical tests may also be used to check for significant difference between groups that may already exist prior to any 'treatment' being applied, and which would invalidate any differences 'after' the experimental treatment has been carried out. As well as the technical difficulties of experimental design, this type of work raises particular ethical issues: especially where there are good reasons to believe that some learners will be deliberately disadvantaged in order to investigate the effect of some intervention. Ethical issues are very important in research, and are discussed in Chapter 7.

Exploring whether modular examinations disadvantage students

One of the studies referred to in Chapter 2 was a paper in the journal *Educational Research*, where McClune (2001) argues that students following modular courses (where some of the credit for final grade is awarded for examination papers taken early in the course) may be disadvantaged compared with students taking linear courses for the same award, and being examined on all aspects of the course in terminal examinations.

Question for reflection

McClune's (2001) study compared the performance of students in the first and second year of an A level course. What factors might need to be 'controlled' to make this a fair comparison?

McClune's study can be seen as an example of working in a positivistic research paradigm (ERP1, see Chapter 3). McClune reviews the 'advantages and disadvantages' of modular assessment, and highlights concerns that students may not be 'ready' for examinations part way through a course, and may need substantial time to consolidate learning before being examined.

This framing of the topic (the author's conceptual framework, see Chapter 3) may be seen as offering an implicit hypothesis – that students examined earlier in their course may be disadvantaged compared to those examined at the end of the course. Such a hypothesis is suitable for 'experimental' testing, i.e. manipulating conditions to compare between the two situations. Such experiments are difficult to set up in educational contexts, but it is possible to use a quasi-experimental design, where instead of a manipulation, advantage is taken of the 'natural' experiment (i.e. that some students were being entered for all their examinations at the end of the course, and others were taking module examinations part-way through).

However, simply comparing examination grades between these two groups of students does not ensure that any differences in outcomes are due to whether students take modular or purely terminal examinations (for example, schools that tend to have less successful examination grade profiles may decide to follow modular courses to see if that helps their students; or students with strong records of examination success may be more likely to opt for courses with terminal examinations).

Designing the quasi-experiment

McClune describes how he set up a sample that was large enough to use statistical testing, and which gave him groups suitable for making a comparison based on whether modular examinations were followed. McClune selected candidates entered for examinations at the same time, in the same subject (physics), and having followed the same subject content specifications. As there were some common questions in the modular and terminal examination papers, McClune was able to look at students' performance on the same questions, assessed by the same criteria (i.e. mark scheme). The sample was selected randomly from all the examination centres (i.e. schools, etc.), and so as to include papers marked by all the examiners marking those questions.

In a truly experimental study, the researcher would randomly assign participants to one of the two conditions (in that case modular or terminal examinations). This would offer some safeguard that there is no systematic difference between the two sub-groups in some factor that might have an influence (and there are potentially many one could consider).

In a quasi-experimental study the researcher cannot assign participants to the two conditions. So although McClune built his sample based on a random choice from those students taking the examination, each student selected was inherently already in the modular (first year) or terminal (second year) condition. There was a random choice of students from within the two conditions, but no safeguard against some systematic factor(s) determining which students were in the two conditions being compared.

Clearly any difference in the marks attained on the common questions among the two groups could be due to (a) chance – due to the particular individuals in the samples; (b) a difference between the groups in terms of the nature of the learning achieved on courses examined by modular or non–modular examinations; (c) a difference between the two groups coincidental to their following different patterns of courses. Only an effect due to option (b) would be relevant to the focus of McClune's study.

To exclude the possibility that any difference between groups was due to factors other than those of interest, one has to be able to identify and control for those factors. In education, we can never be sure of all the possible influences that may be at work, and so it is never possible to be absolutely sure we have excluded all such influences.

Using inferential statistics

To avoid the influence of chance, a large enough sample is needed to be able to use inferential statistics. McClune's sample comprised of 406 students examined on the terminal route at the end of their course, and 346 taking the modular examinations halfway through their two-year course. Inferential statistics can never completely rule out a difference between two groups being due to which individuals were randomly chosen for a sample (rather than reflecting a true difference in the larger population), but they can indicate how likely or unlikely a result is to occur by chance. Generally, a result that is only likely to happen less than once in twenty opportunities ('$p < 0.05$', where p is probability) is taken as being 'statistically significant'. (This means that we have to accept that a proportion of all the many thousands of *statistically significant* findings in the literature are due to random variations. We can reduce the number of 'false positive' statistical tests produced by using a more restrictive measure of statistical significance – but this will reduce the number of significant differences we identify.)

In order to carry out his analysis, McClune had to use a scoring scheme to convert grades on previous GCSE examinations into a numerical score (see Chapter 9). This allowed him to control for the previous academic attainment of the students in the two groups. However, inferential statistics can only give the likelihood of something being so. That an 'analysis of variance' test did not reveal significant differences between the two groups is certainly not the same as saying that the two groups had *identical* GCSE results.

According to McClune's analysis:

> Pupils completing the second year of the course had a higher level of attainment than those taking the examination during the first year of study. Similar differences between upper-sixth and lower-sixth pupils were observed in both boys and girls. ...

> (McClune, 2001: 79)

On most questions the differences in scores between first and second year students were quite small. Often researchers offer an 'effect size', a value which indicates the importance of a difference (it is possible for a very small, and practically irrelevant, difference to reach statistical significance). In this case, McClune does not need to interpret his findings this way: teachers appreciate that the difference between 64% and 69% could be very important in an examination.

Question for reflection

Why would it be difficult for a teacher to undertake the type of study described in McClune's (2001) paper?

McClune's study is an example of research that would have been of practical importance to many teachers (who had to choose between modular and terminal examinations for their students), as well as to policy makers (who decide what type of examination system should be in place, and the nature of the AS level examination at the end of the first year of the A level qualification). However, the classroom teacher is unlikely to be able to carry out such research. McClune worked in a university environment, and his research was only possible with the cooperation of the examination board that allowed him to develop his sample, and access scores for the students from across all the examination centres entering candidates. It is unlikely that classroom teachers would be granted this level of cooperation and access.

Surveys

Surveys look for data from large numbers of people. Some surveys collect information from whole populations of people. For example, a school could survey all its pupils, or all their parents, to find out their views on some issue relating to school policy. In such situations a high return rate, or at least making sure that everyone eligible to respond has the opportunity, may be sufficient for the findings to be of import.

A more complex situation occurs when the population of interest is too large for all members to be asked to respond. In these situations a sample of the population is surveyed. The sample has to be defined to ensure that it is representative of the wider population. One approach is to ask a random proportion of the population. If this is possible, then statistical techniques can be used to estimate how accurately the sample responses are likely to represent the wider population.

Question for reflection

Imagine you are charged with finding out what 13 year-old school children think about the amount and type of homework they should be asked to complete each week. You are required to sample 0.2% of the age range nationally. How might you go about identifying the youngsters in the target population, and then contacting a random sample to carry out your survey?

In practice, it is often impossible to use a random sample. Where the population consists of a broad category such as 'A level students' or 'parents of pupils on the special needs register' it is unlikely that a researcher could ever access the information needed to identify all those in the population. Without this information there is no way to select a random sample.

Sampling populations in surveys

Often research in education (and other social sciences) has to settle for other sampling techniques. The strength of a truly random sample is that it avoids the researcher having to know (or guess) how different people in the population might be influenced by various factors: a large enough sample is likely to be representative (enough) of the influences that might be relevant.

For example, consider a survey to find out which factors have the most influence on whether students apply to study at university. A sample that was comprised of a disproportionate number of students from wealthy backgrounds, or of those with graduate parents and siblings at university, is likely to give distorted results. The problem for the researcher is that to avoid this distortion he or she must be able to both know *which* factors might be relevant (is gender?; is ethnic background?; are there regional factors?; is there a difference between urban and rural areas?, etc.), and be able to build a stratified sample which has representative proportions of respondents matching those in the wider population. This can be a very challenging task.

However, some types of surveys do not need representative samples. The weakest type of sample is based on convenience sampling. So, for example, a survey of primary children may be based on surveying the children in the nearest primary school where access is provided. This clearly leads to severe limits on the extent to which results may be generalised to 'primary school pupils' in the general population.

There are, however, forms of sampling that fall between stratified and convenience sampling. Purposeful sampling builds a sample that includes some representation from certain groups without attempting to build a fully representative sample. So for a survey of staff perceptions of pupil behaviour in a school, the researcher may seek out newly qualified teachers (NQTs), recent appointments and supply teachers to be included in the sample on theoretical grounds (i.e. that these staff are most likely to experience misbehaviour), as well as including some established staff and senior post holders. There will be no attempt to make the sample represent the population in proportional terms, but some members of identified key groups will deliberately be included. It may even be that a decision will be taken to include all the NQTs, even though this gives a distorted sample, if their perceptions are seen to be particularly valuable.

Surveying teacher beliefs about pedagogy

Ravitz et al. (2000) report a study exploring teacher views about pedagogy, and teacher beliefs of student views about pedagogy. Their specific research focus was on the relationship between teacher pedagogy and the use of computers in teaching.

They distinguish 'two overarching approaches to teaching that represent different and somewhat incompatible models of good pedagogy' (Ravitz et al., 2000: 3 – cf. 'Conceptualising constructivist teaching' in Chapter 3, pp. 60). These are:

- Traditional transmission instruction – 'based on a theory of learning that suggests that students will learn facts, concepts, and understandings by absorbing the content of their teacher's explanations or by reading explanations from a text and answering related questions'.
- Constructivist-compatible instruction – 'based on a theory of learning that suggests that understanding arises only through prolonged engagement of the learner in relating new ideas and explanations to the learner's own prior beliefs'.

Question for reflection

The two categories used in Ravitz et al.'s (2000) study seem to offer both a rather simplistic dichotomy of approaches to teaching, and a somewhat caricatured picture of these two approaches to pedagogy:

How would such a conceptualisation fit a study undertaken from a 'confirmatory' or a 'discovery' research paradigm (see Chapter 3)?

Ravitz et al. (2000) undertook a survey to collect their data. Their published report gives details of how, where, and when they went about this. Their study was based on a national survey (the strategy) undertaken through a questionnaire (the tactical instrument) issued in the US during Spring 1998.

Designing a hybrid-sample

Ravitz et al. (2000) explain how they built a sample of schools with three components. As well as schools included on the basis of 'probability', they also deliberately included schools that were known to have a high level of provision of computers, and schools considered to be substantially involved in educational reform (i.e. where it might be expected that teachers will be using more 'constructivist-compatible' instruction). In each school the questionnaire was to be answered by the school principal, the technology coordinator and a probability sample of teachers. Over four thousand teachers responded to the questionnaire, and over half the sample was from the schools selected at random.

Ravitz and colleagues (2000: 11) reported that, overall, the teachers gave similar ratings to both approaches in terms of the student knowledge gains that could be achieved (44% for the traditional approach cf. 42%), although more thought students would gain most useful skills by the constructivist approach (29% for the traditional approach cf. 57%). They also found that most of the teachers surveyed felt more comfortable with a traditional approach (64% cf. 28% constructivist), and most also thought that their students would prefer the traditional approach (53% cf. 37%).

Question for reflection

In another study discussed, Kinchin (2004) reported that secondary level students overwhelmingly preferred a constructivist approach, but Ravitz et al. (2000) found that most teachers believe that students would be more comfortable when taught with a traditional approach. Does this simply mean that the teachers surveyed by Ravitz et al. had incorrect beliefs about their students' views on teaching?

Strengths and weaknesses of a survey approach

The Ravitz et al. (2000) study offers some examples of the limitations and the advantages of a survey as a research methodology. A severe disadvantage of a survey is that responses are limited to the options or categories offered. So this study is undertaken with a confirmatory paradigm (ERP1), where the relevant categories are decided at the outset. The researchers had to characterise the main pedagogic approaches as clearly distinct categories (in this case a dichotomy), and decide upon questions about views and behaviours that would link to these pedagogies – informed by their reading of previous research.

Such an approach produces 'objective' data that is readily analysed, and is suitable for statistical interrogation. The survey approach also allows a sample to be built up that is both large enough to make statistical comparisons, and includes categories of respondent of interest to the researchers. In this case, the carefully built sample provides the possibility of identifying nine groups of respondents, as shown in Figure 4.1.

By making comparisons between responses across different questionnaire items it is possible to uncover statistically significant correlations. So Ravitz et al. (2000) found that teachers conceptualising teaching in certain ways, favouring:

	Principals	ICT coordinators	Teachers
Representative of schools nationally			
Schools with strong ICT provision			
Schools known to be involved in educational reform			

FIGURE 4.1

- an inquiry approach;
- being a facilitator; and
- organising class time around multiple simultaneous small-group activities

were more likely to report doing certain class activities:

- week-long projects;
- student journals;
- designing assignments where students had to 'represent the same idea in more than one way';
- hands-on activities;
- reflective student essays.

The authors were also able to report that respondents selecting responses linked to a constructivist approach were more likely to report frequently using activities considered (by the authors) to be constructivist:

> Overall, those who selected the constructivist belief alternative on each survey question were about one-half a standard deviation higher on an index measuring the sum of the number of constructivist activities engaged in (monthly) than teachers who chose the traditional transmission belief statement (or who selected the middle response).
>
> (Ravitz et al., 2000: 50)

Case study

Case studies are very common in education, and involve the in-depth exploration of a particular case. Defining the case is an important step here, as there is much flexibility. Examples of cases may be a teacher, a class, a group of students who work together, a lesson episode, a unit in the scheme of work, a year group, a school, an LEA, etc. Although cases are often quite limited units of study, such as Duit and colleagues' study based on the 'analysis of one specific classroom discussion episode' (Duit et al., 1998: 1060), this is not always the case:

> The [US] National Institute on Student Achievement, Curriculum, and Assessment ... conducted a Case Study of the entire Japanese school system with particular reference to the teaching and learning of Mathematics and Science.
>
> (Freebody, 2003: 80)

According to Yin (2003), a case study has a number of characteristics. A case study is an empirical enquiry that explores a phenomenon within its context, rather than attempting to isolate the case from its context. This is a useful approach when the boundary between case and context may not be distinct. Case studies are also useful in complex situations where the number of significant variables may exceed the number of cases, making control of variables impossible. We can see how teaching and learning phenomena might well fit into this pattern.

Consider a school where the classes are set in half-year groups, and where the two top maths sets are taught by different teachers (at different times – as one half of the year group has English when the other has maths) in different rooms. The head of department notices that the profile of test scores are consistently much lower in one of the two top-sets although they are meant to be parallel. This could clearly be something to do with the teacher, or the pupils, or the interaction between the two. The timing of the lesson, or the learning environment could be factors. It may be that one class has PE immediately before two of its maths lessons each week, and arrives excited and tired. Or it may be that one of the teachers has a non-teaching period directly before some of her classes with her class and is mentally 'fresher'. There are many possible factors at work, and isolating variables (e.g. move the classes to different teaching rooms) is not likely to be a feasible strategy for understanding what is going on. It is not even clear if the timetable and classroom are merely background context or significant features.

'Triangulation' within case studies

Yin suggests that case studies cope with these situations by using multiple sources of data (triangulation), looking for *convergence*. This is similar to a grounded theory approach (see below) although, unlike grounded theory, Yin suggests that in case-study research 'prior development of theoretical propositions to guide data collection and analysis' are appropriate (Yin, 2003: 13–14). Yin suggests that 'case studies are the preferred strategy when "how" or "why" questions are being posed, when the investigator has little control over events, and when the focus is on a contemporary phenomenon within some real-life context' (Yin, 2003: 1).

A case study of student learning?

In a 1998 study published in the *International Journal of Science Education*, Petri and Niedderer reported their research into one 18 year-old high school student's learning about the atom. Petri and Niedderer (1998: 1075) claim to 'describe' 'one student's learning process in a course on quantum atomic physics in Grade 13 of a German gymnasium (secondary school)'. This description is in terms of what they call a 'learning pathway':

> The student's learning pathway is described as a sequence of several meta-stable conceptions of the atom, starting from a planetary model. His final cognitive element 'atom' following teaching is displayed as an association of three parallel conceptions including his initial planetary model, a state-electron model and an electron cloud model.
>
> (Petri and Niedderer, 1998: 1075)

This is a very interesting study, but we might ask why we would be particularly interested in one particular learner (who is presumably no longer studying at secondary level).

Why do we care about Carl?

In reporting the conceptual framework supporting their work (see Chapter 3), Petri and Niedderer (1998) make a distinction between 'stable cognitive elements' which are fairly permanent features of mind, and what the learner happens to be thinking right now. This distinction is important, but problematic for researchers. Although we may be more interested in the 'stable cognitive elements' we only ever have access to what students (tell us they) are thinking now. The 'stable elements' must be inferred from data based on the 'current constructions'.

This is just one complication of exploring student understanding. Learning is a complex and subtle phenomena, and even when researchers correctly interpret what students say, do and write, each particular datum offers only limited access to current understanding. It is known that students may sometimes hold manifold conceptions of the same topic (Taber, 2000c) so that learning may often be better understood as a shift in the profile of use of 'versions' of concepts in various contexts, rather than as switching between holding different conceptions. In-depth study of individuals, carried out over extended periods of time, are needed to explore the shifting sands of the learners' 'conceptual ecology' (Taber, 2001). For researchers who hold such a perspective, the subtleties of learning are best explored through case studies of individual learners, such as Carl.

Petri and Niedderer (1998) provide contextual information on the course being taught, and when particular ideas were covered in lessons. The authors are interested in developing teaching about the topic of quantum physics at high school level, so it is important that they offer the reader information about the nature of the instruction. They also given an account of the data they collected, and how it was analysed.

Use of multiple data sources in case-study work

A range of data was collected during the course (Petri and Niedderer, 1998: 1078):

- observations and a pre-questionnaire;
- videotapes of the entire unit and the group work of four students;
- short, spontaneous interviews;
- three semi-structured interviews in small groups;
- one semi-structured final interview with all students;
- one semi-structured interview with some students three months after;
- written material from each student.

The collection of different types of data provides the basis for an in-depth qualitative analysis. However, it is important to recognise that in some studies such a
multitude of data sources provides less redundancy (allowing comparison and cross-
checking between different types of data) than may at first seem the case. We need
to be aware of the 'degrees of freedom' inherent in the focus being studied.

If researchers wanted to know if a student knew a simple fact, e.g. whether the let-
ter B is a vowel, it may be sufficient to ask one question. However, we know from
research that student understanding of many concept areas is much more complex
than this: with students holding manifold conceptions that can be elicited in different contexts. To explore student thinking in these areas, it is necessary to ask a range
of questions (or set a range of tasks) varying contextual and verbal cues in the questions. There are more 'degrees of freedom' in what is being studied, so more 'slices of
data' are needed to build an authentic representation.

Studies of learning are attempting to see how already complex phenomena varies
over time – and this requires that a suitable range of probes are used at several points
during the learning process. The 'degrees of freedom' are greater, and so more slices
of data are needed to construct a useful model of the system studied.

Generalising from the case?

No matter how careful and proficient the researchers may have been in producing
their model of Carl's learning about quantum physics, it remains a case study of a single learner. A case study allows a detailed account of a single instance to be formulated. Petri and Niedderer's study tells us very little about the learning of Carl's
classmates, or of students studying the topic elsewhere. We might assume that
students of various ages, studying various other school topics might demonstrate
learning with similar characteristics, but Petri and Niedderer's case study of a single
learner cannot offer any direct evidence to support such an assumption. Not only
that, but the rationale for selecting case study – the complexity of learning processes
and the individuality of learners – suggest that we should be careful about drawing
general conclusions from one case. (This is a general problem of case studies, that
some researchers believe that grounded theory, discussed below, can overcome.)

Ethnography

Ethnography is an approach that is used in anthropology to explore unfamiliar
cultures. The problem facing anthropologists studying a new culture is to try

and find out about 'alien' rituals and customs, in terms of the meanings they had for the people in that culture. So, the type of methodology developed, 'ethnomethodology':

> Is concerned with how people make sense of their everyday world. More especially, it is directed at the mechanisms by which participants achieve and sustain interaction in a social encounter – the assumptions they make, the conventions they utilize, and the practices they adopt.
>
> (Cohen et al., 2000: 24)

At first sight, ethnographic methodology may seem inappropriate when the researcher is exploring aspects of teaching and learning in their own society. After all, ethnomethodology is designed to find out about *other cultures*. However, there may well be situations when those researched can (and maybe should) be considered as members of a different culture, so that an ethnographic approach is appropriate.

This might certainly be the case when the researcher would be considered a member of a different social class for example. A well-educated intellectual in a professional role such as a teacher or an academic researcher should not *assume* that disaffected youths from disadvantaged backgrounds will share the same cultural values and assumptions.

Enthnographic approaches have also been adopted by researchers attempting to explore learners' understandings of curriculum topics. This has been particularly so in science, where many studies have shown that learners commonly hold alternative conceptions of many science topics. Research suggests that 'children's science' may often be coherent, theory-like and highly tenacious. The researcher trying to understand how a student understands a topic area has to try to put aside their own way of thinking and try to 'see' the topic 'through the learners' eyes', to try to 'get inside' the mind of the learner. This is considered to be analogous to the anthropologist trying to learn to think like a newly discovered tribe, to understand the way people in that culture 'see' their world.

Describing the careers of primary pupils

Pollard and Filer (1999) report a study of pupils' primary school 'careers', Their book is based around four detailed case studies of individual primary pupils, based on ethnography. They describe the primary aim of their work as 'to create an accurate description of the perspective, social practices and behaviour' (Pollard and Filer, 1999: 2) of the people they are studying.

Ethnographic approaches rely on detailed observations usually recorded as indepth field notes. Pollard and Filer describe the main methods of their approach as 'discussion, interview, collection of documents and a great deal of "participant observation", with copious fieldnotes describing events, and a 'research notebook' to record analytic ideas and fieldwork experiences' (Pollard and Filer, 1999: 2).

An important feature of this type of research is that it may take a good deal of time to 'immerse' in the culture before beginning to see the patterns of meaning that the informants use to understand their lives. Research notes need to be as 'unfiltered' by existing theories as possible, to avoid imposing some inappropriate pre-existing theory or schemes onto the data:

> Ethnographic studies are carried out to satisfy three simultaneous requirements associated with the study of human activities: the need for an empirical approach; the need to remain open to elements that cannot be codified at the time of the study; a concern for grounding the phenomena observed in the field.
>
> (Baszanger and Dodier, 2004: 10)

It has been noted that ethnography is much better at producing theoretical accounts, than offering ways to validate such accounts:

> Ethnographic methods offer means for generating theory. By the same token, these techniques are poor ones for testing theory, since the data obtained by the researcher were not gathered systematically and do not represent any population of events to which the researcher may wish to generalize.
>
> (Biddle and Anderson, 1986: 238)

To some extent, this limitation is overcome in grounded theory research.

Grounded theory

> Grounded theory methodology…is a specific, highly developed, rigorous set of procedures for producing formal, substantive theory of social phenomena. This approach to the analysis of qualitative data simultaneously employs techniques of induction, deduction, and verification to develop theory. Experience with data generates insights, hypotheses, and generative questions that are pursued through further data generation. As tentative answers to questions are developed and concepts are constructed, these constructions are verified through further data collection.
>
> (Schwandt, 2001: 110)

Grounded theory (GT) is probably a very difficult methodology for a novice researcher to adopt, especially where an enquiry has a limited focus and tight timescales. However, it is important for all educational researchers to *know about* this methodology, because:

- it provides a model for interpretivist research which may overcome many of the limitations of much 'qualitative' enquiry;
- it is commonly used as a referent in interpretivist research.

In other words, many studies make references to using approaches 'informed' or inspired by GT. The reader of such accounts needs to appreciate what is meant by GT research, and to be able to judge whether studies that 'name-check' grounded theory are following the methodology closely enough to be able to claim the benefits of this approach.

The reader interested in GT theory should study some of the methodological texts available, but the following account should give a feel for the key principles of the approach.

Key features of grounded theory studies

Theoretical sensitivity: 'to enter the research setting with as few predetermined ideas as possible … to remain sensitive to the data by being able to record events and detect happenings without first having them filtered through and squared with pre-existing hypotheses and biases' (Glaser, 1978 : 2–3). This is of course similar to the approach taken in ethnomethodology.

Theoretical sampling: GT studies have an *emergent* design, in that the collection of data leads to hunches and hypotheses that inform what data should be collected next, i.e. 'sampling on the basis of emerging concepts, with the aim being to explore the dimensional range or varied conditions along which the properties of concepts vary' (Strauss and Corbin, 1998: 73). This is clearly antithetical to experimental research where the procedures for data collection and analysis need to be established at the outset.

Coding: In GT studies there are well-established procedures for coding data: 'the analytic process through which data are fractured, conceptualised, and integrated to form theory' (Strauss and Corbin, 1998: 3). A key feature is the 'constant comparison' method, whereby new data is compared to existing codes to check fit and look to modify the codes, and where modified sets of codes are then tested back against data collected previously. This iterative process is intended to ensure that the codes used *emerge from* the data, and are *not imposed on* the data. 'Substantive' coding (based directly on describing the data, on a line-by-line basis) shifts to a theoretical level as categories are developed to organise the codes, and a core category of central significance is identified.

Theoretical saturation: GT is only considered as ready for publication once theoretical saturation is reached. That is when new data collection (indicated by theoretical sampling) do not lead to any further changes to the theory, as the scheme of categories and their properties and relationships fit new data without further modification, i.e.:

> The point in category development at which no new properties, dimensions, or relationships emerge during analysis.
>
> (Strauss and Corbin, 1998: 143)

Is the model saturated?

We can apply this notion of saturation to Watts' model of learners' conceptual frameworks for understanding force (see Chapter 3). Watts did not claim to be using GT, and acknowledged that this study produced a model *suitable for further testing*. He claimed his results had similarities with the findings of other studies, but this in itself cannot be seen as strong evidence for the validity of his findings.

TABLE 4.1 **The Watts (1983) sample by age and gender**

Age	11	12	13	14	15	16	17	Total
Females	1			1	3	1	1	7
Males		1		1	2		1	5
Total	1	1	0	2	5	1	2	12

A reader of the research is likely to look for evidence that the model produced is both an authentic reflection of the data collected (i.e. the analysis is careful and comprehensive) and that the findings are likely to be of wider relevance. In this regard, Watts' paper shows that he based his model on a sample of 12 students of a range of ages in several schools in London, England (see Table 4.1).

The question that a reader might ask is that:

- *if* the analysis of data from twelve informants, over a wide age range, from one geographical location, provided evidence of eight alternative frameworks,
- *then* how can Watts (or the reader) be confident that increasing the sample, by interviewing additional students, would not have led to a larger set of frameworks being developed?

This is of course the generalisation issue raised earlier in this chapter: to what extent are Watts' results (from a limited sample) capable of being applied to 'school children learning physics' in general? In quantitative studies, large representative samples offer grounds for trusting that results apply more generally. In qualitative studies, large sample sizes may be avoided by building a sample considered representative of a population by 'theoretical sampling' until a model is saturated. Where studies only offer results from a limited context, the reader needs to judge whether the research is likely to be relevant elsewhere (see Chapter 6).

Watts' study is convincing in suggesting that secondary students do come to class with alternative conceptions of the force concept. However, in reading Watts' research, the reader must question the generalisability of the findings because:

- the sample cannot be considered to be large or representative;
- the analytical procedures do not assure a saturated model;
- the description of the informants and research sites are insufficient for readers to make judgements about degrees of similarity with their own teaching contexts.

Ready for testing?

As Watts recognised, in this sense, the study is 'exploratory'. In this case, this did not prevent the study being published or recognised as significant. Although teachers may not have confidence in the generality of the model of alternative conceptual frameworks presented, the broader finding that the students came to class with their own alternative understandings of forces has important implications for teaching this topic.

A full GT study will produce a theoretical account of a situation which is grounded in the data, is saturated, and which is suitable for wide-scale *testing*. So GT can 'explain what happened, predict what will happen and interpret what is happening in an area of substantive or formal enquiry' (Glaser, 1978: 4). The notion of testing indicates 'ERP1' research, so although the methodology of grounded theory is certainly interpretivist, the full procedure can lead to a 'bridge' between the two main approaches to educational research (Taber, 2000b):

> Of course a theory can be tested. Although validated during the actual research process, a theory is not tested in the quantitative sense. This is for another study.
>
> (Strauss and Corbin, 1998: 213)

Substantive and general theories

In one of the studies mentioned in Chapter 2, Calissendorff (2006) reports a study into 5 year-olds learning to play the violin, where she used a GT approach to data analysis. However, Calissendorff acknowledges that although she has reported what she considers to be a 'substantive theory' of student learning *in her particular focal context*, further theoretical sampling would be needed before it could be developed into a more general GT:

> A substantive theory, based on the study of a small group, does not have the same explanatory scope as a larger, more general theory. For a substantive theory to become formal, it needs to be expanded and compared with other theories.
>
> (Calissendorff, 2006: 94)

A grounded study of teacher mind-sets?

Few studies in education claim to follow the full GT procedures, but many do claim to adopt methods from this approach. The extent to which adopting *some tactics* outside of the context of a coherent GT *strategy* is advisable has to be judged on a case-by-case basis.

Tobin (1990) reported a study of the beliefs and teaching behaviours of two science teachers, and concluded that the teachers held *metaphors* for their roles as teachers that influenced the way they taught:

> Peter's teaching behaviour was influenced by metaphors that he used to conceptualize teaching. Peter described teaching in terms of two metaphors: the teacher as *Entertainer* ... and the teacher as *Captain of the Ship* ... Sandra's teaching was influenced by the metaphor of *Teacher as Resource* ...
>
> (Tobin, 1990: 51, 53)

This fascinating study is reported in great detail in book form (Tobin, et al., 1990), and it is only possible to discuss some key points here. Tobin's study was based on his own belief that teachers have significant metaphors for their classroom work:

> An assumption underlying this study was that many of the teachers' beliefs and knowledge about teaching and learning are metaphorical ... metaphors underlie the understandings ascribed to important concepts about teaching and learning.

> (Tobin, 1990: 35)

Triangulation: the data collection processes used in Tobin's study

Tobin's study offers an example of research where a range of different data–collection techniques were used (i.e. triangulation) to build-up an authentic picture of an educational focus. There was a ten-week period of data collection:

> Participant observer data collecting strategies were employed. These involved observing classrooms, interviewing teachers and students on a daily basis, working with students during class time, obtaining written responses to specific questions, examining student notebooks and test papers and analyzing teacher assessments of student performance.

> (Tobin et al., 1990: 16)

The research team reported that they took care 'to ensure that data were obtained from a variety of sources and that multiple perspectives were represented in the data obtained' (Tobin et al., 1990: 17). A precise schedule for collecting data was deliberately not established at the start of the project. Rather, flexibility was retained to allow the researchers to follow-up interesting leads:

> As the study progressed, the research team made decisions about the aspects of teaching and learning on which they would focus, the data to be collected and procedures to be adopted in collecting and validating data.

> (Tobin et al., 1990: 17)

Question for reflection

Tobin does not claim his study developed grounded theory, although there are certainly aspects of the methodology that reflect grounded theory methodology. Can you identify features of the study that (a) do, and (b) do not match such a GT approach?

Can we consider Tobin's study to be GT?

Although GT is a well-known and much discussed methodology in the social sciences, it is rare to find published studies about teaching and learning that claim to be GT. In part this is surely because the approach is very demanding – being unpredictable and open-ended, and requiring a commitment to a time-consuming and rigorous approach to data analysis.

Tobin and colleagues' study certainly has several features that reflect a GT approach. The collection of a number of different 'slices of data' is one feature of GT research (although this is not uncommon in qualitative studies). The use of an emergent design: where decisions about data collection are made throughout the study in the light of consideration of the data already collected (i.e. 'theoretical sampling') is another feature of this approach to research.

However, at least two features of Tobin's study would compromise its consideration as GT. One factor is the limited duration. Although ten weeks of fieldwork is a considerable commitment for a research team, it still seems to represent a pre-determined window. In true GT studies there is no predetermined time limit on data collection – this should continue until there is 'theoretical saturation' (see above), that is until new data is not offering any more refinements of the model being developed. Secondly, GT research is meant to have an open agenda, where the researchers do not enter the field with preformed notions of what they might find. The extent to which this is actually a practical possibility is much discussed, but it is clear in this study that Tobin was *looking for* the metaphors that teachers held of their teaching roles, and *expecting* to find that these influenced teaching behaviour.

Is Tobin's study ethnography?

Tobin and colleagues' study also shares some of the features of ethnographic work. Their period of fieldwork included a good deal of observation, compiling field notes, and collecting the kind of in-depth data that allows insight into another culture. Tobin and his colleagues were keen to try and understand the meanings that Sandra and Peter gave to their work, and to the interactions they entered into in the classroom. Although Tobin's study would probably not be considered as 'an ethnography', the case studies of Sandra and Peter (like many examples of case study work in education) are certainly built using an approach informed by ethnographic methods.

Action research

Action research (AR) is characterised in terms of purpose: it is 'the study of a social situation with a view to improving the quality of action within it' (Elliott, 1991: 69). Whereas much research is carried out for intellectual reasons – to explore an interesting phenomenon, or answer an intriguing question – *action* research is designed to bring about change in a personally experienced situation.

This makes AR a common approach to *practitioner research* in professions such as teaching. There are many professional problems that teachers may attempt to address through AR:

- poor student behaviour;
- limited understanding of a topic;
- intimidation and bullying behaviour within a group;
- lack of interest in a topic;
- poor quality of homework;
- not enough student involvement in discussion;
- stereotyped gender roles during practical activities.

AR is not characterised by the particular data collection techniques used, but by the attitude to the knowledge developed. AR may well produce reportable new understandings, and these may be applicable elsewhere, but the aim of the research is to solve a problem or improve a situation. Where a solution is found, it will be implemented even if this compromises the collection and analysis of data – if a suspected solution is not helping, it will be abandoned to try something else even though it may not have been rigorously evaluated:

> The fundamental aim of action research is to improve practice rather than to produce knowledge. The production and utilization of knowledge is subordinate to, and conditioned by, this fundamental aim.

> (Elliott, 1991: 49)

AR involves cycles of trying out ideas, and testing them out in practice. McNiff (1992: 38) describes a formulation of the action research cycle:

- I experience a problem when some of my educational values are denied in practice;
- I imagine a solution of the problem;
- I implement the imagine solution;
- I evaluate the outcomes of my actions;
- I re-formulate my problem in the light of my evaluation.

AR is successful if it improves practice, and the researcher needs sufficient evidence to base such a judgement on. However, action research is highly contextualised, and reports may well offer little readily generalised knowledge to inform other practitioners. Indeed, although AR is a very common form of research, very few studies in educational research journals seem to be *presented as being* AR.

Question for reflection

Can you suggest why few genuine AR studies are published in research journals?

An intervention study on pupil literacy

A paper in the journal *Educational Studies* (Lyle, 1999) makes a claim that working in mixed ability groups help pupils develop their literacy. Lyle's paper tells us that the research context was a single primary school that requested the help of education students to support reading in Year 5. Twelve undergraduate students were involved, and each worked with a mixed-ability, mixed-gender group of pupils for one afternoon per week for ten weeks. The pupils were drawn from three school classes, and Lyle outlines the work undertaken (Lyle, 1999: 285).

The study was based in a single school. This raises the question of the extent to which this school may be 'typical', and whether the 48 pupils involved in the study can be seen to be representative of children of this age group (9–10 year-olds, as referred to in the title of the paper). The context of the study was an intervention. Pupils were taken from the normal class context and worked in specially formed groups with second year undergraduates on a specially devised scheme. This type of activity is not so unusual in primary schools, but the reader will wonder whether the study findings would translate to groups working with the normal class teacher (in the busy classroom managing perhaps seven groups at once). Again, this does not negate the value of the study, but it raises questions about the extent to which the research context can be considered similar to other contexts where readers may wish to apply the findings of the research.

Could Lyle's study be considered as collaborative action research?

AR is a very common form of activity in education, along with other professional areas (such as health care). In its purest form, AR involves practitioners enquiring into aspects of *their own* professional context that they consider problematic, or capable of being improved. The key impetus of AR is to improve the professional situation, that is to produce 'knowledge-in-action' to inform the practitioner's own practice. AR often involves interventions, introducing changes, which are then evaluated before being adopted, dropped or, often, modified for further cycles of AR.

Lyle (1999) is not acting as an action-researcher in the usual sense. He is not exploring a problem in his own professional practice, and indeed he clearly has a strong academic interest in the topic. However, the study does discuss an intervention that was introduced to address an issue identified in the school. In this sense we may see this project as a *collaborative* AR study where teachers work with academics to explore an issue of concern to the teachers. When seen in these terms we would expect concern for improving the problematic situation to take precedence over the collection of evidence to make a case for new knowledge in academic terms. If seen in AR terms, then Lyle describes an intervention that does seem to have been very valuable for the literacy development of the *particular* 9–10 year-olds. The problems of reporting action research are considered further in Chapter 10.

Promoting self-regulated learning

In a 2004 study, Corrigan and Taylor (2004) suggest that the requirements for promoting self-regulated learning (SRL) may include:

- offering students choice;
- learning goals and timeframes (within parameters);
- opportunities to reflect;
- a relaxed and supportive environment;
- a hands-on, activity-based, fun learning environment;
- access to a wide range of resources.

Corrigan and Taylor (2004: 49) suggest that SRL is promoted by learning conditions 'where external regulation is minimal', that is, where the conditions of learning are flexible; offer choice; are student-centred; promote active learning; and where learning is project-/problem-based.

Question for reflection

Corrigan and Taylor (2004: 51) describe the methodology they chose to use as 'a qualitative approach within an interpretivist paradigm'. What factors might lead to researchers making such a methodological choice?

Corrigan and Taylor (2004: 51) describe their study as an 'exploratory research inquiry', and such exploratory work would tend to be considered to fit within the interpretivist research paradigm (ERP2, see Chapter 3). Corrigan and Taylor (2004: 51) suggest that such an approach would be most appropriate because (a) a quantitative approach would be 'of limited use' in view of their small sample size, and (b) as they 'wished to gain an in-depth understanding of the effectiveness of SRL as a pedagogy ...'

An in-depth approach is suitable for an exploratory study where it is considered that the existing knowledge about the field is sketchy, or of limited relevance to the context being explored (see Chapter 7). Collecting data in-depth often means working closely with a small number of informants instead of obtaining data from a larger sample. Quantitative methods are indeed of little value in these situations where there is no specific hypothesis to test, and a modest sample size. Presenting the decision-making in this way fits the 'ideal' way of undertaking research, with methodological decisions determined by the type of study being undertaken, which is in turn determined by the way the research conceptualises the field and formulates questions (see Chapter 3).

However, Corrigan and Taylor's wording can also be read to imply that their choice of a qualitative approach was determined by the practical constraint of working with a small sample. Research decisions are often constrained by pragmatic considerations such as this. This is especially the case when *practitioner* researchers enquire into aspects of their practice: as the research site and potential foci for enquiry are often fixed by the practitioner's institutional and teaching context.

Question for reflection

Corrigan and Taylor (2004) are working in the context of higher education: to what extent can their study be seen as action-research?

Corrigan and Taylor (2004: 52) describe their sample as 'purposeful': '6 volunteer participants (5 female and 1 male) … intended to reflect the views of a range of students with different performance levels within the SRL project'. In their paper the authors are quite clear that their focus is 'the effectiveness of SRL as a pedagogy for use with pre-service primary teachers' (Corrigan and Taylor, 2004: 51), and their data derived from one sample drawn from one cohort of trainee teachers in one institution.

Are the findings from AR context-bound?

Corrigan and Taylor refer to their informants as being *pre-service primary teachers*. It would have been possible to design a multi-site site study with a much more robust sample, that could allow knowledge claims to be made which derive from a much more diverse group of *pre-service primary teachers*. However, Corrigan and Taylor's decision-making in their research makes more sense if considered as an example of action research (AR).

Corrigan and Taylor are *practitioners* (in higher education) looking to make improvements in *their* professional work. They had introduced changes to *their* teaching to attempt to encourage stronger SRL in their students, and so the main focus of their research was evaluating that intervention. AR takes place within the problematised context, and seeks understanding for the practitioners involved in that context. AR:

- *empowers* practitioners to develop as teachers; but
- *constrains* research design as data collection is limited to the specific context of the intervention, and must be planned around the opportunities that intervention allows.

This is something that teacher-researchers need to be aware of when planning their own research studies (see Chapter 7).

Section 2
Learning from Educational Research

This section considers some key ideas that can be used to *evaluate* educational research. There are at least two different ways in which we might wish to judge a report of educational enquiry:

- are the claims made justified?
- are the claims made relevant?

In other words, as readers and potential users of educational research, we wish to know whether a study has been competently executed, so that we can have confidence in its findings, and also whether what was found in the research is likely to have implications for our own professional context or area of concern. These are different issues as there may be very good reasons why an extremely competent piece of research should not be assumed to apply 'here' – just as there may be potentially relevant findings in poorly conducted research.

It is very important to appreciate this distinction, as publication of research in an international peer-reviewed research journal *should* suggest that the study has been competently carried out and carefully reported, but does not give any assurances that the findings are transferable. Chapter 5 considers how we can evaluate the quality of research studies, and Chapter 6 explores how we might judge the relevance of research to our own professional context. Both of these chapters will draw upon some of the key points about educational research discussed in Section 1.

5

Teachers Evaluating Research Quality

Three metaphors for thinking about research writing

For the reader new to research writing, and perhaps apprehensive about the task, it may be useful to adopt three metaphors that can provide guidance: the author *as story-teller*, *as advocate*, and *as teacher* (see Box 5.1).

Box 5.1   The research author as story-teller, advocate and teacher

Effective educational research writing can be seen in terms of:

The *literary* analogy: A good research report has a narrative that leads the reader through 'the story' of the research.
The *legal* analogy: The author needs to make the case by a careful, logical argument, drawing upon convincing evidence.
The *pedagogic* analogy: The author is a communicator, charged with informing readers about the research.

Different types of research require different types of evaluation

A key point to be taken into account when judging research reports is that different types of studies set out to do different types of things, and it is not appropriate to judge them all in exactly the same way. This is closely tied to the idea that educational research is usually undertaken within a 'paradigm' that informs all aspects of the research process, and determines the nature and significance of the claims being made (see Chapter 3). It is strongly suggested, therefore, that the present chapter should be read after the previous chapters (which introduce and explain the main distinction between different types of educational research).

So, in research undertaken within ERP1 the researcher is attempting to find out about, and record, some aspect of an objective reality. The researcher attempts to uncover that reality whilst having as little influence on the researched situation as possible. The informants in such research are often considered as 'research subjects' in the very real sense that in many studies the individual subjects are assumed to represent members of a wider population, and to be interchangeable with other members of the population.

However, research undertaken within ERP2 is likely to see informants as participants in the research, perhaps even co-learners in the research (Taber and Student, 2003), and jointly involved in the process of constructing the research account. There is no assumption that the researcher merely reports what was there, as the researcher has entered the research context and is interacting with the other participants. There is often a deliberate attempt to collect data from individuals in such depth that the accounts developed reflect the personal history and unique character of the informant. Such research does not assume that participants could be non-problematically swapped for other members of some wider population without changing the findings of the research. The issue of generalisability, whether findings might apply elsewhere, is often a key concern when reading this type of research.

Judging whether educational research claims are justified

There are several issues that will influence whether we consider research reports to offer justifiable findings. When reading a research report, especially one that claims to demonstrate that major changes in professional practice are needed, we need to ask ourselves a number of questions:

- is the account detailed enough to make further judgements?
- is the account honest?
- is the focus appropriately conceptualised in the research?
- is the methodology appropriate?
- are the techniques applied in a technically competent manner?
- do the conclusions logically follow from the findings?

A failure in any one of these stages may invalidate the conclusions and make any recommendations dubious. (This should be borne in mind when planning and carrying out classroom research – see Chapter 7.) A further question we should consider is:

- Has the research been conducted in an ethical manner?

Question for reflection

Should it matter to the reader if research findings have been obtained by unethical means as long as all the criteria for offering justified knowledge claims have been met?

The peer-review process

An initial question that can be usefully asked about any study we read is 'Where is it published?' Research reports can be published in research journals, professional periodicals, at conferences and on personal web-sites, for example. In general, if a study is published in a recognised international research journal, it can usually be assumed to have some worth.

Publishing in academic research journals

Such a journal will normally be published by a commercial academic publisher, or a recognised research institution; will have an editorial board and/or advisory board drawing upon experts in the field internationally; and will require all submitted studies to undergo 'peer-review' by several 'referees'. This means that the editor sends papers for comment to recognised experts in their field, and bases decisions on what to publish on these recommendations. The most prestigious journals reject most of the material they receive. Most importantly, most papers that are published have to be revised by the authors to meet the criticisms and suggestions of referees – so peer review is a process that improves as well as selects what is published.

   Journal websites will provide information on editorial boards and procedures. Normally submitted papers are read and evaluated by at least two experts in the field before being accepted for publication. The reviewers are usually anonymous (to avoid them being subject to pressure from authors) and often the authors are asked to submit a version of their manuscript that disguises their own identity so that the work must be judged on its own merits. The system is not perfect – it is often possible for a referee to realise who the author of a paper must have been, and editors have to rely on referees making judgements objectively rather than allowing personal friendships or antagonisms to influence their recommendations. However, the system provides a safeguard that the community can trust that most papers published have sufficient merit.

Publishing in practitioner journals

Some practitioner periodicals also use peer review procedures. However, the criteria used to evaluate papers may be less stringent. For example, accounts that are considered to provide useful illustrations of good practice may be accepted for publication in such periodicals, without needing to demonstrate any substantial contribution to new knowledge. Such periodicals often also publish 'opinion' based pieces meant to stimulate discussion that need not be based on wide readings of existing literature, nor new empirical evidence. It is often quite acceptable for such articles to be based on selective literature and anecdotal evidence. These contributions may indeed stimulate useful discussion among readers, but should not be confused with reports of research. Where researchers do publish articles about their empirical work in practitioner journals, they are often required to simplify their theoretical background and limit the number of academic references made in order to meet the style of the publication (and the assumed preferences of the professional readership).

On-line Journals

Most international research journals allow papers to be accessed via websites (through electronic subscriptions or payment per article downloaded), and the research reports are no different to those in paper copies of the journals (and so have the same status). Often these journals publish the paper 'on-line first', sometimes many months before the paper copy.

There are also journals that only publish on-line. These may be most reputable. For example, the author is part of the International Advisory Board of an electronic-only journal called *Chemistry Education: Research & Practice* (CERP). CERP has an editorial board, and advisory board drawn from recognised experts internationally, uses the accepted peer-review process and is published by a learned society (The Royal Society of Chemistry).

However, it is important to bear in mind that anyone could start and publish a journal on-line, and if unsure a reader should looks to see who the editors and board members are (and whether they are based in a range of countries).

The 'grey' literature: conference papers

Material presented at conferences is often also published in one form or another. The status of conference papers is variable. Some prestigious conferences review papers according to the same type of peer reviewer process used in journals. However, as one of the advantages of conferences is allowing reports of recent and on-going work, it is more usual that only an abstract written months before the conference has been reviewed. When formal books of proceedings are published, there may be peer-review and revision of papers after presentations. However, paper copies of papers collected at conference, or made available by the author later, may have been through a minimal peer-review process.

Sometimes conference papers, and other such literature – discussion papers and position papers that may be distributed without being through formal peer-review processes, are referred to as 'grey literature'. This reminds us that the quality and status of such papers is very variable.

The 'grey' literature: publishing on the web

Publishing papers electronically on web-sites has become very common. Individual researchers sometimes publish papers on-line. However, as researchers are judged by their publications in research journals, some caution is needed in considering these papers. Usually such papers are reprints (i.e. making available writing previously published) or pre-prints (making available papers due for publication in journals or books) or conference papers. If papers appear to have no information about where they have been published, submitted or presented, then one may suspect that they either fall short of publication standards, or report work-in-progress not ready for formal reporting.

Various organisations may also publish research through the web. This can include reports commissioned from reputable researchers by charities and other organisations; and research digests commissioned by organisations such as education authorities. The status of the hosting organisation, the independence and reputation of the authors, and the extent to which reference to other relevant literature is included can all help the reader make a judgement about the quality of the 'research' reported.

Teacher research on the web

In recent years, there has been encouragement for teachers and other professionals to carry out small-scale research, with limited funding support from sponsoring organisations. The UK government offered 'Best Practice Research Scholarships' (BPRS) for some years, requiring those receiving the support to produce a report for publication on a website. A good deal of classroom research of this type is now available. The BPRS scheme required the practitioner-researchers to have a research mentor to advise on the project, but the level of research training available within such schemes is usually limited, and the detail required in reports is often minimal. This is quite reasonable, as award holders may well have been deterred by the thought of having to produce a lengthy report at the end of the project, and the research was often of an action research nature where the main aim was to improve practice rather than create new public knowledge (see Chapter 10). There must be a question over the extent to which such limited reports of 'best practice' can inform teaching and learning more widely, but this source of literature can certainly provide ideas and examples for other teachers.

Is the account detailed enough to make further judgements?

The reader of research papers needs to be able to make judgements about the nature, quality and significance of the research reported. Making such judgements requires the report to include sufficient detail of how the focus was conceptualised, what data was collected, and how it was analysed, to be able to decide whether the researcher's findings seem justified.

Data analysis always involves some level of data *reduction*. In studies using quantitative analysis we have to assume that counting, coding and calculating have all been carried out carefully. There are equivalent technical procedures involved in analysing qualitative data. The reader has to trust that coding has been carried out carefully and sensibly, and that fragments of data used to illustrate categories and themes are representative of the wider data set. It is never possible to know for sure how well this work has been done, and so we usually have to assume that researchers are technically competent in these matters if they appear to have followed appropriate procedures.

Box 5.2   When reading an ERP1 study, we need to have enough information to answer questions such as these

Questions we may ask about ERP1 studies might include:

- is the sample size large enough?
- is the sample representative of the population?
- does the data collected address the research question/hypothesis?
- is the statistical test used appropriate for this type of data?
- have the outcomes of statistical tests been clearly presented?
- is it clear how statistical findings are interpreted?
- etcetera

Box 5.3   When reading an ERP2 study, we need to have enough information to answer questions such as these

Questions we may ask about ERP2 studies might include:

- were interviews long enough for in-depth discussion?
- what types of questions were used in interviews?
- did the researchers record informants' comments verbatim?
- how much of the data collected was transcribed?
- how was the data sorted and coded?
- how did the researcher(s) decide when they had sufficient data?
- how did the researcher(s) decide when they had undertaken sufficient analysis?
- etcetera

The reader should, however, be given enough detail in an account to decide whether the types of procedure applied are appropriate. Some examples of the types of questions that the reader should be able to answer from the information given in a paper are given in Boxes 5.2 and 5.3.

Any paper that does *not* allow these types of questions to be answered restricts our ability to judge its quality, and so limits the weight we should give to its findings. Journals are often under pressure to keep papers short (to publish more studies in the available pages), and so editors often look to see if they can persuade authors to make papers concise – and there are often stringent guidelines on paper length (4–6000 words for many journals). This makes it difficult for an author to give a full report of a major research project in the space available. Whilst recognising these constraints, a research report should give sufficient detail to allow readers to know:

what was done;

and why

and how.

If this is not clear, the paper is of limited value as a contribution to knowledge.

Is the account honest?

The reader of educational research has no real way of safeguarding against fraudulent accounts of research, which are occasionally identified. A famous example concerns very influential research on the 'nature versus nurture' debate, where studies into twins who had been separated soon after birth were used to attempt to determine the extent to which such characteristics as 'IQ' were determined by genetic inheritance, and how much by upbringing. Years after these studies became widely reported in textbooks, doubts over the research surfaced. There were questions over how so many pairs of separated twins had been identified for use in the research, why the statistics did not shift in the ways expected as the sample size was increased, and why there was no trace or reliable records of the research assistants who had supposedly collected much of the data.

This type of fraud is probably very rare, as professional researchers who are caught out are likely to lose their jobs, reputations and careers. Studies that are undertaken by researchers from established universities or institutes of similar standing, and that is published in recognised research journals with international editorial/advisory boards, and which use peer-review procedures, are very unlikely to be deliberately dishonest. It would not be impossible to prepare a paper with fabricated data that might seem genuine to reviewers, but this would go against the values and 'epistemological hunger' (or desire to understand and know) that brings most researchers into academic work.

Bias in educational research

A more insidious type of dishonesty concerns the extent to which researchers allow their biases and expectations to flavour their findings. In ERP1, carefully followed procedures should minimise the effects of researcher bias. Although the choice and definition of concepts and categories will limit what could be found in a study, these choices should be clearly stated. This is a much more difficult issue in interpretivist research. One suggestion is that researchers do not assume they can be totally objective, but make their assumptions and expectations explicit, so the reader is aware of the direction that any bias would shift findings. A grounded theory methodology (see the previous chapter) should provide the same types of safeguards against bias as the procedures used in ERP1 research, but only if the full GT process is carefully carried through.

It should also be recognised that many interpretivist researchers would argue that when dealing with the world of ideas, feelings, beliefs etc., there is no objective truth, only the understandings constructed in human minds and through their interactions.

This is a fair point, but where such research claims to explore the ideas, beliefs or understandings of teachers or learners, the reader has a right to expect the research account to be an interpretation that owes more to the informants than the beliefs and opinions of the researcher.

Is the research paper a fraud?

The Nobel prize winning immunologist Sir Peter Medawar (1963/1990) posed the question of whether the scientific paper is a fraud. Medawer was raising the issue of how research in the natural sciences is often reported as if it is a straightforward, linear process. Hypotheses are proposed, tested, supported or refuted – and a neat account is published. The messy reality of crazy conjectures soon ditched, false starts, mistakes, laboratory mix-ups, data lost to contamination, power-failure, computer crashes, or researchers being delayed returning from lunch, and so forth, seldom appears in the account. The result is that the final paper presents a very convincing argument for the smooth path to the findings: how can it have been otherwise?

The contexts of discovery and justification of findings

Interestingly, Medawar did not feel that any of this actually mattered in terms of the findings (although research papers may offer a very poor image of what doing science is actually like). Medawar was drawing upon a recognised distinction between *the context of discovery* and *the context of justification*. In other words, it does not matter how ideas came to be formed, or what false moves were made in exploring them, as long as there is a sound argument for why we should be confident in them.

So, it does not matter (to take an almost mythical example) if the chemist Kekulé came up with the idea for the molecular structure of the compound benzene when he dozed off and had a dream about snakes. This has no significance for whether the structure should be accepted. What does matter is the eventual evidence that led to chemists accepting the structure that Kekulé (quite literally) dreamed-up. Scientists must report *this evidence* accurately and honestly, and in enough detail for it to be checked by other scientists replicating the work. As long as this is done, stories of how they may have started off with a different hypothesis, or perhaps dropped a flask part way through an experiment and had to start again, are not considered relevant and are not reported.

Question for reflection

Medawar was a scientist: can his analysis be applied to research in classrooms?

Subjectivity in research accounts

To a natural scientist (or the teacher with a background in the natural sciences), some research reports in education and other social sciences must seem rather personal compared to the dry, third person, accounts they are used to reading. Many research papers in the social sciences are written in the first person, and have an almost biographical nature. These accounts may include personal feature of history that 'explain' research interests, or include anecdotal material to indicate how hunches arose. False starts, rather than being omitted may even seem to be celebrated in some reports.

This type of writing is not ubiquitous in educational research, but is common in studies from ERP2, where it is recognised that research has a subjective element. If a researcher sees him or herself as an integral part of the context being studied, interacting with the informants in a process of co-constructing data (see Chapter 3) then it makes sense to write an account where the researcher's role is recognised rather than obscured.

Potential conflicts of interest

Question for reflection

Would you believe a study that claimed a computer programme was effective in supporting student learning, if that study was sponsored by the company selling the software?

One related issue is when researchers may be seen to have a 'conflict of interest'. For example, one of the studies mentioned in Chapter 2 (Macaruso et al., 2006) found that computer-based supplementary phonics software enabled students considered to be 'low performing' to catch-up with their classmates. The second author of the paper, Hook, was a consultant involved in the design of the software. The third author, McCabe, was actually the Director of Research and Product Management at the company that developed the software. This is something the reader may wish to bear in mind when reading the study. However, these affiliations are reported at the end of the study, so that the potential 'conflict of interest' is acknowledged. Whilst ideally we might prefer an evaluation of the software that can be seen as independent, the developing company is both prepared to support research into their products (which may not happen otherwise), and presumably highly motivated to use the findings from research to improve and develop their software.

Is the focus appropriately conceptualised in the research?

There are many different ways that a project can be conceptualised. Any research paper will have specific focus (and/or research questions), and the first part of any research account is usually setting the scene for the research by offering a way of thinking about the research context. This introductory section of a paper will explain key ideas that are being used to think about the research, and will discuss existing literature the author thinks especially relevant (see Chapter 3).

The reader may also have a view about how the topic is best understood, and which existing literature provides useful insights into the topic. It can be very thought-provoking to read the work of researchers who see things very differently from yourself, but you may decide not to be influenced by the findings of research which derives from a very different way of understanding the research focus.

Validity

The notion of *validity* is often used to judge research, especially in ERP1. There are different flavours of validity, but basically this is about measuring what you believe you are measuring. For example, a study of boys' and girls' involvement in lessons might measure how often pupils answer the teachers' questions. If it is found that girls answer fewer questions, this could be used to suggest they are less involved in lessons: if we believe that we have used a valid indicator of involvement. A survey of pupils' attitudes to school science might include a question about 'do you think science is interesting?'. Pupils responding might think that the question was about the science they hear about in the news, and not have school lessons in mind when answering. School science is at best an imperfect reflection of Science (Kind and Taber, 2005), so this would invalidate the question as a means of finding out about attitudes to *school* science.

The role of the conceptual framework in making the case

Part of the reason that the conceptualisation stage (see Chapter 3) is so important in research is because of the imperative in writing up studies to 'make the case' – providing readers with a coherent argument that convinces them that the conclusions drawn from a research study (and so the implications for practice that may be recommended) are based on sound logic. It is in the nature of a logical argument that any one single flawed link undermines the whole argument. Yet most research studies are in themselves only able to explore and report a single aspect of an issue.

For example, in Kinchin's (2004) study of students' preferred type of learning environment offered respondents a choice of two caricatured classroom styles. Kinchin (2004: 310) argues that 'a mismatch between teachers' and students' epistemological views is likely to perpetuate problems in the classroom'. This is a reasonable opinion, but is not supported purely by the data presented *in this study*. As is necessarily the case with so many studies, the evidence actually presented offers support for part of an argument, the rest of which relies on findings from other work (and which are built into the conceptual framework for the research presented at the start of the study).

One key way that educational researchers think about their own enquiries is from within a much more extensive conceptual framework (based upon previous research and scholarship) that provides the wider context for their research. It was the physicist Isaac Newton, one of the archetypes of science who (in a seemingly atypically modest comment) suggested that if he had seen further than others it was because he had stood on the shoulders of giants. In this sense, at least, natural science can provide a useful model for research in education – even if within the educational community there may be somewhat less agreement on who our giants actually are.

Is the methodology appropriate?

Decisions about methodology derive from fundamental (paradigmatic) assumptions about the nature of what is being researched, and how knowledge may be generated through research. These assumptions will normally be apparent (either explicitly or implicitly) in the way a topic is conceptualised in the introduction to a research paper. However, if the reader feels that the methodology chosen is inconsistent with the way the topic has been set out in the introduction to a paper, this will limit the degree to which any findings are likely to be considered as addressing the initial research questions/focus.

Are the techniques applied in a technically competent manner?

As suggested above, one has to assume that much of the data handling in a research project has been carried out carefully and proficiently. However, there are technical issues that will be addressed in research reports that should be carefully considered. Statistical tests are usually only applicable to certain types of data, and may require minimum sample sizes. A test that is only valid where a population has a normal ('bell-shaped') distribution may not be informative if applied to bimodal ('two-humped') distribution.

In a similar way, an in-depth analysis of interview data would normally assume that the informants' words were recorded verbatim, and another approach (e.g. the researcher making notes of the interview after the event) may not be considered rigorous enough.

Reliability

There are ways to increase the reliability of some research techniques. For example, in ERP1 research, it is usually assumed that the researcher measures some aspect of a pre-existing reality. In principle, the researcher can be substituted by another without influencing the findings. One way to test this assumption is to check inter-researcher consistency. For example, two researchers could independently use the same observation schedule in the same class, or code the same data into the same categories. This can lead to reliability coefficients, which are closer to 1 when the observers agree. It would normally be expected that although there is inevitably some variation, there should be substantial agreement between researchers.

In some research, the checks of inter-researcher reliability are also used as a way of improving reliability. For example, in coding data, the researchers may all code the same sample independently. They then meet to discuss any disagreements, and argue out which coding category they should use, until they feel they have developed a common understanding of the coding scheme. This is similar to the moderation process used by examination boards to ensure similar standards across examiners.

This type of checking is not possible in a study with a single researcher. It is also less significant in studies where the researcher considers they are co-constructing data with informants (ERP2 approaches), as here the data would be expected to be influenced by the researcher, and inter-researcher reliability is not a relevant consideration. This type of research account is not *fiction*, but it is a personal construction of the researcher – and so as long as we appreciate that, then the personal element does not invalidate the account.

Alternatives to validity and reliability

Indeed, it is sometimes suggested that traditional notions of validity and reliability are not appropriate in interpretivist research, where accounts instead need to be trustworthy and authentic. Although these approaches use different techniques, there are still issues of technical competence in the way that data is collected and analysed.

One important technique often used in ERP2 is 'triangulation' (see Chapter 4). As with validity, this is a term that has many variants of meaning. However, the key point is that data from different sources, and if possible different forms of data, are collected and compared. The researcher would often expect these different sources to offer a coherent picture, and when this is not the case, then the researcher should comment and try to explain the discrepancy. There may be good reasons, for example, why a teacher and learners have different understandings of what happened in the same lesson – or indeed why a 'bully' construes an episode rather differently to the 'victim'. Although consistent interpretations of several 'slices of data' (to use a GT term) do not *ensure* the researcher has made a good job of making sense of the data, the effective use of triangulation gives the reader *more confidence* that the researcher has produced an *authentic* account.

Where research aims to explore the understandings, beliefs, views or experiences of others – such as teachers and learners – it may be possible to show these informants draft accounts of the researcher's reports to get them to comment. This is not always feasible, and there is clearly no assurance that informants will be able to give objective feedback on the extent to which an account does reflect their original contributions. However, it is a useful technique in some studies.

Do the conclusions logically follow from the findings?

A report of research needs to offer a logical argument. The findings of the research need to follow logically from the results – from the analysis of data. Any recommendations (for further research, for good practice) should then follow from the findings in a logical manner.

It might seem a fairly trivial matter to check this, but much educational research has a strong rhetorical flavour (see Chapter 1). It is not unusual for the discussions and conclusion to research papers to mix a consideration of the results of the paper with a range of other considerations (beliefs, opinions, viewpoints). It may well be that recommendations at the end of the paper do logically follow from accepting the presented findings AND all the assumptions leading up to them (about the way the field is conceptualised AND the choice of methodology AND the decisions made when collecting and analysing data) AND other assumptions or beliefs introduced and argued in discussing the findings. The use of capitals here implies that the conclusions are only sound if *each* of the components of the argument are accepted. A reader who is not convinced by these additional considerations could logically accept *the findings* of the study, but still not accept the implications drawn and recommendations made.

The rhetorical function of research: the value of mixed-ability teaching

In a 1999 paper, Lyle reports research that argues for the value of mixed-ability grouping in teaching. In the abstract of Lyle's paper (1999: 283), two claims are made:

1. In analysing the children's comments, it is argued that mixed-ability teaching provides a setting in which both low- and high-achieving students value the opportunity to work together where both groups believed they benefited.
2. The study suggests that interactions among peers can facilitate literacy development in individual children.

Interrogating knowledge claims

There are several points worth noting about these claims. Claim 1 is about the pupils' perceptions: Lyle reports that children of this age value working in mixed groups, and believe they benefit. However, the wording of the claim is noteworthy – it *could be interpreted as meaning that an analysis has been designed to illustrate an existing thesis. This would be a much weaker claim (i.e. if evidence was selected and arranged for such a purpose).*

Claim 2 is about learning, and is somewhat firmer, although phrased with the careful term 'suggests'. However, this is not a claim about the value of mixed-ability groupings. Knowing that peer interactions can help individual children develop their literacy *in itself* tells us nothing about whether we should set up such interactions by organising pupils into mixed ability groups within the class.

As reported in Chapter 4, Lyle's study was an intervention that might be seen as Action Research (AR). There are inherent difficulties in writing up AR, as the 'action' to improve the educational practice takes precedent over a rigorous research design (see Chapter 10). Lyle (1999: 288) provides a good deal of evidence in the form of quotes from two focus group interviews – with those students in the class identified as low attaining pupils, and those identified as 'high-fliers'. The comments made by the pupils quoted in the paper are summarised in Table 5.1.

TABLE 5.1   **Pupil observations in Lyle's 1999 study**

Group	Reported
Both groups	• having someone to break down words, explain word meanings, and suggest words was useful • making new friends
Group 1 (below average attainment)	• group reading was helpful • sharing ideas in group work was useful • the specific activities in the intervention were helpful • that writing activities helped reading and spelling • they had learnt content in the intervention (i.e. geography content related to the materials used) • discussion was a useful way of deciding upon the best idea • group work involved skills such as listening and taking turns
Group 2 ('high fliers')	• the student teachers helped them • helping others can consolidate new learning • helping others may lead to developing strategies that will be useful in one's own learning • helping others may initiate new learning if you need to find out new things to help them • the intervention activities were enjoyable • having an audience in mind is useful when writing • their writing improved during the intervention • they had learnt new curriculum knowledge • learning new concept/concept words • skills such as listening etc., were needed for effective group work • group work helped them achieve more than they could alone • pupils who they had considered stupid were actually nice once you got to know them • group discussion can help identify good ideas

Question for reflection

Which of the reported pupil beliefs provide strong evidence for the effectiveness of mixed ability groups in developing literacy?

This listing of Lyle's findings necessarily paraphrases and simplifies a long section of Lyle's paper offering detailed material from his data, but essentially covers the points made. The evidence presented seems to strongly suggest that the pupils quoted generally found the intervention valuable, and that these pupils did indeed benefit from the mixed-gender, mixed-ability group work with the undergraduate students.

Does Lyle's study demonstrate the benefits of mixed-ability grouping?

There were at least four significant aspects to the intervention:

- the pupils worked in small groups;
- special activities were devised;
- the groups had full-time support of an informed adult helper;
- the groups were mixed-ability.

Many of the positive outcomes could relate to the special activities devised for the group, or the presence of a 'teacher' assigned to the group, or the value of groupwork itself. The mixing of 'abilities' probably *was* valuable as it becomes more likely that weaker readers will have someone who can help them, and the more able can reinforce and consolidate learning by taking on the 'teacher' role. Yet, the study was not set up in a way that enables the reader to know how much additional benefit the grouping strategy provided:

- Perhaps similar ability groups might have had similar or better outcomes?
- Perhaps the use of mixed-gender groups facilitated the smooth running of groups more than the mixing of attainment levels?

The report of the study does not enable the reader to do any more than speculate on these issues.

Question for reflection

Would it be appropriate for a researcher who has strong grounds for believing that students learn more effectively when organised in mixed-ability groups to use similar-ability groups (to compare with mixed-ability groups) in his research?

To what extent must ethical considerations compromise methodological decisions?

In a study such as this, a believer in the educational value of mixed-ability grouping has to balance the ethical imperative (to 'do no harm') against the methodological imperative (a rigorous research design). This issue is discussed further in Chapter 7.

Research writing as rhetoric

In absolute terms Lyle's paper tells us that a particular intervention organised in a particular way, with some pupils in one particular school, was thought by the pupils to be helpful in their learning. The intervention used groups that were judged to be mixed-ability, and that may be a factor in some of the findings. The critical reader may well wonder how Lyle expects to convince the article's audience, given the limitations of the study, that the evidence presented leads to the conclusions offered. Certainly, in terms of the empirical evidence, the logical chain supporting the author's conclusions is delicate.

However, Lyle has not set out to present an account of a rigorous test of the value of mixed-ability grouping, and his study should not be judged in this way. Although the paper reports a research study, it makes little pretence at being an objective, in the sense of disinterested, investigation. Lyle begins the paper by suggesting that government guidance encouraging setting is not supported by research, and then reviews literature that demonstrates limitations and problems of grouping pupils in this way.

Lyle's study (1999: 294–5) is conceptualised (see Chapter 3) from a socio-cultural perspective, where learning is seen in terms of facilitating conditions where teachers and students can co-construct meaning. Lyle argues that collaboration with peers changes the contributions of the individual children in the class, and recommends that when planning their lessons teachers should consider how they will group children as well as which activities they will provide. The gist of Lyle's argument is that teachers should 'adopt practices that allow children to use talk as a meaning-making tool in collaborative settings'.

The study is then set within a *rhetorical* context that is designed to make an argument that government preference for setting may be ill informed, and that schools and teachers should not accept this view uncritically. The author sees his task as one of persuading readers of the potential value of mixed-ability grouping despite official guidance suggesting grouping by ability improves achievement.

So Lyle does not present disembodied findings, but rather interprets his data in terms of theoretical ideas from the underpinning conceptual framework supporting the research. In other words, Lyle makes claims that cannot be directly shown to follow from the data presented:

> As the children either read, or listened to each other reading, each was involved in actively construing and interpreting the text. Subsequent discussion mediated the higher function of reading for meaning, as the children reflected on their thinking together.
>
> (Lyle, 1999: 293)

Lyle did not collect data to demonstrate these points *directly* (the pupils' comments were not framed in terms of 'construing', 'higher cognitive functions' and 'reflection'), but rather he presents this as a reasonable interpretation from within the conceptual framework used in the research.

Caveat emptor

The reader of educational research is invited to 'buy into' the story being told by the author of the account. It is the author's responsibility to make the case for any conclusions offered. However, it is the reader's responsibility to check the argument proposed. Inevitably any argument presented in an educational research study will in part depend upon data, and in part upon the interpretation of that data – an interpretation that draws upon the author's conceptual framework.

In some examples of ERP1 research, where hypotheses are tested, research writing is expected to be largely objective, following the model idealised (if not always achieved) in the natural sciences. In natural science, research is influenced by values relating to objectivity, accuracy, transparency in reporting, etc.

However, much writing in education is not disinterested, but is informed by other values, for example relating to social justice. It is quite legitimate for a researcher to take such a stance (if education is not based in our values, then it may be considered to have little value), and to use research in support of their own beliefs. As a reader of educational research, it is important that we are aware when this is happening, and can learn to identify the chain of argument for any research claim. Lyle's study would seem substantially flawed from the standards of experimental research. However, Lyle is quite open about his own beliefs, and allows the reader to clearly see the extent to which his interpretations derive from the data or from his own conceptual framework. This is common in ERP2 studies, where it is considered difficult for a researcher to be an objective observer of phenomena (see Chapter 3). The important criterion here is that the research should present the work honestly, making the subjective elements as explicit as possible, so that the reader can make up their own minds about the soundness of the underpinning values supporting the work. Where this is done, such as in Lyle's study, it is perfectly legitimate to write rhetorical papers.

What makes for effective teacher development?

Garet and colleagues (2001) report an American study, published in the *American Educational Research Journal*, which explored teachers' perceptions of the type of professional development courses that were effective. They claimed in their paper that certain 'structural features' of the courses were important, including the form of the activity, the collective participation of teachers who shared professional concerns (e.g. teachers of the same subject, or grade level, or from the same school), and the duration of the activity (Garet et al., 2001: 916).

Garet et al. (2001: 916) claimed that the core features of 'professional development activities that have significant, positive effects on teachers' *self reported* increases in knowledge and skills and changes in classroom practice' were:

- a focus on content knowledge ('our results confirm the importance of professional development that focuses on [subject] content');
- opportunities for active learning;
- coherence with other learning activities (Garet et al., 2001: 936).

(It is interesting to note that we might well make the last two points about children's learning in schools.)

Garet et al. (2001: 919) report that their study was based on a 'Teacher Activity Survey', where they 'surveyed a nationally representative sample of teachers' who had attended professional development (PD) activities supported by a major sponsor. They reported 'receiving responses from 1027 teachers…an overall teacher response rate of 72%'. The findings were based on 'self-reports of teacher experiences and behaviour'.

Garet et al.'s (2001: 919, 929) report of their study explains:

- How they selected their sample;
- How they designed the questionnaire to elicit information about 'structural' and 'core' features of PD activities;
- How they identified effective PD activities ('We asked each teacher in our national sample to indicate the degree to which his or her knowledge and skills were enhanced … to what extent they made changes in their teaching practices…').

Question for reflection

How would you position Garet et al.'s (2001) study in terms of the two educational research 'paradigms' introduced in Chapter 3?

Garet et al.'s knowledge claims are based on a statistical analysis of teacher responses to different items in the questionnaire used for the survey (2001: 915–16). By comparing responses to items related to various aspects of the types of PD received, and the perceived effectiveness of the PD activities, the researchers were able to conclude that certain types of features made the professional development activities more effective.

In considering Garet and colleagues' claims we need to consider both strengths and limitations of the study. The sample size and the response rate are both encouraging features. The published report offers a good deal of detail about how the sample was constructed, and how the questionnaire was designed and how the analysis was undertaken. All of this gives the reader confidence that this was a competently undertaken study, i.e. one that should be considered to offer valuable knowledge.

Input constrains output

However, there are two *inherent* limitations in this study. The first concerns the overall epistemological stance of the authors. Their research is clearly situated in the educational research paradigm described in Chapter 3 as 'confirmatory' (i.e. ERP1). Garet and colleagues built into their questionnaire items that asked teachers about specific, specified features of the PD activities they had attended. These features had been selected by a reading of the literature, and so were limited to features that had already been identified as potentially being important. Such an approach is not able to identify any other features teachers considered significant, but which they were not asked about in the questionnaire.

Links in a chain

The second limitation is that the survey did not include any independent measure of the effectiveness of the PD (e.g. such as an Inspector or school principal judging any change in teaching). The perceptions of potential key features of PD were related to the teachers' own perceptions of any changes in their teaching. So the survey was able to relate features of PD to teacher perceptions of PD effectiveness – but the survey only informs the reader about the effectiveness of PD activities *to the extent that teachers reported perceptions* are reliable (and honest) indicators of changes in their thinking and teaching.

This is not to suggest that teachers are not offering accurate judgements – but (as we often find) a particular research study is only able to offer evidence for part of the chain of logic needed for a convincing argument. In this study the reader has to make assumptions about links that are not directly addressed (the availability in existing literature of the most relevant factors to include in the survey; the correlation between teacher reports and actual changes in teacher skills and classroom behaviours) to be convinced that the findings do tell us about the most significant features of effective PD activities – at least in the US context where the survey was undertaken.

Interpreting statistical findings

McClune's (2001) paper indicating that modular examinations may put students at a relative disadvantage (see Chapter 4) offers a detailed account of how he went about his research, and designed his sample, and accessed and analysed data. McClune demonstrated differences between the attainment of first and second year A level students in his sample that, overall at least, were unlikely to be due to chance. He took reasonable measures to ensure that the two groups were not wildly different in terms of previous academic success.

Although McClune's study took care in sampling students, the findings relate to the common questions in one year's examinations for one examination board, in one A level subject. (Even in this limited context the study represented a considerable undertaking.) Despite the careful way the study has been conducted and reported, it cannot be considered to have *proved* that in general that students following modular courses are (always) disadvantaged compared with students taking linear courses. It is still possible that:

- significant results are due to the random sampling (unlikely, but therefore by definition *possible*);
- the academic abilities of the two groups were different in some way not uncovered;
- there may be other relevant differences between the two year groups that have not been considered;

- the findings were an artefact of the particular common questions in that year's examination;
- the findings may relate to some aspect of the way this particular examination board sets and marks papers;
- the findings may not be generalisable to other subjects.

This is not a criticism of the research, which is presented here as an example of a well executed and documented 'experimental' study, but an observation on the inherent limitations of any single research enquiry.

Has the research been conducted ethically?

Educational research should follow ethical guidelines (such as those provided by the British Educational Research Association – BERA, 2004). It is important that educational research does not harm or distress students, teachers or others who may be asked to help with out research. Ethical issues are especially sensitive for teachers who are conducting research in their own classrooms as the dual role of teacher-researcher complicates the relationship with informants (Taber, 2002). Key aspects of undertaking ethical research are discussed in Chapter 7. In terms of reading research, readers must take a view about any paper they find which they consider includes data obtained unethically. Disregard for ethical standards tarnishes research, and some would argue that anyone using knowledge obtained in this way is implicitly condoning the unethical approach, signalling that such ways of working are acceptable. Others would argue that disregarding knowledge obtained through such research is to confuse means and ends, and that the inconvenience or discomfort of informants is compounded if the research outcomes are discounted. Readers are not offered direction on this point, but should consider these matters when reading material they consider to have been created through unethical procedures.

6

Teachers Evaluating Research Relevance

This chapter looks at how teachers can learn from reading research, especially in terms of informing their own classroom practice.

In Chapter 5 it was suggested that when evaluating studies, we need to ask ourselves a number of questions:

- is the account detailed enough to make further judgements?
- is the account honest?
- is the focus appropriately conceptualised in the research?
- is the methodology appropriate?
- are the techniques applied in a technically competent manner?
- do the conclusions logically follow from the findings?

If the answers to these questions are 'yes' then the teacher who is interested in *applying* research findings will also want to know:

- 'does it apply here?'

Readers have to be able to judge the extent to which the findings from studies may be transferred from the context of the study, to the context in which the reader is working.

Transfer of knowledge – does it apply here?

A key issue in reading an account of a research study is deciding whether it is relevant to our own context. In Chapter 5 some key questions were suggested which will help judge the quality of research accounts. However, even a high-quality study may have little to offer to inform a very different educational context.

The term 'generalise' is often used to describe how research applies beyond the specific original context. There are different ways of interpreting generalisability, and two common concepts will be discussed.

Question for reflection

How do approaches to building samples (or selecting cases) influence the generalisability of research findings?

The reader may find it useful to review the ideas about sampling in Chapter 4 before proceeding.

Statistical generalisability

Research studies that sample larger populations look for statistical generalisability. This means that the sampling techniques used are designed to ensure that the results obtained when analysing data collected from the sample allow inferences to be made about the wider population.

So, for example, a survey of teenage girls' attitudes to participating in PE lessons in school would collect data from a sample of teenage girls. If the sample was large enough, and representative enough of the wider population, then it is possible to make statistical generalisations. If it was found that 12% of the teenage girls wanted to avoid PE lessons because they found them embarrassing, then (given a representative sample, etc.) it would be possible to assess how precisely that sample figure would be reflected in the larger population. Similar techniques are very common in public opinion polls, for example near elections, when the actual percentages of the sample giving different responses are quoted with a likely sample error (e.g. ± 2%). The larger the sample size used, the more precisely the sample results should respond to the results that could have been obtained had it been possible to ask the whole population of interest. However, this always assumes there are no biases in the make up of the sample. A sample comprising girls who had all brought notes to excuse them from PE lessons could not be considered representative of teenage girls in general.

Reader generalisability

Individual teachers or students, particular classes or schools, are like many other teachers or students, or classes or schools in *some* senses. Yet, each teacher or learner or class or lesson is also in many ways unique. Statistical techniques are used to help draw general conclusions about typical, average or common aspects of specific populations (maintained 11–16 city schools; gifted pupils in French classes; special needs coordinators in secondary schools, etc.). Where these studies attempt to balance out individual differences, interpretivist studies (see Chapter 3) may deliberately emphasise them.

Many interpretive studies do not work with large sample sizes, and indeed may select participants to study for theoretical reasons (because they provide interesting cases) that value the uniqueness of the individual case rather than see them as a representative of a larger population.

A case study of a lesson, for example, will present a detailed account of that lesson, hoping to provide the reader with as much of the context as possible to provide an *authentic* account that helps the reader understand that lesson. Conclusions drawn from the lesson may help us understand other lessons that may be similar. The difficulty is in knowing *how similar* that lesson may be to our own lessons.

The researcher needs to provide enough context ('thick description') – of the students, of the physical environment, of the teacher–class rapport, of the subject matter, etc. – for a reader to make a judgement about how likely it is that insights drawn from that particular case may be useful in understanding the lessons that we are interested in (as teachers, as researchers, as appraisers of teachers, etc.). This is called *reader generalisability*, because the reader has to decide. Both the researcher and the reader have responsibilities in this process.

Judgements of relevance rely upon the person making the judgement having a good understanding of both contexts. The researcher cannot be expected to know about the reader's context of interest, and so it is only the reader who can make the judgement. However, the researcher has a responsibility to provide a detailed, balanced and carefully composed account of the research context that can provide the reader with the basis for making a judgement.

Transfer between contexts: SRL

In a 2004, study Corrigan and Taylor suggested requirements for promoting self-regulated learning (SRL). They described their sample as 'purposeful': '6 volunteer participants (5 female and 1 male) … intended to reflect the views of a range of students with different performance levels within the SRL project'.

Developing self-regulated learning is an important goal for schools, and this is closely linked with the currently popular 'assessment for learning' and 'pupil voice' movements. School teachers will want to learn from research about how to best encourage their students to develop more independence as learners. Studies on this topic are therefore to be welcomed.

Corrigan and Taylor offer some suggestions for the conditions that are likely to encourage self-regulated learning; however, the reader looking for research to support evidence-based practice has to decide whether this study offers any relevant findings. Even though we may believe (a) that Corrigan and Taylor are highly competent and skilled researchers, and (b) that their findings do represent a valid interpretation of the data they collected, the critical reader will still wish to ask about the extent to which these findings could apply elsewhere – i.e. can they be generalised?

Degrees of separation?

In their paper the authors are quite clear that *their* focus is 'the effectiveness of SRL as a pedagogy for use with pre-service primary teachers' (Corrigan and Taylor, 2004: 51), and their data derived from one sample drawn from one cohort of trainee teachers in one institution. Although the study cannot possibly be considered to demonstrate beyond doubt that these conditions would work with other trainee primary teachers (in other cohorts, in other institutions), none the less it would seem reasonable for other teacher-trainers to consider that the findings *may well* also apply in their own professional contexts.

The further a context is removed from that of the original study, however, the less confidence we might have in the findings being relevant. Trainee teachers are mature individuals, highly motivated in their studies, who have previously learnt to be successful students in school, who clearly value learning, and are in the process of learning a lot more about learning itself. This does not apply to students in primary or secondary schools, or even to many students in further education. Teachers working with students at these levels might well consider Corrigan and Taylor's study to offer useful ideas for testing out in their own classrooms; they would, however, be ill-advised to assume that the types of strategies recommended in this study can non-problematically be transferred to very different settings and applied to 'learners' in general.

Findings, generalisations and mechanisms

As a reader of educational research it is important to be able to distinguish between three types of information that researchers will present through their papers.

Many research papers present:

- Findings: what we found out in this context from these informants;
- Generalisations: what we think this might tell us about a wider set of contexts or the wider population we think our sample represents;
- Conjectured mechanisms: what we think is going on here.

These are all perfectly legitimate features of a research report: they all contribute to the author telling the story of the research; making the case; and teaching about their understanding/models of the phenomena studied. However, sometimes authors (inadvertently or deliberately) do not cleanly separate these features, and the reader must be alert to the transitions from what had been found, to what this might suggest, to why we think this could be going on. (It may be useful at this point to review the discussion of Lyle's study in Chapter 5).

Why are modular exams a bad idea?

One of the studies referred to in Chapter 2 was a paper in the journal *Educational Research*, where McClune (2001) argues that students following modular courses (where some of the credit for final grade is awarded for examination papers taken early in the course) may be disadvantaged compared with students taking linear courses for the same award, and being examined on all aspects of the course in terminal examinations.

McClune's research design is considered in Chapter 4. Here it was reported that he found a difference in the average examination scores on a set of questions between 406 students taking their terminal examination and 346 students answering the same questions during a modular examination half-way through their course.

McClune had built his sample so that the two groups were considered to be comparable (see Chapter 4) and inferential statistics suggest that the differences in average performance found can be assumed to represent differences that would probably apply to the wider populations (statistical generalisation). This means that we would expect that – all other things being equal – a student would be likely to get a better score on these questions if taken as part of a terminal rather than a modular examination.

Theoretical generalisation ...?

However, there is a second, different type of generalisation being made. Statistical techniques can tell us that different samples from the wider populations were likely to give similar results, but statistics cannot tell us whether similar findings would have been found:

- on different questions;
- in an examination set by a different board using different styles of questions; or
- in a different examination subject.

Yet McClune writes about his research findings as though they tell us something about terminal and modular examination *in general*. We can consider this to be a kind of 'theoretical' generalisation, as it is based upon the conceptual framework supporting the research design.

This type of transition is very common in research reports, and is quite appropriate: it is important that researchers offer the bigger picture that shows readers why their findings might be important for our practice. (But *the reader* needs to be careful to recognise this shift.)

... is supported by a feasible mechanism

This transition is linked to something else McClune offers in discussing his results: an interpretation of what might be going on. McClune suggests the differences found (between the examination performance of the two groups of students in the analysis) could be due to the increased maturity and examination skills of the older students, and/or the increased opportunities to consolidate learning about the examined material during the two-year course.

This is not something that could possibly be supported *by the findings themselves*: the data collection and analysis does not concern these matters. Rather the author is offering feasible mechanisms as a conceptual framework within which the results make sense. Indeed, these considerations may be considered as part of the initial conceptualisation of the research: concerns that led to the hypothesis being tested.

All of this is perfectly valid and proper. The author has a responsibility to give enough detail, and a clear enough account, to enable the reader to distinguish what was found in the specific research context, what the author thinks this might mean more widely, and how the author makes (sic) sense of the findings.

We should also be aware of the rhetorical value of the suggested mechanisms in generalising the significance of the research. If we accept that McClune's suggestions may well explain *why* there was a difference between the two experimental groups, then we are more likely to accept (on theoretical rather than purely 'logical' grounds) that we can generalise his findings to other contexts where increased maturity, increased examination skills and greater opportunities consolidating learning may apply. In other words, it helps McClune make his case that his specific findings may have *general* relevance when comparing modular and terminal examinations.

Section 3
Learning through Educational Research

As pointed out in Chapter 1, there is an increasing expectation that teachers should be able to undertake small-scale empirical classroom studies to inform their own practice. Research students on MEd, MA, MPhil and PhD courses are expected to show they can competently carry out all stages of such research – but increasingly trainee teachers on PGCE courses are also expected to undertake small research projects.

This section offers advice on the process of undertaking small-scale classroom research, building on the familiarity with educational research provided by Section 1, and an awareness of how we judge the quality of studies, that draws upon the principles discussed in Section 2.

This section has four chapters concerned with planning the research, and ensuring it meets ethical standards (Chapter 7); collecting the data (Chapter 8); analysing the data (Chapter 9); and reporting research (Chapter 10). As earlier in the book, key points are illustrated by drawing upon examples from published studies. It is not possible to offer a thorough handbook for carrying out research in an introductory volume, and I would advise research students to consider this section (supported by the prior reading of Sections 1 and 2) as your *initial* guidance, to help you plan and conceptualise reading of more detailed texts on matters such as data collection and analysis techniques.

For practising teachers, looking to make the first tentative steps towards practitioner-research, the following chapters should offer sufficient guidance for the moment. However, if you 'get the bug' and come to view being a fully professional teacher as implying being a teacher-as-researcher (with classroom enquiry as an intrinsic part of teaching), then you will find there are many more detailed books available to help you develop into a more sophisticated classroom practitioner-researcher.

7

Teachers Planning Research

Approaching practitioner research

This chapter offers advice to the teacher looking to undertake their own classroom enquiry, whether purely for informing their own practice or as part of course requirements at higher degree level (PGCE, MEd, etc.). In Section 1, we saw how research should always start from a consideration of basic assumptions, as these inform decisions about the type of research strategy (methodology) to choose. It will have been clear from the examples of published studies discussed in the book that our basic assumptions influence all that follows in the research process. This chapter then takes the reader through the stages of planning their classroom research, and highlights the various decisions that need to be made during the planning process.

The focus

The first stage of any research project is to identify the focus (see Chapter 3). This will be an issue that is considered to warrant close attention. For professional educational researchers, the research focus often derives either from suggestions in the existing published literature, or from their own previous research. Such researchers are often working in a 'research programme', where individual studies both derive from and lead to further research (see Chapter 1). Each study is one part of an ongoing incremental programme gradually exploring and developing understanding of a theme. This is one reason why many small-scale educational research studies that are published in the literature can seem to be highly flawed when considered individually. Often an individual study depends heavily for its rationale on other related studies. Findings from any individual study may seem tentative and highly contextualised *unless* seen as a single piece in a large 'jig-saw'.

For the teacher-researcher, the focus often seems to suggest itself. Certainly, *action research* (AR, see Chapter 4) is often considered to be research that is undertaken to explore and ultimately improve some aspect of the professional context. So for a classroom teacher undertaking research, there is often a very strong professional motivation as the research is about solving a perceived problem, or improving some aspect of professional work which is considered to be sub-optimal. Even if a study is being undertaken as part of course requirements (e.g. for a PGCE or masters course), it makes sense to identify an area where there are clear grounds for believing that research could potentially inform improvements for the teacher(s) and learners involved.

There are many possible foci for practitioner research, but there are few examples of the kinds of issues that might motivate research:

- test results indicate that understanding of a particular topic is disappointing;
- learners indicate that they find the materials used to teach a particular topic to be uninspiring (they are more likely to use the term 'boring');
- the teacher feels that boys in the class volunteer answers to questions much more than the girls;
- learners in a class are very competitive about marks/scores received, but make little effort to act on specific feedback given;
- the teacher is concerned that lessons are insufficiently differentiated to both support and challenge the wide-range of abilities present;
- published research indicates that learners are likely to misunderstand key concepts in a topic as many come to class with existing intuitive beliefs that are inconsistent with curriculum knowledge;
- very few students wish to continue studying the subject once it ceases to be compulsory.

What do we already know about this?

Whatever the focus selected, it is unlikely that a body of research does not already exist that would seem to be relevant. Clearly, it is usually helpful to find out what is already known about a topic, before starting out on research. Even if we believe that the focus is contextualised in such a way that findings from elsewhere may not be applicable, it is useful to look at what others have done, and what they have found, to inform our own work.

Ideally we would search out, read and evaluate all relevant prior research. This is certainly expected (in principle) at doctoral level, although will normally be considered unrealistic in smaller-scale research. For the busy practitioner, there may be problems of access to libraries and time for reading: none the less, time spent identifying, reading and considering the most relevant studies can be invaluable in informing practitioner-research.

Keeping records of material read, and summary notes of key points (e.g. developing an annotated bibliography of sources) is useful, but if a report is needed with a literature review then time will need to be spent developing an overview or synthesis of the research. (See the section on research conceptualisation in Chapter 3.)

Forming research questions

A common approach to moving from a research focus to planning a research study is by the development of one or more research questions. These research questions should be informed by the conceptual framework developed from reading previous research, and will inevitably be informed by our understandings of the nature of the phenomena being studied and the type of knowledge educational research can develop (see Chapter 3).

It is worth pointing out here that there are two basic types of questions that can be asked, reflecting two main types of approach to educational research (as discussed in Chapter 3).

Question for reflection

How might you expect research questions in ERP2 studies to differ in form from those in ERP1 studies?

A good research question guides your research plan and gives you a basis for later evaluating whether your research has been useful, and so needs to have some level of specificity. However, in some ('provisional', 'exploratory') studies, research questions are quite open-ended.

Hypotheses and research questions

ERP1 research which is 'positivistic', following the experimental model derived from the physical sciences, will often be set up with the kind of question that looks for a definitive 'yes'/'no' response. For example, consider one of the issues given above:

- the teacher feels that boys in the class volunteer answers to questions much more than the girls.

It may be that there are at least as many girls in the class as boys, and that it is so rare for the girls to put their 'hands-up' to volunteer to answer questions that the teacher has little doubt there is a real issue here.

However, we might ask what if the situation was less clear-cut, and the teacher *had a strong feeling* that girls were under-represented in volunteering answers to questions, but could not be sure if this was a real issue. One possible approach in this case might be to consider the teacher's belief as a testable hypothesis:

- girls in the class volunteer answers to my questions significantly less often than the boys.

Alternatively, the same point may be phrased in terms of what is called the 'null' hypothesis:

- there is no significant difference in the extent to which the two genders volunteer answers to my questions in class.

When put in this form, the hypothesis can be tested, although this may not be straightforward.

Question for reflection

Before reading on, it may be useful for you to consider how this question might be tested, and what the difficulties associated with this might be.

Exploratory research questions

If the teacher was sufficiently convinced that there was indeed an issue of girls not volunteering answers in class (either because the difference is so obvious, or because the hypothesis has now been tested), then this raises further questions:

- why do the girls volunteer answers significantly less than the boys?
- what can I do to ensure the girls are contributing in lessons as much as the boys?

These are much more open-ended questions, that do not invite 'yes'/ 'no' type answers, and cannot be set up as testable hypotheses. (Of course, a study that explored '*why* do the girls volunteer answers significantly less than the boys?' might well identify a range of candidate factors, which might *then* lead to further research questions that could be set up as hypotheses.)

Notice that the first question here is about *understanding* the teaching–learning context, and the second is about *improving* it. For a study to be considered as action research it would usually be expected to be intended to change the research context for the better, but it may only be possible to answer the 'what can I do?' question once the 'why?' question has been explored.

Question for reflection

Imagine you were undertaking a small-scale study and had chosen this issue as your focus. Your project advisor has strongly warned against taking on too much, and advises that in the time available you should limit your study to the 'why?' question and not also investigate what might improve the girls' participation. Does this negate the value of the study? Does it become a completely 'academic' exercise without any useful outcomes?

We might even see this sequence of questions as a mini-research programme: moving from confirming there is a problem, exploring the nature of the problem, and testing possible solutions.

The middle stage of this 'programme' is about exploring why girls in this particular class do not volunteer answers in class. There may be a range of answers to this question, and we should bear in mind that:

- just because girls are offering to answer questions less in this class, that does not mean this is a gender issue *per se* – it may relate to some other characteristic that happens to correlate with gender in *this particular* class (see the discussion of generalisation in Chapter 6);
- just because girls are participating less in terms of offering to answer questions in class, that does not mean that the girls are participating less overall – there may be different patterns of participation for the boys and girls, with the reluctance to publicly give answers compensated in other ways (Taber, 1992).

As always, classroom teaching and learning are complex phenomena. Finding out why the girls are volunteering to answer questions less than the boys would help us re-examine whether this really is a problem of girls' lack of participation, and will suggest ideas about how to respond to improve participation if that is still deemed appropriate.

At this point it could be that the teacher and class part company, after the focal issue has been explored, but before there is a chance to try out any kind of intervention. In this situation, the research programme comes to an unfortunate stop. If the teacher-researcher is undertaking the study as an *academic* course requirement then the data collected will still support the assignment or thesis. However, it could be asked whether the research has any value if there is no opportunity to apply what has been found out in the classroom.

This is a genuine concern. Research has costs. The teacher's time and effort may be considerable, and often (if not always) a study makes some additional demands on students. If learners have given up time to act as informants then there is an ethical dimension that needs to be considered, i.e. how does a teacher justify asking students to provide information for research purposes if that research is unlikely to have benefits for those informants?

A key consideration here would be the extent to which the new knowledge developed through the study was likely to be of value in another context:

- If what has been found out about the class is only likely to be of practical value to that teacher when teaching that class, then the value of the research is limited;
- If the insights gained can be of value to another teacher taking over the class, or to the teacher-researcher in working with 'similar' classes in the future, then the research can have more value;
- If the research uncovers insights that are likely to be relevant to a wide range of teachers and classes, then it has *the potential* to be useful well beyond its initial context.

Ethical concerns are important in education, and for teacher-researchers are complicated by the dual-role. Ethical issues are discussed in more detail later in this chapter.

Where a study has wider relevance, its value remains 'potential' unless and until it is disseminated. For research to be transferred to new contexts, then other teachers have to know about it, and appreciate its usefulness. So, no matter how *potentially* transferable a study may be, it can only have an impact if it is communicated. The issue of reporting research is the theme of Chapter 10.

From questions to research plans

A good research question (whether a formal hypothesis to test, or a more open-ended question) provides a focus that should inform the research plan, and any subsequent evaluating and reporting of the research. However, even an apparently clear question may need some additional clarification. For example, considering how to test the hypothesis used as an example above ('there is no significant difference in the extent to which the two genders volunteer answers to my questions in class') leads to a number of complications.

In everyday life, language is used flexibly and in a fluid way – with word meanings taking on nuances depending on context. Each individual person has a unique variant of their language – none of us have exactly the same vocabulary, or the same precise understanding of what shared words means. In conversation this can lead to misunderstandings, but the very inter-subjective nature of conversation – what Bruner (1987) calls constant transactional calibration – *usually* allows us to communicate meaning *well enough*. In a legal context, when drawing up contracts, that would *not* be considered sufficient, and it is important to ensure different parties appreciate exactly the same meanings. This is done by using a technical formalism with well-established terms, and by defining anything that might be ambiguous.

Similar considerations apply in research. (Remember, one of our metaphors for writing-up research is the legal advocate.) Even in a simple statement there are likely to be potential areas of ambiguity. These need to be clarified by using accepted formalisms, or defining terms. For example, Petri and Niedderer (1998) used the term 'learning pathway' in their research, and needed to explain to their readers exactly what they meant by this term (see Chapter 3).

We all know what we mean by saying something is 'significant' in everyday usage, but when reporting research findings this is usually expected to imply *statistical* significance (see Chapter 4).

Some problems with testing hypotheses

The term 'significant difference' has a technical meaning when used in research. In effect, it means that some accepted statistical technique has been used, and has suggested that any differences between two sets of data are unlikely to be due to chance alone. Usually the meaning is actually more specific than that – that the difference is only likely to occur less than once on twenty occasions by chance (often represented as '$p < 0.05$').

Much educational research (i.e. from ERP1) uses statistical approaches to test hypotheses in this way, but there are a number of pitfalls that the teacher-researcher should be aware of:

- there are a range of common statistical tests, and all have to be applied following strict procedures for any results to be valid;
- for some tests these procedures include randomisation (e.g. of students to different 'treatments') that may be difficult to follow (see Chapter 4);
- different tests are appropriate for different kinds of data, and some tests only apply if data has a certain type of 'distribution' so that the test is only strictly valid if the data have been shown to fit the pattern (by using other tests);
- a statistically significant result can still be due to chance: if a study involved a great many comparisons and identified many significant results it is quite likely that some are just due to chance (and there is no way of knowing which);
- a result which does not reach statistical significance may still be important, even though it is not unlikely enough to be judged 'significant';
- a *statistically* significant result may be a very small effect which has minimal importance;
- large data sets are often needed to identify statistically significant outcomes.

Inferential statistics: powerful, but specialised

This is not to say that there are no situations where the classroom teacher can use inferential statistics: but such an approach does require an understanding of the available tests and their ranges of application, and is only likely to be of value where large enough data sets are available to make identifying any significant factors possible. If in doubt, it is best to avoid inferential statistics. Although statistical tests may be carried out with pencil-and-paper (supported by a calculator with basic statistical functions), it is more common these days to use a computer-based package such as 'SPSS' (Muijs, 2004). When using such a tool it is useful to bear in mind the adage 'garbage in, garbage out': the machine will perform calculations but cannot do the thinking for you, and the computer should only be used to analyse data according to your research design. In particular, student studies that involve testing for relationships between every possible combination of variables almost invariably lead to the machine producing 'false positives' (see Chapter 4) and suggest research that is not informed by a strong conceptual framework.

Descriptive statistics: straightforward, but less informative

Descriptive statistics (such as reporting means, ranges, percentages) are much easier to use, but do not allow inferences to be drawn. For example, if a teacher kept records of when students volunteered answers in class over a two-week period and found that 41% of the time it was girls offering answers, and 59% of the time it was boys, then this would allow the teacher to report that in absolute terms the boys volunteered answers more often. This descriptive statistic is of interest, but cannot *in itself* tell us anything about whether this might have just been a chance effect that is likely to be reversed if the study was repeated. This could still be indicative enough to encourage the teacher to investigate why pupils in the class did or did not tend to volunteer answers, perhaps looking to see if any gender-related effect could be found. If follow-up work found that a number of the girls reported being intimidated by the boys in the group, then the descriptive statistics would have been useful as part of the 'programme' of research.

Defining terms

Even if the meaning of the term *statistically significant* is defined for us, we still have to ensure we are clear about what we mean by other terms in our research question. For example, it may seem obvious what we mean by 'the teacher's questions' and 'volunteering answers', but if we are to collect data that rely on these terms we should spend time clarifying them. In a study where several researchers collect data it is important that they all know what such terms mean, but even in a single-researcher study we need to be precisely clear about what 'counts' as 'a question' (for example), before we set out to collect data. (You may feel we all know how to recognise a question: but time spent observing classroom interactions is likely to demonstrate that this is not so clear-cut.) This will also help us communicate to others in due course exactly what we have done.

This is not simply a pedantic matter. If when classifying classroom interaction, we limit 'volunteering an answer' to cases where students put their 'hands-up' we may come to different conclusions than if we include 'calling out'. (This is avoided when we've persuaded all the students to always put their hands up: otherwise it is quite conceivable, for example, that girls and boys could put hands-up to a similar extent, but classroom interactions could be dominated by boys if they call out answers more.) We would also need to decide if we wish to define a boundary around the context of the 'questions' we are counting: are we interested in all questions ('can anyone see the board rubber?'; 'was that the bell?'; 'didn't I tell you to stop chatting?'; 'are you chewing?') or are we actually only interested in questions relating to the subject-matter of the class. In different research studies, we might take a different view of this.

This is not a minor point: a significant proportion of teacher–student interactions in some classrooms can concern administrative, procedural and social agendas rather than the 'academic' content of the lesson (Taber, 1992). This is not a criticism, as such interactions may have important functions supporting teaching and learning, but it is quite possible that participation in these different aspects of lessons may vary according to gender. A class where girls answered less questions purely because they were less often the focus of disciplinary enquiries ('are you paying attention?') raises different issues to one where the girls are less involved in discussing the subject matter. Similarly, if the girls 'participate' in teacher–student interactions to the same extent as boys, but a much higher proportion of these interactions concern 'housekeeping' matters (distributing books and materials, tidying-up) there may still be reason for concern.

Exploratory research

This may lead the reader to ask how they will know how to define the key terms in their research question(s). Often this comes from reading the literature reporting studies of similar phenomena. However, it may often be the case that it is not possible to be sure what exactly one is looking for until one has started looking. Research that is looking at a topic that has not been well studied (or at least not in comparable contexts) may be *exploratory* – looking to see how to best refine and define research questions.

In their 2004 study into self-regulated learning (SRL) Corrigan and Taylor describe their work as an 'exploratory research inquiry' (2004: 51), and suggest that such an approach would be most appropriate because (a) a quantitative approach would be 'of limited use' in view of their small sample size (six trainee primary teachers), and (b) as they 'wished to gain an in-depth understanding of the effectiveness of SRL as a pedagogy…' (2004: 51).

This type of research can be very useful (for example, at the start of a research programme), although it may not always be an advisable approach when classroom enquiry is undertaken as a course requirement. The danger of exploratory research is that it is difficult to know in advance what, if anything, will result. An enquiry with a more specific focus, and a pre-defined research question, is more likely to lead to a suitable assignment report (if not always being the most productive way of learning something useful about the classroom).

Whatever approach is taken, it is usually a good idea to undertake some *pilot* work to try out data collection and analysis techniques and make sure that the research plan will provide the type of data needed. This allows the opportunity to revise the plan before too much time and effort have been committed to an approach that does not lead to the type of data needed.

The research plan

The identification of a focus, and the framing of a research question, informs the development of a research plan. Such plans vary considerably in their level of detail.

Question for reflection

How would you expect research plans for ERP1 and ERP2 studies to compare?

Well-specified research designs

At one extreme, hypothesis-testing should follow a well-specified procedure. The research plan should show exactly what data is to be collected (the type of data, how much, how collected, the schedule), and how it is to be analysed (the specific statistical test(s) to be applied). There is limited flexibility in such a plan, as any attempt to change procedures once the process is underway may be considered to undermine the validity of the research. The type of test to be used will depend on the nature of the data, and the amount of data needed will depend on the test to be used. When used properly these techniques are powerful, but – as pointed out above – results are only of any value when the researcher has the technical competence needed. Widely available software can be used to do the calculations, but the output only has any worth if an appropriate test is being correctly applied to suitable data – and the computer has no view about that!

Emergent research designs

The other extreme is an emergent design. As the phrase suggests, this is an approach to research where one has a starting point and sees where that leads. This is an important feature of grounded theory (GT) approaches (see Chapter 4). GT is a powerful research approach when exploring an issue where there is little available background to guide research. However, when done properly, a GT approach is an open-ended commitment, as the researcher has to follow leads indicated by the data collected ('theoretical sampling') and can only consider the study complete when the data analysis suggests that the model being developed (the 'grounded theory') has reached saturation, i.e. when further data collection is unlikely to offer any further insights to refine the model. Although GT is a very valuable research approach *it is totally unsuitable* for anyone needing to know they can complete a study within a limited time period. So GT is not a sensible choice for the teacher-researcher with limited time to draw conclusions and produce a report of their findings. (However, it may be a very sensible way of exploring an issue of burning interest over many years with a succession of classes.)

Allowing for the things that will go wrong

Generally, a sensible approach to most classroom research is to have a fairly complete but robust plan. Such 'robustness' should include the inclusion of some contingency:

- allow time to pilot data collection, whilst there is still time to amend the plan;
- allow enough time for data analysis and (where appropriate) for writing–up within the schedule. It is best to assume that these stages will require a lot more time than you initially expect;

- plan the type of data to be collected, and how this will be done. (The next chapter talks about data-collection techniques.);
- have a schedule of when data will be collected; but
- always assume that some of the expected opportunities for data collection will be lost (due to illness, unforeseen timetable changes, students going on unexpected school trips, school closures due to heavy snow, general elections – or some other factor beyond your control).

As a general rule, any schedule that does not allow for things going wrong is most unlikely to be met, so 'play safe'.

Designing a case study

It will be clear from the descriptions of methodology provided earlier in the book that some approaches require specific technical expertise (e.g. using inferential statistical tests) or require extended periods of time (such as grounded theory – GT). Teachers planning research to improve their own practice and solve problems in their own professional context may well undertake action research (AR). However, AR is a cyclic process that requires interventions to be implemented, evaluated, modified, implemented in their new form. ... As with GT, setting out on AR is an open-ended commitment to enquiry. AR also implies making decisions about when to move to the next stage of an intervention determined by the needs of classroom practice (based on judgements of the balance of evidence), which usually means before there is sufficient evidence to 'make a case' that would satisfy the demands of academic rigour.

For students required to undertake an empirical study in a restricted period of time, it is important to select a focus, and methodology, which allow such a study to be completed, and to be based on sufficient evidence to convince an examiner that the findings are sound. This usually means investigating something because it is interesting, rather than trying to solve a particular problem: in this situation the aim is *to demonstrate an understanding of and competence in small-scale classroom enquiry*, not make a major contribution to knowledge. Nevertheless, these small projects can still bring useful insights about teaching and learning to the student completing them.

One suitable approach to meeting this type of course requirement is to set out on a case study. This means having a specific focus in theoretical terms, and limiting the empirical phase of the research to a particular context. There are many possibilities, but a key feature will be to collect enough detailed information from a variety of sources (see Chapter 8) to provide the basis for analysis and preparation of an authentic account of the case.

Question for reflection

What data would you collect to undertake a case study of the following?:
Language use during a single lesson;
Student understanding of the concept of 'revolution' before teaching;
Student learning about climate over a two-week topic in Year 10 geography;
Students' affective responses to a range of learning activities in a topic;
The nature of teacher questioning during a week's lessons with a class;
The effectiveness of new teaching materials;
Student dialogue during group work over a two-week period;
Exploring whether analogies help students learn about electrical circuits;
The influence of students' religious beliefs on their learning about cosmological theories.

Teachers who wish to undertake AR for their project for a higher degree should check with their university whether an account of AR would be an acceptable basis for a thesis. Where the focus of the degree is on reflecting on, and developing, professional practice (as is the case on some MEd – EdD routes), this may be possible. However, the usual expectations of an MPhil/PhD thesis would not be met by an account of a typical AR study. It may be possible to undertake AR and still meet academic requirements: Tripp (2005: 457) suggests that 'a dissertation cannot be achieved through performing action research, but through completing a case study of the action research performed'. However, this may mean a good deal of extra work, and/or compromising on AR principles to ensure the rich data needed for a case study.

The ethics of educational research

Educational research is undertaken to increase knowledge and understanding of educational processes. This would seem to suggest such research is worthwhile, as it can inform educational activities – teaching and learning – that are generally considered to be important. The potential of educational research to improve education, and so be beneficial to the quality of human life, justifies the allocation of time and other resources.

The basic premise of this book would certainly support this general position: enquiry into teaching and learning can help teachers and learners and so is a worthwhile activity. However, as we have seen, individual research studies often only make a small contribution to knowledge; much research may seem to lead to only 'academic' outcomes, with no immediate and obvious transfer into the classroom; and research makes use of valuable, limited resources.

This does not negate the *potential* contribution of educational research, but does suggest that it is sensible to weigh-up the costs and benefits of studies. Research is worthwhile, but research studies are *not automatically* going to produce benefits that justify the time and effort involved.

Ethical principles

As well as this general consideration of the resource implications of any enquiry, there are other more substantial ethical concerns that need to be carefully considered by researchers setting out on a study.

In the UK the British Educational Research Association sets out ethical guidelines for educational research (BERA, 2004: 4), and these suggest that all educational research should be carried out 'within an ethic of respect' for:

- the person;
- knowledge;
- democratic values;
- the quality of educational research; and
- academic freedom.

The BERA guidelines are a useful starting point for anyone planning a research study.

Do no harm

In the medical profession, doctors are required to 'do no harm', and this is clearly a general principle that should apply to education. It is clearly not acceptable to plan any research where there are reasonable grounds for believing that some of the research participants may be harmed by the process. Clearly, no educational researcher should want to deliberately harm someone through research, and this principle has consequences for methodology and the development of knowledge.

Consider for example the following two hypotheses:

- lower secondary students learn more when classrooms are organised to alternate boys and girls around the class;
- students need to take in fluids during the day to function effectively as learners.

We could imagine that it would be *possible* to test both ideas by some kind of quasi-experimental approach. To test the first idea in a school with eight (mixed-ability) form entry, we might randomly assign four form groups to the treatment (sitting children boy–girl–boy–girl, etc. in class) and four forms to the existing practice (e.g. allowing pupils to sit with friends). There might be a case for saying that boys and girls generally have single gender friendship groups in the lower secondary years, and requiring them to sit with pupils of opposite sex either side is likely to decrease the proportion of student interactions which are off-task. (Some schools have implemented such arrangements for similar reasons.)

If a school were to carry out such a study, and intended to run the 'experiment' for a year, but found after a term that it seemed very clear that learning outcomes were significantly better in one arrangement than the other, then it might well be considered inappropriate to continue the study, and require half the pupils to continue studying in an arrangement that seemed to disadvantage their learning. In this example, provisional findings may well indicate that a study should end early.

This assumes, of course, that there were not other considerations. A school might well take the view that children need to learn to regulate their own learning and behaviour, and their own social interactions, and so believe that gains in learning of subject matter following from forced seating arrangements need to be balanced against limiting the opportunities for learning in other important areas.

In our second example, it would be possible (in theory) to organise a similar sort of study: randomly assigning students to conditions where they are required to drink fluids regularly through the day, or where they are asked not to drink at all during school hours. As there are good reasons to believe that not taking in fluids for long periods of time is detrimental to learning, and indeed health, this would be an unethical study and totally inappropriate: ethical considerations would not allow the most 'scientific' approach to be used.

In this extreme example, it is possible to imagine students could be *physically* harmed by unethical research. If we are to respect participants in research studies we should not only avoid any procedures that might harm them physically, but also those that might embarrass them, make them feel stupid, make them doubt their self-worth, etc.

Question for reflection

Consider a researcher who has strong grounds for believing that students learn more effectively when organised in mixed-ability groups, and who wished to explore this issue and undertake research that could potentially inform teaching (i.e. producing findings that would encourage teachers to adopt more mixed ability grouping in their classes). Would it be appropriate for this researcher to use similar-ability groups (to compare with mixed-ability groups) in his research if he strongly believed that learning is less effective with such groupings?

Ethical concerns may compromise research design

In his 1999 paper, Lyle reports research that argues for the value of mixed-ability grouping in teaching. The argument is supported by an empirical study of an intervention that provided literacy support for students in mixed-ability groups. Lyle's claims that the intervention was effective, and his suggestion that the mixed-ability aspect was an important feature are undermined by the lack of any type of comparison group. This can be seen as methodologically problematic (see Chapter 5).

However, Lyle (1999: 285) informs his readers that 'the decision to use mixed-ability groups was a principled one. The benefits of collaborative classroom learning have been well documented'. For a researcher who already believes there are strong grounds to think that students will 1benefit more from a mixed-ability context, requiring some students to work in similar ability groups (purely for the sake of the research design) may be seen as ethically questionable.

Voluntary informed consent

The area of consent is potentially a difficult one when undertaking research in schools, as most participants (the children) are by definition vulnerable. Teachers act *in loco parentis* (i.e. take on the parent's legal responsibility for the child during school hours), and in some situations a class teacher will act as a careful 'gatekeeper' who will not allow his or her charges to be part of inappropriate research. There is clearly a potential for conflict of interest if the researcher is *also* the teacher (see below).

In some studies this may not be enough, and it may be necessary to explicitly seek parental consent for pupils to be involved in research projects. Even when parents and/or teachers approve the research, if it involves children individually (rather than something being done at a class level) it will usually be appropriate to seek the permission of the individual children to take part.

Research participants can only meaningfully give consent if they know what they are being asked to approve. Generally the researcher needs to explain *why* they are doing the research, and *what* they will ask the participants to do.

Question for reflection

A researcher has a duty to obtain informed consent from participants in research. Consider a researcher who wishes to explore whether teachers interact differently with students according to gender, i.e. interacting more often with boys than girls (or vice versa), or interacting in a different way with boys and girls. The researcher needs to get permission – informed consent – from teachers to undertake observation in their classes. How much detail of the purpose of the observations should the researcher reveal in advance?

Is it ethical to revisit research data for a new purpose?

Harrop and Swinson's (2003) study of the nature of questions used by teachers, was discussed in Chapter 3. Interestingly the data analysed was not originally collected for the study reported in this paper, but consisted of recordings of lessons made as part of 'an investigation into teachers' uses of approval and disapproval in infant, junior and secondary schools' (Harrop and Swinson, 2003: 51).

Question for reflection

Is it appropriate to use data collected for one study for substantially different purposes in another study?

There is no *absolute* requirement that data used in a study should have been *specifically* collected for that study. However, there are two important caveats that should be considered. From a *methodological perspective*, any study is based around one or more research questions, or some similar focus, and ideally details of the methodology should be designed accordingly. This includes such matters as the type of data to be collected, the amount of data needed, and the sampling technique for collecting that data. These steps are all short-circuited when data is re-used for a different purpose. It is important therefore to be confident that *a data set is appropriate* for use for the new purposes. Re-using a data set in this way probably means some compromise over research design features, but does provide considerable savings of time and effort.

Question for reflection

How much detail of the purpose of classroom observations should a researcher reveal in advance in order to obtain informed consent from teachers?

Balancing the methodological and the ethical imperatives

From an *ethical perspective*, data that are collected in schools are a gift to researchers from teachers and pupils. These individuals are the original 'owners' of their feelings, ideas, beliefs, utterances and a researcher must get permission for the use of such material in research. (It is normally the parents who give consent for pupils under the age of 16.) For this to be *informed consent*, the informants must be told the purposes of the research. This in itself may be problematic, as people may well change their behaviour (if not always intentionally) when they know someone is scrutinising them, and so researchers will often be deliberately vague about their precise purposes.

If teachers gave Harrop and Swinson specific permission to record their teaching to explore their use of approval or disapproval, then the researchers should have sought renewed permission to then analyse the data for new purposes. However, it is unlikely the researchers' original request would have been this specific in case the teachers' behaviour had been modified in recorded lessons. It is more likely that the teachers gave consent to the recording being used for more general purposes, e.g. to 'investigate aspects of teacher's classroom talk' or to 'explore aspects of classroom interaction'. If this were the case, then that would have covered Harrop and Swinson's 2003 study as well as their original research with the data.

Balancing costs and benefits

All of these ethical safeguards have potential to compromise research design. The researcher also has a duty to any sponsors of research (such as a funding agency, or a school that has safeguarded non-teaching time) to attempt to undertake a methodologically robust study, so that findings are more likely to be of value to inform future practice (and further research). There is clearly a balance here. Deception (misrepresenting the purposes of research) is generally considered unethical; however, it is often necessary to be deliberately vague about the *precise* purposes of research as research participants are likely to (deliberately or otherwise) change their behaviour when being observed. Any teacher being observed (whether by a researcher, senior colleague, trainee teacher) is likely to be more careful than usual to demonstrate good practice – however, knowledge of the precise focus of research may well lead to the observed teacher significantly changing their typical behaviour in relation to that focus.

Confidentiality and anonymity

Participants should also know that they are free *to withdraw* from the research at any time. Usually it is also appropriate to promise *confidentiality* in the research, to give assurances that research data will only be shared within the research team, and anonymity – to assure participants that it will be written-up in such a way that readers will not know the real names of the people concerned. (This may not be straightforward in studies that present 'thick description'.) It is often also appropriate to offer to let participants see, comments on, or even veto drafts of any writing about their contributions to the research.

Difficulties in ensuring anonymity

The study by Tobin and his colleagues (discussed in Chapter 4) raises important ethical issues. A key ethical concern is to do no harm (including psychological harm, such as damaging an individual's self-esteem), and a common safeguard is to make sure that the true identity of informants is not revealed in any reports. It is also common practice in research with a collaborative nature, as here where two teachers volunteered to be subject to close scrutiny, to offer informants the chance to read, comment on, challenge and perhaps veto drafts of material that relates to them.

In the Tobin et al. (1990) study, the two teachers, Peter and Sandra, were involved in reading and responding to the researchers' field notes and draft reports:

> When the field notes were written, we gave them to the teachers so that they would not feel anxious about what we were writing and so that they could give us

feedback on their accuracy. ... Each teacher was provided with written reports of
the study and the findings were discussed with them in depth. Feedback from the
teachers about the written reports of the study was used as another data source.

(Tobin et al., 1990: 16)

Although 'Peter' and 'Sandra' are assumed names, and the real names are not given,
it is clear that colleagues (and students) who know these teachers will be aware of
who they are: after all, not many teachers have been followed around school for an
extended period in this way (and not by this particular group of researchers). Sandra
and Peter are not presented as representing 'good' and 'bad' teachers: but there is little
doubt that Sandra comes out of the study rather well, at least compared with Peter.
Beside his 'mind-set' being clearly considered by Tobin as less suitable for effective
teaching, the study also suggests that Peter ('not a particularly popular member of the
staff', Tobin et al., 1990: 21), often behaved inappropriately for a teacher:

Peter frequently was sarcastic and some of his remarks, which sometimes were
belittling and sexist, could have discouraged some students. ... At times, Peter
seemed to project himself in a manner that was slightly risqué and suggestive.

(Tobin, 1990: 59)

It is not possible to know how such descriptions may have been greeted by 'Peter',
or his colleagues and senior staff (or any parents of students in the school), but it is
perhaps not surprising that Sandra (and not Peter) contributed the participating
teacher's foreword to the book. Of course, researchers not only have a responsibility
to protect their informants, but also to report their findings, and it may not always
be easy to balance these expectations.

Responsibilities to report research

Researchers are also under an ethical responsibility to report research as fairly and as
completely as possible. This has a number of features:

- providing enough details of methodology and context to ensure readers can
  make judgements about the quality of the research, and of its relevance to other
  contexts;
- not selectively reporting some studies over others because outcomes better fitted
  expectations of personal commitments;
- not selectively reporting data within papers because some data seems to better
  support preferred findings;
- highlighting recognised limitations in the study.

Each of these points are potentially problematic. For example, it is important to highlight the limitations in research studies – both because this contributes to a developing

programme of research (by indicating how further research should look to improve or supplement existing studies) and to avoid findings being over-interpreted. However, researchers will clearly also wish to make the strongest case for the significance of what they have found. These demands are not inherently incompatible, However, it is clearly a challenge for any researcher to 'stand back' from their research to write a balanced account which both argues for the study making a genuine contribution to knowledge, *and* explains the inevitable compromises and limitations of the research.

A major problem for academic research is that most research journals limit authors to a modest word length (e.g. 4500–6000 words), which is a severe limitation on reporting a complex study in detail. The British Educational Research Association (BERA) suggests that researchers should prepare detailed research reports that can be made available for anyone who wishes to find out further details after reading an account published in a research journal. The Association also recommends that researchers should consider writing-up for different audiences – short, teacher-friendly accounts highlighting evidence and recommendations for practitioner journals, as well as more technical accounts for the research literature (BERA, 2000).

Avoiding bias in reporting research

The requirement that one should not merely select data that fits one's preferred outcomes may seem an obvious principle. However, in practice this is not so straightforward. In much interpretivist (ERP2) enquiry, the researcher has to sift through and organise a good deal of material, and even make decisions about which data is significant to the purposes of the study, to develop a model suitable for reporting.

In writing-up, the most cogent segments of data are often chosen to clearly communicate the categories and ideas that have been developed through the analysis. It is normal practice, and quite *appropriate* to selectively use data in this way – assuming all material collected is carefully considered whilst the model is being developed. The key question is the extent to which data is selected in terms of the emerging models rather than in terms of the researcher's pre-existing expectations and prejudices.

This is a difficult area as in many published studies the rigour and open-mindedness of the researcher has to be taken as given by the reader. Whilst it is reasonable to assume that academic researchers are not generally deliberately distorting research findings, it is much more difficult to know the extent to which analytical processes are inadvertently channelled by the researcher's existing ideas and beliefs.

Grounded theory (GT, see Chapter 4) methodology is designed to offer techniques which safeguard against this problem, by setting out procedures that ensure that all data is fully considered, and re-considered, and never prematurely dismissed. The rigorous application of a full GT methodology requires a good deal of time, and an open-ended commitment to looking for what is called 'theoretical saturation'. However, many studies using qualitative data report the data-analysis to have been undertaken with 'iterative procedures' or using a grounded-theory approach.

Question for reflection

It is suggested that educational researchers are under an ethical obligation to report their findings – as selective reporting allows bias in
which results reach the public domain. To what extent should this
obligation apply to teacher-researchers: should those doing practitioner research be under an ethical obligation to publish their findings?

The particular ethical issues facing the teacher-researcher

All educational researchers, and especially those working closely with children as
informants, have to be aware of their ethical responsibilities. The situation is even
more sensitive for the practitioner-researcher. Teachers who wish to research their
own classroom need to be aware of the complications that can raise additional
ethical dilemmas.

Question for reflection

How are the ethical responsibilities that any researcher must accept
complicated when the researcher is also the teacher of the class being
studied?

Universities, and their education faculties, will have their own procedures for
ensuring that their research students plan their research in the light of ethical considerations. This may simply be based on including ethical advice in the research
training, or may involve more formal recording and approval of research designs. In
any case, research will be discussed with supervisors who have experience as
researchers. A teacher planning research as part of their professional practice will not
have their research plans subject to this external scrutiny.

The teacher-researcher is subject to the same expectations of high ethical standards as all researchers in education. However, having the dual role of class-teacher
and researcher, and so having a more complicated relationship with the learners,
raises the potential for the teacher-researcher to abuse the privileged position of a
teacher with responsibilities to students.

The teacher-researcher's dilemma

All researchers have ethical responsibilities towards those they research. For a teacher-
researcher wishing to enquire into teaching and learning in their own school, there

are complications in the way ethical responsibilities are resolved. The complications arise from the potential abuse of power of the privileged position the teacher holds. Consider three examples:

- if the teacher-researcher is a head of department or senior member of staff, and asks to observe less senior colleague's teaching, or to interview students in a range of classes within the department;
- if the teacher-researcher wishes to carry out an intervention study by using some form of innovative approach, or novel teaching materials, in his or her own class;
- if the teacher wishes to enrol volunteers from among his or her students to take part in interviews about their learning.

Gatekeepers for research access

In each case the research may well be appropriate, and potentially worthwhile. There is nothing in principle wrong with any of these scenarios. However, in each case, if an *external* researcher wished to do this work there would be the safeguards of additional gatekeepers. An external researcher would normally need to first get permission from the Head Teacher to work in the school (unless the researcher was already known to the school through an existing partnership arrangement), and then arrange informed consent within the department for the work that was to be undertaken.

The approach to obtaining research access to schools may vary if undertaking work abroad. In some countries requests to undertake educational research in schools need to be made at the level of district education offices. If the work is approved at that level, the schools may well be *expected* to co-operate with the researcher. If undertaking fieldwork abroad, it is important to check the procedures that would apply in the particular country.

Any teacher who had doubts about the nature or value of the research, or considered it potentially disruptive or uncomfortable for the students, would refuse permission. The head of department and/or teacher acts as a gatekeeper with the power to refuse permission to the researcher.

However, if the researcher is the person who would normally act as gatekeeper, then that safeguard is missing. The teacher-researcher who wishes to undertake the research must be able to also consider the research from an independent perspective to see how it might disrupt the normal teaching–learning in the class. Any research has the potential to complicate classrooms, as well as the potential to improve them: but it may be difficult for one person (especially if under pressure to undertake research, for a university course for example) to judge the balance between the potential value and costs of the research.

For example, if an outside researcher wishes to interview volunteer students about their learning, and the class teacher believed this was a worthwhile activity, she might well encourage students to help the researcher. However, if the teacher was also the researcher, and keen to collect the data, the students might feel under pressure to give up their free time and take part in an activity that may potentially make them uncomfortable.

This is not a good reason to discourage teachers from undertaking research into their own classrooms (which is often likely to be a valuable activity), but it does mean that the teacher-researcher should think about the safeguards for those who might be asked to participate in research. Schools *could* establish ethics committees that vet requests for research access (whether from external or internal researchers). However, this would require additional administrative structures, and would not encourage teachers to see classroom enquiry as a core part of a teacher's work. It would also be very difficult to know which types of innovations counted as *sufficiently innovative* to require such vetting: classroom action research is only a systematic application of processes of improving teaching that all teachers are involved in all the time.

What is suggested here is that the teacher-researcher needs to think very carefully about the way one's students (or junior colleagues) are invited to participate in any research activity, to ensure there is no abuse of power. Whenever researching one's own students, it is important to prioritise the 'ethical imperative' and try to contextualise the enquiry within an ethical framework that ensures students know their involvement:

- is voluntary;
- is safeguarded by confidentiality;
- is not linked to any kind of formal class assessment; and
- may be cancelled at any moment by their choice, and without detrimental consequences.

Ultimately, we have to ask why others give us the gift of acting as informants in our research, and offer them the chance to decline or withdraw at any point where they feel participation is not in *their* interests (Taber, 2002).

8

Teachers Collecting Evidence Through Research

This chapter offers some introductory advice to the teacher-researcher on data collection. The type of data collected in any enquiry should be determined by considering the information needed to answer the research questions. Two general considerations are:

- the 'subject' of the enquiry;
- the unit of analysis.

What is the 'subject' of the research?

Studies that are concerned with finding out what people *do* in classrooms will look for different data to those exploring what is going on in their minds. These latter studies will collect different data if the focus is what people (think they) know, rather than on what they believe is right, or what interests them. The following questions have different types of subject:

- what proportion of a students' time is spent on task?
- do the students understand Newton's laws of motion?
- do the students believe copying homework is a valuable activity?
- why don't the students in this class seem to enjoy poetry?

What is the unit of analysis?
Studies also differ in whether they are focused on isolated individuals or interactions and groups. So, for example, research based on a conceptual framework (see Chapter 3) which includes a model of 'knowing' as a solitary activity is more likely to favour collecting data from individual learners. However, research based on a conceptual framework which views knowing as a social activity might chose to explore student understanding by working with pairs or groups of students. Similarly, research from a view of teaching which sees the central relationship as being between teacher and student may focus on the interactions *between* teacher and individual learners, where

a different view of classroom learning might lead to a focus on the interactions *within* groups when working on tasks set up by the teacher.

Data collection

There are a range of data collection techniques that are open to classroom teachers exploring teaching and learning. Some of these are more problematic if a teacher is trying to research her own classroom. Available techniques include:

- interviewing;
- observation;
- questionnaires;
- tests;
- learner products;
- documentary evidence.

Each of these can have a range of 'flavours', and so can be fine-tuned for particular types of study.

Documentary evidence

Classrooms and teaching are often well-documented. A range of documents may be useful in answering research questions. These include attendance records, mark-books, schemes of work, and teacher feedback on work. Other documents that are less centrally focused on a particular classroom but which may well be significant for what goes on there include departmental minutes, school policy documents (on marking, inclusion, literacy across the curriculum, etc.), inspection reports, papers presented to the governing body, school strategic plans, school brochures, etc. Such documents may in themselves only be sufficient to answer limited questions (e.g. 'do cross-curricular school policies make reference to needs of those students identified as gifted and talented?'), but documentary analysis can play an important part in enquiries comparing actual classroom experience with the intentions (or gloss) presented in school policies.

A particular area of documentary evidence that has traditionally been called upon for assignments on teacher training courses is that of lesson plans and evaluations. Although all teachers are expected to plan and evaluate their teaching, there is usually no requirement for qualified teachers to keep detailed paperwork (DfES, 2003).

Question for reflection

To what extent are lesson plans and evaluation likely to be reliable as evidence in classroom research?

However, trainee teachers are usually expected to make detailed lesson plans, and to evaluate their lessons in writing.

Lesson plans represent the pedagogic intentions of the teacher (or trainee teacher). Their lesson evaluations attempt to identify what went according to plan, and why, and what did not go as expected – requiring the plan to be changed *in situ* and/or for teaching that lesson to a future similar class. To be useful, lesson evaluations have to be honest ('it went okay, I think it was a good lesson' is of little value to informing future practice), and analytical (so that impressions are supported by evidence and are consistent with the models and theories of teaching and learning that the teacher uses to make sense of the classroom).

However, the teacher can make a very poor objective observer of the classroom – being intimately involved in the action, and often having a great deal invested in the outcomes. This can lead to lesson evaluations that miss key events, and are much too self-critical or self-forgiving.

The validity of sources depends upon the research focus

Given this, it may seem that such teacher documentation is of very little value as research evidence. However, this again depends upon the research questions being investigated. By themselves, a teacher's lesson evaluations must be treated as having limited reliability in reporting the effectiveness of teaching. However, if the research questions concern teacher thinking (e.g. 'does the teacher think about the needs of the full ability range when planning lessons?'; 'does the teacher consider she is meeting the learning needs of the full ability range?') then these documents may be a very useful source of information.

Teaching diaries

If a teacher is concerned with such an issue, and wishes to explore it in her own teaching, then it makes sense to focus thinking on this particular issue. This could take the form of a reflective notebook or diary, focusing on the matter. The teacher can use this notebook as a record of thoughts about the topic, including ideas that feed into planning, and any relevant notes made when evaluating lessons. Such a reflective diary provides a record of the teacher's developing thinking as she explores the issue, and its significance and manifestations in her classes.

A diary or set of notes in this form remains largely subjective – the thoughts, impressions and interpretations of one individual. This is a particular form of research data that has its value and limitations. This type of record can be useful in later explaining why certain ideas were used to plan actions – for example, why certain types of classroom interventions were undertaken rather than others. It may also record critical incidents that can provide useful clues for following up in other research. A student comment about why a particular activity was too difficult or too simple or uninteresting may provoke a new research question.

Attitudes to the use of this type of information as research evidence vary. Where research is carried out for the professional development of the individual teacher, this can be a valuable record of critical reflection, and can help systemise and organise thoughts. If teacher-research is viewed as being primarily about the development of the teacher-researcher, an account of the research based on such documentation may be considered appropriate (Whitehead, 2000).

If, however, research is expected to produce new knowledge for the profession as a whole, then the personal reflections of one individual may not be considered to provide rigorous evidence. However, even here such accounts may provide useful starting points for the collection of other, more 'objective' types of data.

Tests

Teachers commonly associate testing with formal assessment, and that is quite appropriate, but we should recognise that if classroom assessment was a new invention it might well be considered a form of teacher-research. After all, tests are ways of collecting evidence about student knowledge and understanding.

Indeed formal examinations (such as SATs, GCSEs, etc.) provide immense amount of data that have been used as the source of a great deal of educational research. Such research can provide substantial data sets for exam boards and others to use (for example, McClune's study discussed in Chapter 4).

In the 1980s an organisation called the Assessment of Performance Unit (APU) was set up in the government's education department, and tested large representative samples of the school population against some of the things they were expected to learn in school. For example, in science, the APU tested large numbers of students at ages 11, 13 and 15. The data from these surveys were made available to researchers, and was the starting point for major research programmes exploring student understanding of key science concepts.

Classroom teachers use assessment at the end of modules to evaluate student learning and their own teaching; during learning sequences to inform teaching and learning; and at the start of a topic to check identified prerequisite learning is in place and to look for the presence of known common 'misconceptions'. Just because these processes are part of the normal work of the teacher, this does not exclude them as being part of a research plan. If undertaken in a systematic manner, to address a specified research question, summative, formative or diagnostic testing could all be used in classroom enquiry.

Validity of test items

As with all assessment work, the validity of outcomes will in part depend upon the test items actually testing the knowledge or understanding they claim to test. Indeed the validity of assessment items could be a suitable focus for classroom research (for example, comparing written answers given on tests with the knowledge and understanding students are able to demonstrate in interviews).

Examination boards are responsible for setting papers which lead to assessments that will have public confidence (and are used for course progression, in evaluating job applicants, etc.) and so invest considerable amounts of time and effort developing and pre-testing examination papers – but still occasionally find themselves severely criticised when something goes wrong.

Teachers (and researchers) should be aware of the difficulty of producing tests that are both valid (testing what they claim) and reliable (giving reproducible results). Examination boards may have their own research units where they explore various aspects of setting and grading formal assessments. This is a complex area with many pitfalls. For example, the introduction of contextualised questions (where the question is framed in a familiar context) was meant to be helpful to learners by making questions seem less abstract and unfamiliar. However, this also introduces new complications (Taber, 2003): students have to 'process' more information, dis-embedding the principles behind the question from the context; the context may trigger everyday 'life-world' ways of thinking that do not match academic learning (which may also be present); and any context will be more familiar to some students than others (and so may introduce a cultural or gender bias).

Assessments may be a useful source of information for the teacher and the researcher, but it is important to appreciate that a poorly designed test will produce information of limited value. One should be especially wary of using any assessment for research purposes if it has not at least been carefully piloted with similar groups of students to those being tested in the enquiry.

Learner productions

A source of information about classroom teaching and learning is the wide range of outputs produced by learners as a normal part of the work of the classroom. Student's class-work (and homework) can be analysed to provide information about learners' knowledge and understanding; work rate; ability to follow instructions; skills; etc.

In principle, any work that a student produces individually or collectively that could be assessed in the normal course of teaching could be used as data. This should not be surprising, as teachers assess work to obtain evidence of learning, and to guide teaching. In the same way, the difficulties inherent in assessing work as part of normal teaching apply when we use this material as research data.

Question for reflection

What might be the difficulties of using 'work' produced by students as evidence of learning?

Complications of interpreting learners' productions

The things that students write (or draw, or perform, etc.) only provide *indirect* evidence of what they think, know and understand (and need not be reliable guides to what they believe). So:

- whatever has been written or said (or acted-out) has to be interpreted by the teacher or researcher to find what the learner(s) 'meant';
- unless work is closely supervised, the teacher (or researcher) cannot be sure about the extent to which a product is the learners' 'own' work;
- if learning is seen as a socially mediated process, we might wish to reframe that previous point: unless work is closely supervised, the teacher (or researcher) cannot be sure about the extent to which learners interacted in producing a 'group' product;
- 'correct' answers can be guesses – for example on 'objective' items such as those used in multiple-choice tests;
- 'incorrect' answers can be due to an ability to get thoughts into writing, or misinterpreting what the question required, or lack of concentration (or motivation) or due to pressures of time;
- 'correct' answers may demonstrate new learning, or pre-existing understanding that was already in place before teaching;
- responses reflect one way of thinking available to the learner, which may just be one facet of a repertoire of available ways of thinking ('manifold conceptions', or 'multiple frameworks');
- answers may reflect what the learners think they are meant to write, rather than what they actually think or believe.

Given all these potential problems, it may seem that students' work (or records of it, such as a video-recording of a performance or role-play) has a limited role to play *in research*.

Question for reflection

Given the potentially flawed chain of associations between students' knowledge and understanding, and the teachers' assessment of their work, how can teachers justify using such 'data' to make judgements about learning?

Indeed it seems reasonable to suggest that students' work (or records of it) should only have a limited role to play in *informing teaching* – whether as part of everyday practice or in the context of a research project.

'Fuzzy' data and iterative analysis

In everyday classroom practice, teachers *are* informed by their assessment of learners' work, but seldom put too much emphasis (or 'weight') on any particular 'product'.

Teachers usually consider student work (the products) collectively, and alongside their observations of the students working (the process), and their responses to oral questions, in class. We might say that teachers acknowledge that they are working with 'fuzzy' data where an individual datum offers a limited basis for drawing inferences. However, over an extended period of time, *teachers* naturally use an informal iterative process to learn from such data: for example, noting an especially poor response, or an unexpected insightful one, forming tentative hypotheses about what might be indicated, and looking for opportunities to test out these ideas. (We might refer to this as 'grounded practice' cf. grounded theory; see Chapter 4.)

Researchers should see this type of data in a similar way. Student work outputs can be useful when seen as one 'slice of data' to be triangulated against other informative data sources.

Setting up teaching/learning activities to generate data

As well as the normal sorts of tasks that students regularly undertake in class, it is possible to set up particular activities that provide useful information. There is clearly an ethical issue here (see the previous chapter), as students should not be asked to put a lot of time and effort into creating material that is only intended as data for the benefit of the teacher's research. However, when planning teaching, it is often possible to incorporate activities that can be useful *both* for student learning and teacher research.

Learner diaries

Given the importance of reinforcement in learning, and the value of learners developing metacognitive skills to work towards becoming self-regulated learners, it may be appropriate to ask learners to keep diaries of:

- what they have done in class;
- what they have learnt;
- whether they enjoyed activities;
- what they need to put more effort into, etc.

The precise questions would clearly depend on the focus on the enquiry.

Concept maps

Concept maps (e.g. see Figure 8.1) have been widely used to collect data about learners' developing understanding of topics. They are also promoted as useful tools for planning teaching, and for helping students both as a learning tool and as way of monitoring their own developing learning about a topic (Novak and Gowin, 1984). Some (not all) students enjoy producing concept maps. Concept mapping can be scaffolded (as the task can be set from a blank sheet of paper, or with various degrees

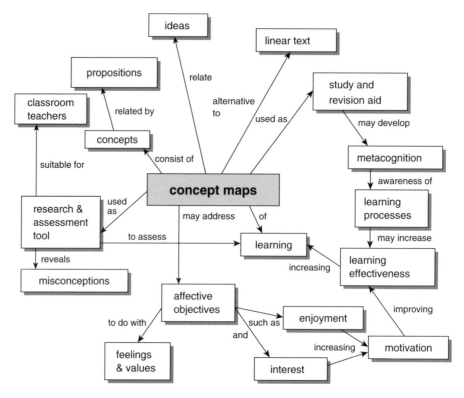

FIGURE 8.1   **An example of a concept map (from Taber, 1994)**

Reproduced with permission of Institute of Physics Publishing.

of structure and information already provided) and may be organised for individual study or a group activity.

Concept maps, then, offer great flexibility, and it is certainly easy to justify asking students to complete them. Interpretation of how concept maps reflect learners' ideas and understanding can be problematic (with a number of the problems listed above coming into play), but can potentially be very informative when used alongside other techniques such as interviews ('right, Pritpal, I wanted you to talk me through this concept map you drew for me').

Questionnaires

Questionnaires comprise sets of questions that are answered by an identified group of people (new first year students; girls in the year 9 class; my form group; pupils on the gifted register; anyone in school sports teams).

Questionnaires are usually paper instruments that respondents complete in writing. Questions may be of various types (e.g. see Box 8.1). Questionnaires do not, however, test learning, but provide questions that all respondents should be able to respond to.

Box 8.1   Some types of questions that may appear in questionnaires

Questions may be:

closed	e.g. *how many nights a week do you normally do school work?* ☐ *less than 3/*☐ *3–4 /*☐ *more than 4*
or open	e.g. *what do you most enjoy about your French lessons?*
about factual matters	e.g. *how many older brothers and sisters do you have?*
or opinions	e.g. *what are the good and bad things about having to do homework?*

Various types of scales may be used in questions (e.g. how much do you enjoy your maths lessons: ☐ *a lot;* ☐ *a little;* ☐ *not really bothered;* ☐ *I dislike them*), and attitudes may be explored by asking about agreement with given statements (e.g. *school is the highlight of my life:* ☐ *strongly agree;* ☐ *agree;* ☐ *disagree;* ☐ *strongly disagree*).

Question for reflection

How might the nature of interview questions differ in an ERP1 study compared with an ERP2 study?

There are advantages and disadvantages to different types of items and scales. Closed questions only find out which *of the offered options* respondents chose, but are simpler to analyse. Open questions provide the opportunity for respondents to give an answer that better matches their views, but need to later *be categorised* if they are to be reported in an economic way. (Analysis of data is considered in Chapter 9.) Selection of illustrative comments always raises questions as to *how representative* such examples are. Sometimes a mixture of open and closed questions is useful, allowing the researcher to report proportions of responses in different categories, supported by selected quotations (see the comments on Kinchin's study in the following chapter).

Designing questionnaire items

There are techniques for increasing the *validity* and *reliability* of questionnaire items. One suggestion is that scales should *not* have central points as this forces the respondent to make a decision about how they feel – but this may be an artificial choice if they genuinely have neutral or mixed feelings about a topic. The inclusion of several equivalent statements, or opposite statements, may help check the consistency of responses.

Similarly, reversing the sense of some statements (e.g. I like French: ☐ *strongly agree;* ☐ *agree;* ☐ *disagree;* ☐ *strongly disagree;* I dislike German: ☐ *strongly agree;* ☐ *agree;* ☐ *disagree;* ☐ *strongly disagree*) is considered to encourage respondents to think about each item.

Such advice is commonly given because it is recognised that questionnaires comprising of many scale-type items may sometimes be completed with little thought. For any questionnaire it is important not to ask too many questions, as this will increase the chance of respondents losing interest, concentration and good-will towards the researcher.

Questionnaires as providing one slice of data

Although questionnaires are limited as a means of eliciting in-depth information of the type usually needed in ERP2 studies, they may be a useful adjunct to other techniques. For example, in their study of 'the experiences and understandings of a group of full-time further education trainee teachers', Avis et al. (2003: 191) report that:

> Our findings are based upon a series of focus-group discussions with the students, followed by in-depth individual interviews. A questionnaire was also used to seek information on the background and experience of the trainees.
>
> (Avis et al., 2003: 191)

How valid are questionnaire responses?

One of the severe limitations of questionnaires is that they only (at best, assuming honest responses) elicit information about people's thoughts, beliefs and recollections: not actual behaviour. That teachers claiming to have constructivist views also report more frequently using pedagogy consistent with constructivist beliefs is not surprising, but does not necessarily demonstrate these teachers *actually do* use these teaching activities as often as they think they do (or should).

It is interesting that Ravitz and colleagues (2000) found that most teachers in their survey thought students were more comfortable with traditional approaches, although Kinchin found most secondary students had a strong preference for learning in constructivist classrooms (see Chapter 2). This could indicate that teachers are 'out of touch' with their students.

Another issue worth considering, though, is the way that particular questions, and forms of questioning, may channel respondents' thinking. Ravitz and colleagues found that although most of their sample selected response categories that were not 'constructivist' in response to simple requests to select statements reflecting their views, a somewhat different outcome was elicited by a different approach. Ravitz (et al., 2000) found that

> Given a brief argument made between support for a philosophical position consistent with constructivist instructional reform and one reflecting a more

traditional viewpoint, many more teachers will select agreement with reform than with traditional teaching practice.

(Ravitz et al., 2000: 12)

It is important for the researcher (and reader of research) to remember that some-times it is not just the questions asked, but the ways they are posed, that in part deter-mine the responses elicited.

Classroom observation

Observation has been used in classrooms to collect information about teaching and learning for a long time. Classroom observation can vary in a number of ways. As always, our decisions are influenced by our basic (paradigmatic) assumptions about the research.

Question for reflection

Classroom observation is a technique that can be used as a component of methodologies that fall within both main educational research para-digms (see Chapter 3). How might classroom observation be different in character within these two paradigms?

In principle, observers can be as unobtrusive as possible and avoid interacting with the class at all. The ultimate observer aims to be 'invisible' so that their presence does not influence what happens in the class (but when discretion becomes covert obser-vation this raises ethical issues in relation to 'informed consent'; see Chapter 7). At the other extreme an observer might choose to be part of the classroom interaction being observed. A participant-observer would certainly observe something different from the lesson that would have taken place in her absence, but that may not be a problem (depending on the purpose(s) of the research).

Participant observation

An observer wishing to take an ethnographic approach might want to avoid altering the researched situation by becoming a participant-as-observer, by going 'under-cover' as one of the class and not being spotted as an observer. This raises similar ethical issues as the pure observer who is hiding from the class. It is an approach that could be used in some contexts (a parents' meeting, a class in an adult education college) but few teacher-researchers are likely to be able to go undercover with a typical class of 11 year-olds!

Whilst this may be a ridiculous image, a viable (if risky) compromise might be for the researcher to tell the class that she wishes to be treated as one of them in the lesson. The class teacher and students obviously know the researcher is just taking on this role, so the situation is artificial, but nonetheless it could be a useful approach with some classes. If kept up for some time, the researcher may indeed come to be accepted at some level as one of the class, and may even have to keep in mind the dangers of 'going native' by coming to identify too closely with the new role.

More commonly, researchers may be present as adult participants: something that students may readily accept if used to teachers working in teams, or regularly having trainee teachers and/or learning assistants in lessons.

The type of observation undertaken by Tobin and his colleagues (1990) in their study of teacher mind sets (see Chapter 4) involved going into classes as participant observers: people known (at least to the teachers) to be undertaking research, but choosing to get involved in the lessons and talking to the participants openly, rather than sitting quietly at the back making notes without interacting.

Types of classroom observation data

Another key dimension of classroom observation concerns the type of data collected. This can vary from free-form notes, where anything that might prove to be of interest is noted, to the use of a formal observation schedule with clearly defined categories (where the observer's job may be to keep a tally of events identified as being in these categories). Again, the type of data collected depends upon the purposes of the research. A research question of the form 'what is it about 8F that leads to all their teachers judging them a 'pleasure' to teach?' needs a different approach to data collection than the question 'do the boys in 8F shout out answers to the teachers', questions significantly more often than the girls?'

The latter question derives from a pre-formed hypothesis that is going to be investigated within ERP1, by collecting quantitative data suitable for statistical testing. The observer enters the field with preformed observation categories, and hopes that her presence does not lead to the teacher or students behaving any differently than they would do in lessons without observers. The former question requires a more exploratory approach from ERP2, and the observer tries to free his or her mind from prior assumptions, and is looking for any useful clues.

Both types of approaches have limitations. Structured observations will only find out about the categories that have been built into the schedule. Open-ended observations are likely to produce useful hunches, but there are likely to need to be *triangulated* against other data sources (see Chapter 4), or developed through more structured observations.

Piloting and developing, or adopting and adapting an observation schedule

As with assessment papers, observation schedules need to be *piloted* before they can be used in research. This piloting has two purposes:

- checking the validity of the schedule in collecting the data needed;
- providing practice in using the schedule to make observations reliable.

In small-scale research where structured observations are chosen to collect data, it may be sensible to use a pre-existing schedule that has already been shown to be useful in answering similar research questions (and adapting it where needed), rather than constructing a new instrument that may need several stages of development. Ideally the *reliability* of the data collection should be tested through inter-observer agreement – several observers using the schedule to observe the same classroom episodes, and then calculating how well their data matched. This is seldom possible in small-scale research carried out by classroom practitioners, so practice in using the schedule before collecting the research data is important.

Degrees of structure in observation schedules

Simple schedules may require the observer to check off each instance of certain events (teacher questions, pupil call-outs), perhaps for different groups within the class (e.g. by gender); or may ask the observer to classify what is going on (teacher talk, teacher questioning, group work, students working individually) at regular periods in the lesson (e.g. every two minutes).

There are intermediate formats between highly structured schedules, and a blank sheet of paper. For example, an observer could have a form with several categories or themes, and be looking to make notes on any instances that seem relevant. So for example, if the research focus was the way a teacher responded to the needs of different learners in a class, the observer could be looking to identify *and describe* instances of where the:

- teacher differentiates by task;
- teacher differentiates by degree of teacher support;
- teacher differentiates by organising groups for peer support;
- teacher differentiates in evaluating outcomes.

How can we observe without seeing?

In Harrop and Swinson's (2003) study of the nature of questions used by teachers, the research was carried out using data collected on the teaching of 30 teachers, 10 each from infant, junior and secondary schools. Harrop and Swinson describe how the data was collected, with teachers being 'recorded by a radio microphone for 30 minutes whilst teaching a lesson'. The analysis was based on the recordings of the classrooms. Understandably, perhaps, given this mode of data collection, certain types of lessons and lesson activities were excluded from the study:

> The lessons recorded were all classroom based, with literacy hour and numeracy sessions excluded, as were practical/activity sessions (e.g. physical education, craft, art).
>
> (Harrop and Swinson, 2003: 51)

Recording classroom dialogue can be a very useful way of collecting data, but only where an audio recording is able to 'capture' the information needed. Recordings of teacher-led classroom dialogue often only clearly pickup the teacher's voice. Recordings of group work often have a good deal of background noise (from the other groups in the class) and even when talk is audible it may be difficult to identify the different speakers in the group. Again, this is a technique that may often be best used as part of a battery of data collection approaches, providing one slice of data complemented by evidence from other sources.

Video-recording may provide richer data than audio recording, but is more obtrusive and difficult to set-up.

Feedback from mentors/colleagues

The discussion above has assumed the researcher is the observer. However, when enquiring into *our own* teaching practice it can be very useful to get feedback from *other* suitably informed observers. Teachers in training will be used to receiving regular written feedback about their teaching. The feedback will be tied to specific issues that have been identified as the focus for development in trainee–mentor sessions. Focused feedback of this type can certainly be seen as suitable evidence in classroom research, especially when used alongside other 'slices of data'.

Being observed by colleagues is now part of the normal procedures in place for quality assurance and staff development in most schools and colleges. This type of observation is however usually infrequent, and undertaken to a pre-existing agenda. Nonetheless, this contributes to a professional ethos in most schools and colleges where observing colleagues is seen as acceptable and healthy, and a teacher-researcher may well find that a colleague will be prepared to help by observing teaching (although time commitments are unlikely to allow this to be more than occasional). The same considerations apply when we ask someone to observe our classes, and when we observe other teaching. If we wish to collect specific data about particular aspects of teaching and learning, then the observer has to be well briefed, and provided with a schedule with both appropriate headings/categories and a suitable level of structure.

Interviewing

Interviews are special kinds of conversations (Powney and Watts, 1987): conversations designed so that the interviewer can find out information from a privileged informant. The interviewee is privileged in the sense of having access to information. This may be because the interviewee was present at some time and place when the researcher was not around. However, often in educational research, the informant is intrinsically privileged as the information being sought is about some aspect of the way that the person thinks, understands, values or believes. The best way to find out what someone thinks can be to ask. This is not a guaranteed approach: both questions and answers can be misunderstood; the interviewer may be interested in some aspect of thinking or belief that is tacit (and so not consciously available to the informant); and sometimes interviewees may not give careful, complete or even honest answers. Despite these limitations, interviewing is often the *most direct* and reliable way to find out what someone knows, believes or thinks.

One strength of interviewing is its flexibility: allowing the interviewer to rephrase questions, clarify answers, seek elaboration and so forth. Although most research interviews have an agenda or schedule of questions, this is often used as a guide rather than a strict set sequence of questions. A skilled interviewer can often obtain valuable data from an informant who is in a position to provide information and is prepared to do so. As Bruner (1987) has pointed out, conversation allows 'constant transactional calibration', allowing us to check that we are understood by, and understand the intended meanings of, people we are talking to. Whilst not a perfect means of communication, a conversation allows us checks that are absent from questionnaires, for example.

Question for reflection

Is it more important for an interviewer to be able to be responsive to the informant's comments, or for the interviewer to follow the same procedures and schedule with each informant?

This flexibility has costs. An interviewer who takes advantage of the flexibility of this ('semi-structured') interview format will not be interviewing all subjects in identical ways. This would be a problem in some enquiries. For example, if one was testing the hypothesis that 'girls are just as likely to experience bullying as boys', then one would wish to make sure that the same question was asked in the same way, so that the respondents judgements were not influenced by different phrasing of the question, or differently cued by the question sequence. (Asking the question 'can bullying be verbal, or must it always be physical?', just before asking 'have you ever been the victim of bullying?' could well lead to a different response to the second question.)

Types of interviewing and interview data

In this situation, an enquiry likely to be identified as within ERP1, a fully structured interview schedule would be appropriate. However, a study with a similar focus, but from a more interpretivist perspective, would indicate a different type of interview. A study to enquire into 'how boys and girls construe bullying and feel about with bullying' would be situated within ERP2. Here it is more important to uncover in-depth data about how individuals make sense of their experiences, than it is to ask a large number of people identical questions. Both types of research question may be important, and may use interviewing as an appropriate technique, but with different types of interview to collect (or 'construct') different types of data.

The distinction between data collection and construction is significant here. The researcher in the ERP1 interview is acting as a technician, to collect responses to precise, predetermined, questions as effectively as possible. Indeed, in professional research, the individuals employed to collect the data may be trained-up for this purpose, and have little knowledge of, or other involvement in, the research.

Co-construction of interview data

This is not an approach a researcher in ERP2 could take: here the text produced in an interview (an 'InterView'; Kvale, 1996) – the dialogue, the recording of the interview, the transcript of the interview – is a creative production of two authors. The text is constructed through the interviewer and informant interacting. (Note: this is anathema to the 'positivistic' assumptions of ERP1.) The researcher needs to be highly skilled, and have a good understanding of research purposes to help shape the data produced. The researcher brings those professional skills, and the interviewee brings their own understandings or views.

In this type of interview, the researcher is an intimate part of the data construction process, and it is neither reasonable, nor perhaps even desirable, to believe that another interviewer would have elicited exactly the same information. It is also worth noting that although the interviewer may feel that he or she owns the text constructed, the other author (the interviewee) might be considered to share ownership (Taber and Student, 2003). As has been pointed out by Limerick et al. (1996), this type of interview, and the text constructed through it, is a gift from the interviewee. The interviewer gives of their time and opens up their ideas to examination (and potential ridicule) for the benefit of the researcher who hopes to benefit professionally. There is clearly an ethical issue (and potential for abuse of trust) – and researchers need to make sure they are comfortable with the way they obtain information from informants, and use that information afterwards.

Group interviews

Group interviews, where several informants are interviewed together, have a number of advantages. Some students are much more comfortable talking to a researcher in pairs or groups, especially where they are interviewed with friends. Group interviews also allow the comments of one student to act as stimulus for another, perhaps eliciting information that would not otherwise have been revealed. Sometimes the closer match in levels of knowledge and language (compared with that of the researcher) may help the flow of the interview. This arrangement also takes some pressure off the informants, who can take 'time out' for thinking as a peer contributes.

The obvious disadvantage to this type of interview is that the responses that individuals give cannot be assumed to be the same as they might have offered if interviewed alone. This is particularly true if one of the respondents feels intimidated, embarrassed or uncomfortable 'opening-up' in front of a peer.

This is no clear preference for individual or group interviews. The former are clearly appropriate in some situations where the presence of other learners would 'contaminate' the data being collected. However, for a study of student learning which viewed the learning process as primarily mediated through interactions within a class, a researcher might well feel that group interviews give more pertinent data.

Focus groups

Focus groups (which are set up more as observed discussions than interviews) have become common in market 'research', and often involve quite large groups (half-a-dozen or more) people talking through ideas. In this situation discussion is encouraged, and the researcher might be more interested in any consensus positions that derive from the debates, rather than individual viewpoints fed in. Focus groups are clearly not helpful in looking at individual learners' ideas in any depth, but are a useful way of involving more people as informants without significantly increasing the time available for interviews.

In Lyle's (1999: 288) study of mixed-ability grouping in the primary school, evidence of the effectiveness of the intervention was collected when 'two groups of 12 children were interviewed on separate occasions. The interviews were video-recorded and later transcribed'. Interviewing a group of 12 pupils might well help overcome reservations children might have at being interviewed and videotaped by someone who is presumably not well known to them. However, this raises questions about the extent to which all 24 children contributed to the interviews and whether each felt able to freely give their own view. As always, research decisions involve weighing up the 'pros' and 'cons' of the available alternatives.

Probes

Probes may be used in interviews to focus a student's thinking, and provide a starting point for the dialogue (e.g. White and Gunstone, 1992). For example in Watts' (1983) research of student thinking about forces (see Chapter 3), he used line diagrams as a focus to elicit student ideas. This has been called 'interview-about-instances' as the starting point for each diagram would be 'is there an example of a force (or whatever) in this diagram?'

In Sade and Coll's (2003: 102) study of the views of some Solomon Island primary teachers and curriculum development officers on technology education, the main source of data was 'semi-structured interviews – typically of about 40–45 minutes duration, in which both the teachers and the curriculum development officers were asked non-leading, open-ended questions'. However:

> During the interviews, a picture quiz questionnaire was given to the participants
> and they were asked to identify which pictures they associated with technology.
>
> (Sade and Coll, 2003: 102)

A similar approach is called interviews-about-events, where the interviewer uses a simple demonstration (e.g. a candle burning), and asks the interviewee to explain what they think is going on during the event. For example, García-Franco (2005) reports an interview-based study 'based on semi-structured interviews with secondary students in English and Mexican secondary schools (Year 8 – Year 11) using for the analysis a grounded theory approach'. The research was looking at the types of explanations students use and, in particular, whether they consistently adopt the curriculum models of 'particles' (molecules). During the interviews she demonstrated simple phenomena (dissolving, mixing, burning) and 'students are asked to describe the phenomena, to explain "why does it happen that way?", and if they do not use particle theory in the construction of their explanation, they are then specifically asked to think about particles'. This 'hierarchical focusing' approach (Tomlinson, 1989) approach allows García-Franco to see first if the students *spontaneously* introduce particle ideas in their explanations, and – if not – whether they *are able* to build explanations using particle models.

Concept cartoons as stimuli

Kinchin (2004) used 'concept cartoons' as stimuli for collecting his data. A concept cartoon is a simple line diagram of a situation, usually including a number of people (often children, as the cartoons are used in teaching) offering different views about a phenomenon (Keogh and Naylor, 1999). In teaching, the cartoon is used as a stimulus to group discussion, with students asked to consider the range of ideas, and to offer reasons for agreeing and disagreeing with them.

Kinchin, in the spirit of 'student voice' involved students, 'a focus group of Year 10 (15 year-old) secondary students' (2004: 304), in designing the cartoons. This might be seen to increase the validity of the instrument, as the ideas and language used should be suitable for secondary students. Kinchin then used the cartoon to collect his data:

> Secondary students in Year 7 (12 year-olds) and Year 9 (14 year-olds) from two
> schools in south-eastern England were asked to examine the dialogue in each of
> the cartoons (A and B). They were then asked in which of the two classrooms
> each of them would rather be a student and to offer reasons for their choice in
> the form of a written free response. Responses were collected during form time
> on one day.
>
> (Kinchin, 2004: 304)

Kinchin reports that the 'these cartoons were intended to trigger talk among students about their epistemological beliefs' (2004: 304). In his conclusion Kinchin (2004: 310) reports that 'it seems that secondary students are capable of commenting upon their learning. ... Concept cartoons may provide a convenient starting-point for such classroom discussions'.

The data collection instrument also differed from more familiar context cartoon approaches (that some students are likely to be familiar with) as instead of alternative views being presented within one cartoon, the instrument comprised two line diagrams: each one offering an exchange between an adult (presumably the teacher) and child (looking somewhat younger than those responding to the instrument). However, as the images are different (a computer features in one, a chalkboard dominates the room in the other), there is a danger of student preferences being influenced by the difference in apparent nature of the classrooms, as well as the dialogue. Kinchin was aware of this, and reports that the images were swapped on 'some question sheets' without making any difference to the results.

Collection and analysis of data

This chapter has described some of the techniques that can be used to collect data in the classroom. These different techniques can provide a range of different types of data for our research. However, before we can draw any conclusions from the data, we need to carefully and systematically analyse them.

9

Teachers Interrogating the Evidence from Classroom Studies

Collecting data is clearly an important part of the research process, but the analysis of data is just as important. This may seem obvious, but what many students and teachers new to empirical research do not realise is that the analysis of data *needs to be planned*, just as much as the collection of data.

Analysing data

In much ERP1 research, data is collected that is basically quantitative, and suitable for analysis in statistical terms. This may be using statistical tests, *if* the research has been designed to allow inferential statistics (i.e. hypothesis testing). For example, in Button's study of pupil perceptions of music (see Chapter 2), he reports that the difference between the proportions of boys and girls in his sample that reported having access to a musical instrument at home was statistically significant.

According to Button (2006: 426), in his sample of students there were:

- 86 girls who said they had access to an instrument;
- 29 girls who said they did not have access to an instrument;
- 50 boys who said they had access to an instrument;
- 51 boys who said they did not have access to an instrument.

Button used a statistical test (known as χ^2, or chi-squared), which compares such 'observed' frequencies with what might be expected if there was no significant gender difference. So in this case, there were 216 students, and 136 (i.e. 63%) had access to an instrument. All other things 'being equal' we might therefore have expected that about 72/115 girls and 64/101 boys would have had access to instruments.

Clearly in this sample there was a *higher proportion* of girls reporting access to instruments, but this could just be a reflection of the particular young people in the sample, rather than being true about 'boys' and 'girls' in general.

Button (2000: 426) presents the statistic that he obtained from using the χ^2 test, which tells him that the probability (p) of getting such a skewed sample by chance is less than one in a thousand ('$p < 0.001$'), so it seems very likely that this gender difference would be found in the wider population of KS3 students.

However, it is sometimes (and often, in small-scale practitioner research) sufficient to use descriptive statistics to summarise findings. For example, findings are often in the form of the frequencies (often as percentages) of data falling into different categories. Results are tabulated, with means, standard deviations, etc., presented. Results may be presented graphically, i.e. using pie-charts or bar charts to communicate findings visually.

Presenting quantitative results

McClune's (2001) study of relative achievement in modular and terminal examinations used quantitative methods of analysis, and his results are summarised in tables in his study. There were three compulsory questions common to the modular and terminal examination papers. When the three questions were considered together it was found that the second year students averaged 22.7 marks (out of 33 available) for these questions, whereas the first year students scored 21.0 on average. This difference was statistically significant. In Table 3 (McClune, 2001: 84) the probability value of this outcome is given as $p < 0.001$, meaning that such a difference would only be likely to be found by chance in a sample this size less than once in a thousand opportunities.

The scores of boys and girls are also considered separately. The average score for second year boys was 23.0 compared with 21.3 for the first year boys – a result likely to happen by chance less than once in a hundred opportunities by chance (i.e. $p < 0.01$). Among the girls, the second years also attained a higher average score on these questions, 22.8 cf. 21.8: however, this difference was considered non-significant (usually shown as 'n.s.'). This means that such a difference would happen more than once in twenty opportunities by chance, and *by convention* this is not considered a statistically significant finding. So among this group of girls, the average score was slightly higher for the second years: but we should not assume this would be repeated if we had compared the scores of all the girls who took the examination rather than just a sample.

McClune also presents the statistics for the three questions separately. Among the boys, the second year students outscored the first years on all three questions, averaging 11.9 marks out of 17, compared to 11.1; 4.0 (/5) cf. 3.8; 7.0 (/11) cf. 6.2. Two of these differences (the first and third) were statistically significant (both reaching $p < 0.01$). For the girls, the first years attained a higher average score on the first question (11.6, cf. 11.3), but had lower average scores on the other two questions (3.8 cf. 4.0; 6.4 cf. 7.5). Only one of these three differences (the last) was statistically significant ($p < 0.05$). Taking both genders together, this final question was the only one where the difference in scores reached statistical significance ($p < 0.001$).

Question for reflection

McClune (2001) obtained findings that were *statistically* significant: but how much significance should we assign to such findings?

So, overall there was a statistically significant difference between the performance of first year students (taking modular examinations) and second year students (taking terminal examinations) – but this did not apply to the girls as a subgroup, and was only found in one of the three common questions. McClune summarises the findings:

> ... pupils in upper sixth (group 1) had a mean score which represented 69 per cent of the marks available, while those in lower sixth (group 2) gained 64 per cent of the available marks. Pupils in the lower sixth have not performed as well as those in the upper sixth when attempting these questions under the same examination conditions. This may seem to indicate that ... pupils opting for modular assessment midway through the course may be at a disadvantage compared to those who opt for assessment at the end of the course.
>
> (McClune, 2001: 83–4)

Statistics can only tell us about the specific data collected. Statistically significant differences become easier to identify in larger samples, and it may be that the smaller size of the girls' subgroup (205, less than half the 490 boys) is partially responsible for finding a significant overall attainment difference only among the boys.

Using scoring schemes

Sometimes quantitative data is obtained by direct counting of instances of different categories. However, sometimes scores are assigned to data according to where they appear on some perceived scale. McClune (2001) argues that students following modular courses (where some of the credit for final grade is awarded for examination papers taken early in the course) may be disadvantaged compared with students taking linear courses for the same award, and being examined on all aspects of the course in terminal examinations.

McClune assumed the major factor that would indicate if the two groups were comparable would be their previous examination success. He compared the students' GCSE (school leaving) grades and reported that there was no significant difference between the two groups. In order to make the comparison, examination grades have to be processed in some way. McClune chose to:

- only consider examination grades in three subjects;
- weigh the three subjects as being equally important;
- convert grades to a numerical scale: $A\star = 6, A = 5, B = 4, C = 3$, etc., to give each student an overall numerical score.

Each of these decisions is reasonable, but clearly it is possible that making different decisions (such as including more subjects; giving most weight to science and maths; giving greater differentials between the highest grades, e.g. $A\star = 10, A = 7, B = 5, C = 3, D = 2, E = 1$) could have led to a different outcome.

Classification schemes

Frequency data is obtained when it is possible to assign data to a limited set of categories. For example, Harrop and Swinson (2003) used a classification scheme to characterise teacher questions. The type of scheme (or typology) used offers mutually exclusive categories to cover the full range of teachers' questions. That is, any question a teacher asks must fit into one, and only one, of the categories on the scheme.

Question for reflection

What are the limitations and potential problems of using a classification scheme to analyse classroom data such as teacher questions?

As we have seen in other studies, researchers have a responsibility to produce a simplified account of their data which is readable and readily appreciated by readers, although this can never reflect the full complexity of the educational phenomena studied. This is usually achieved either by selecting analytical categories from existing knowledge during the conceptualisation stage *before* collecting data, or by a process of 'induction' – of identifying 'emergent' categories that seem to represent the main patterns in data once it is collected.

In Harrop and Swinson's case, their initial conceptualisation of the field in terms of previously published research meant that they started the research with categories to use in analysing data – the types of questions identified in previous work. In this situation, the researcher would normally have a recording sheet in the form of a table set up to record instances of the different types of questions observed whilst listening to the lessons. In real time observation the observer would identify the appropriate category and place a mark in the appropriate place on the recording sheet. If working from transcripts of lessons, it may be more sensible to use a set of codes for the different question types, and to code the transcripts. In either case, the result makes it easy to tally-up the instances and enter the tallies into a summary table, showing the total number of examples of each category observed.

Developing categories

Working with predetermined categories is more likely in studies from within ERP1. Research that has a more interpretivist nature is likely to delay establishing categories until after data collection. In ERP2 approaches, the researcher develops the categories by interrogating the data, and deciding which classifications will best 'fracture' the data set in ways that represent the patterns in the original data.

For example, in their 2004 paper on self-regulated learning, Corrigan and Taylor (2004: 52–3) outline the way they collected data (a 'semi-structured interview protocol was constructed to detect perceptions, experiences, dilemmas and problems faced by students … student reports … were [also] examined'), and how they then analysed it ('all interviews were audio-taped and transcribed. After reading the transcripts, a number of categories were developed …').

The categories are said to 'emerge' from, and be grounded in the data (cf. grounded theory, GT; see Chapter 4). Of course, the categories really emerge from the researcher's mind, and will be influenced (often subconsciously) by the analyst's own prior belief and ideas about the topic. This is inevitable, and is a possible source of bias in interpreting data.

However, there are ways of minimising such bias. Although the creative process of coming up with categories ('induction') is outside of conscious control, it is certainly possible to carefully *check the fit* of categories against the data, and only retain those which fit well ('post-inductive resonance'). Iterative processes have been developed in GT that involve constantly checking (and modifying) the analytical codes against the data being collected. In effect, codes and categories are hypotheses being tested against new data. Given such safeguards through the *context of justification*, the rather mysterious and subjective nature of the *context of discovery* is not problematic (cf. Chapter 5).

Identifying themes

In a paper in the journal *Teachers College Record*, Aldridge (2006: 680) offers an account of how US history textbooks misrepresent the life of Martin Luther King Jr., offering 'a sanitized, noncontroversial, oversimplified view of perhaps one of America's most radical and controversial leaders'.

In his study, Aldridge identifies three 'master narratives' about King:

- as a Messiah;
- as the embodiment of the civil rights movement; and
- as a moderate.

This claim is based on the analysis of six American history textbooks that Aldridge (2006: 664) characterises as 'popular and widely adopted' high school texts. He identifies the texts and justifies their selection for the study.

Aldridge (2006: 664) describes his main methodological approach as *literary analysis*. This is described as a simple process of reading materials to identify evidence *to support* a perspective or argument. The approach, followed in the paper, has four stages: reading; identifying themes; discussing the themes identified; and offering examples that support the case being made.

Aldridge outlines his perspective early in his paper:

> History textbooks often presented simplistic, one-dimensional interpretations of American history within a heroic and celebratory master narrative … a teleological progression from 'great men' to 'great events', usually focusing on an idealistic evolution toward American democracy.
>
> (Aldridge, 2006: 662)

The starting point for the study (Aldridge, 2006: 663) was a belief that 'The dominance of master narratives in textbooks denies students a complicated, complex, and nuanced portrait of American history'. Later in the paper, Aldridge (2006: 66) 'illustrate[s] the master narratives that history textbooks present of one of America's most heroic icons, Martin Luther King, Jr'.

The rhetorical nature of Aldridge's study

This study is particularly interesting in terms of some of the points raised earlier in the book, about research writing as rhetoric (see Chapters 1 and 5), and about the importance of a researcher's conceptual *frame*work for *framing* research studies (Chapter 3).

> ## Question for reflection
>
> Aldridge (2006) clearly expected and intended to find 'master narratives' about King in the books analysed, and his expectation was realised. Does this undermine the findings as being influenced by the researcher's biases?

It is clear that Aldridge sets his study within a rhetorical context – an argument that history teachers in the USA should teach in ways that compensate for the limitations of the commonly adopted textbooks. Yet (as with Lyle, see Chapter 5) Aldridge is always totally explicit about this position, and his description of his methodology makes it clear that the case of King is being used as an example to support his beliefs.

Indeed the methodology might be seen as inherently self-fulfilling, as 'identifying themes' is seen as unproblematic. However, this methodological approach did not preclude the possibility of finding nuance and complexity (e.g. that the same books could have presented 'King as moderate' and 'King as radical' in interwoven themes.)

If Aldridge's study had been set up as a test of the hypothesis that US history books presented history through oversimplified meta-narratives, then the methodological approach would be significantly deficient. However, Aldridge's acknowledged conceptual framework for the research was that such narratives *were* present, and the study sought to identify them. In these terms his study must be judged on how well the three proposed narratives reflect the texts he analysed.

Following the leads to a core category

One of the papers referred to in Chapter 2 was Calissendorff's (2006) study of 5 year-olds learning to play the violin. This study used a GT approach to data analysis, and the author clearly explains the stages of the process in her account.

For Calissendorff (2006: 85), 'leads' emerged during her study, as she interviewed and observed the young musicians, their teacher and their accompanying parents. A 'lead' derived 'from an interesting event, statement or observation. It is followed up, and eventually either forms a category of its own, is placed within an existing category or is rejected'. As well as reporting the 'leads' which emerged through her study, Calissendorff describes how some of these were modified or combined over the period of data collection to give a set of categories that organised her data: motivation, perception, time, etc. Calissendorff then describes how she adopted the core concept of 'learning style', drawing heavily on an existing learning style model she had read about.

Question for reflection

Is it acceptable in a GT study to organise the data around a core concept that is taken from a literature review, rather than one that emerges from the data?

Calissendorff (2006: 91) adopts a concept from her reading to structure her findings, because she found a strong match between her own categories, and key elements of the published model ('what has been presented earlier is now integrated within the core category … it includes everything'), However, she points out that her core concept is an *adaptation* of the published model, modified to fit the details of her own findings. This is within the spirit of GT (see Chapter 4).

Selecting a case for case study

Petri and Niedderer published an account drawing on a case study (see Chapter 4) of one 18-year-old high school student's learning about the atom. Although they report the case of a single learner, Petri and Niedderer (1998) collected data from a class of nine students taught by two teachers. The researchers collected data over 12 weeks of the course. The authors then made a selection of Carl as the subject for a case study. They offer the reader two criteria that were used (Petri and Neidderer, 1988: 1078). They wanted a case study where the student made verbal contributions in class, and where the student was not at either extreme of the attainment range for the level.

The authors also give an overview of the main steps in the process of developing the case study (Petri and Niedderer, 1998: 1078–9):

- data were analysed using an iterative … interpretation procedure;
- data were transcribed selectively, using previous research results;
- hypotheses were formulated;
- further transcriptions were undertaken as indicated by hypotheses formed;
- transcripts were repeatedly read to (dis)confirm tentative hypotheses;
- the data on Carl's learning pathway were compared to selected data on other students.

Petri and Niedderer collected a good deal of data in their study, although in their analysis they 'transcribed selectively' and focused on the material relating to their selected 'case', Carl. It would not have been sensible to have identified a case to study at the outset, as they could have made a poor choice of subject (perhaps a student who said little in class, and offered little in interviews, perhaps an atypically able learner) or even selected a student who dropped-out or became ill and missed much of the course. By delaying their selection they safeguarded the study.

They used an iterative process that involved developing hypotheses during data analysis, which then directed which other data should be interrogated in detail. Though the use of triangulation, a range of different 'slices of data' provides the richness of evidence to allow such an iterative process to be possible.

'Mixed methods'?

In his study of student preferences of learning environments, Kinchin (2004) reports his results in two forms: he presents both quantitative and qualitative data. In Chapter 3, it was suggested that educational research tends to be associated with different traditions, based upon different assumptions about how useful knowledge about educational contexts may be generated. ERP1 (positivistic, nomothetic, confirmatory) was considered to be basically a quantitative paradigm, whereas ERP2 (interpretivist, idiographic, discovery) tends to rely more on the use of qualitative data.

Studies that collect both quantitative and qualitative data are sometimes referred to as 'mixed methods' (although it is of course quite possible for a mixture of methods, e.g., interviews, observations and document analysis, to produce purely qualitative data). In Kinchin's study, students selected their preference for what Kinchin characterised as a constructivist (student-centred) or an objectivist ('traditional') classroom, and offered their reasons.

The quantitative data consists of raw numbers that have been tabulated (Kinchin, 2004: 305): 310 of 349 respondents selected option B (the constructivist classroom) and the other 39 chose the option representing the 'objectivist' classroom. Kinchin reports that the response patterns were similar in the two age groups.

The qualitative data presented in the paper was a small selection of quotations from the justifications students offered. So, for example, in his analysis of responses from those favouring option A (the 'objectivist' classroom) Kinchin identifies two themes. His analysis of the data suggests that there were two main reasons for students making this preference:

- feeling this was an easier way of studying;
- it offered a more suitable basis for revising for examinations.

Kinchin's analysis of the responses from those preferring option B (the constructivist classroom) identified three main themes among student justifications:

- feeling that this type of classroom made learning more interesting;
- that it was more effective at supporting learning;
- that it gave them greater ownership of their own learning.

Again, these categories were supported with a small sample of quotes from the data collected.

Question for reflection

Would you consider Kinchin's (2004) study to be in the positivistic or interpretivist tradition – or is it an example of a distinct 'mixed methods' approach?

The form of data analysis reflects the type of study being undertaken

In Chapter 3 it was suggested that the decisions made at the start of a research study may have implications throughout the enquiry (i.e. see Figure 3.4.). The type of data analysis appropriate to a study depends upon the type of data collected, which should reflect the researcher's beliefs about the type of research (e.g. exploratory or confirmatory) being undertaken.

There are some features of Kinchin's study that are positivistic. The main one is that he began the study with an assumption that the categories of constructivist and objectivist classroom, as he conceptualised them, were a suitable basis for exploring students' views. An alternative approach would have been to have undertaken research to explore student thinking about their preferred style of 'classroom' without preconceived categories. This might have produced a more authentic account of 'student beliefs about their preferred role as learners'. However, Kinchin's own conceptualisation of the project was in terms of official guidance supporting 'constructivist' teaching approaches, so setting up his research in terms of a dichotomous preference (with constructivism as one pole) better fitted his purposes.

Given that teaching and learning are complex phenomena, the educational researcher has a responsibility to produce findings that are a simplification: simple enough to be readily understood, and to provide the basis for teachers and others to act on them. Inevitably this means reporting results in terms of categories (or at least headings). In ERP1 it is usual to formulate categories at the outset, so that during data collection 'forced choices' are made (by researcher, or respondents) in relation to the permitted categories. In ERP2 it is usual to collect data in a more open-ended way, but to identify categories during analysis, which best reflect the main patterns in the data (inevitably filtered through the pre-existing conceptual structures of the analyst who interprets the data).

Kinchin's study shows that he felt that there was sufficient basis in existing research to support a simple model of classroom styles that could be used to force choices when collecting data about student preferences. However, he was more open-minded in terms of the reasons for those choices, and allowed categories for reporting student reasoning to emerge during analysis.

The presentation of quantitative data is often associated with ERP1, but Kinchin does not offer an explicit hypothesis to be tested, and so does not present any inferential statistics (to show the *statistical significance* of findings). The discussion of the findings from student justifications is certainly presented as being closer to an interpretivist approach to educational research. Kinchin does not report bringing preconceived categories to his data analysis here but suggests the categories 'emerged' from his analysis of the data. Presumably, Kinchin's reading of the relevant literature provided him with a conceptualisation of the field suggesting that the way students might justify their preference for an 'objectivist' or 'constructivist' classroom was still very much an open question.

10

Teachers Making the Case Through Reporting Research

Should all research be reported?

There are two contrary opinions about reporting research, which need to be considered when deciding if, and how, to report classroom-based research:

- research is not of value until it has been put in the public domain so that it may be considered, replicated, criticised and become subject to professional dialogue;
- practitioner research is intended to improve the professional context for a teacher and her/his students: time and effort formally reporting the work is unnecessary and a distraction.

Question for reflection

Consider your own research project: which of these opinions more closely fits your own views about writing-up your work? How would you argue against the other opinion?

The view taken here is that both of these (opposite) opinions are essentially correct! To appreciate how it is possible to agree with both of these contrary opinions, we should consider the purposes for which research may be undertaken, and so *the form of knowledge* that is being sought.

Academic researchers

Traditional 'science' research is about creating 'public knowledge' that is shared by the community. In the natural sciences, new 'discoveries' are only usually considered to be due to the person who *publishes* the ideas first, as only once published are findings open to scrutiny, and available to help develop the field. In these fields, ideas become part of a consensus and come to be considered reliable knowledge (Ziman, 1991), but only after due processes. This involves other scientists critiquing methods and findings, and checking that the published results are reproducible, i.e. that other competent investigators can confirm the findings. (This is a rather simplistic description of a complex and sometimes highly contended process, but offers the essence of what happens.)

Although social science knowledge is often viewed differently to natural science knowledge, so that there is less expectation of consensus or potential for *direct replication* of studies, similar academic norms operate. The gatekeepers of knowledge are the journal editors, referees used by academic publishers, professional bodies, etc., and publication in peer-reviewed research journals is considered the minimum requirement for claiming the production of new knowledge in a field. *Academic*, professional, researchers are judged by their ability to contribute to the development of knowledge in their field by publishing in appropriate forms.

Publish or be damned?

For such researchers, the *intellectual* purpose of their enquiries may be primarily in terms of a desire to know more, to understand, etc., but the *professional* purpose of research is to contribute in the expected ways: to produce academic publications. For the professional researcher (in education or another field), publications are the sign of acceptable knowledge creation – and to some extent, of professional worth.

These researchers must report their research, and they must report it to a designated audience, and in a *format* that is considered acceptable to their peers. Their research must be written-up in such a way that others in their field will judge that they have reported their work in a way that contributes to the field – knowledge that others can engage with. The criteria for acceptable writing are the norms established in the relevant journals.

Question for reflection

What are the criteria that are likely to be used to decide whether a research report submitted to an academic journal should be published?

In particular, a contribution to the academic literature has to offer some originality. This may be just a slight modification of existing ideas, or the finding that previously reported outcomes may (or may not) also apply in a slightly different context: from modern language teaching to geography teaching; from primary to lower secondary level, etc. The journal editor will wish to be convinced that by publishing the researcher's paper the readers will have access to something that was not previously available, whether a major new insight, or just increasing understanding of the properties of something that is already well-known. (The status of the journal, and the ratio of submitted to accepted papers, will largely determine where the line is drawn on *how* novel something has to be before it is likely to be accepted for publication.) As will be discussed below, the onus of *making the case* rests on the author.

Practitioner researchers

At the opposite end of the scale to the professional academic researcher is the practitioner, perhaps a newly qualified classroom teacher. The professional priority here is not to publish research, but to effectively teach students. The teacher will not be judged by publishing accounts of professional work. The research may be no more than trying out an idea that is already well reported in the literature to find out if 'will it help here?' The purpose is to support teaching, and so help students learn. The teacher wants to be able to evaluate these new approaches to find out if they improve professional practice.

Question for reflection

Research was described above in terms of knowledge-creation. Is this practitioner – who is using research as a systematic way to evaluate ideas used in teaching – actually creating new knowledge?

It was suggested above that knowledge does not 'count' until it is published. Do you think anyone doing research in this way should feel obliged to publish their findings?

Let us assume that this teacher is competent in planning the research, in collecting the data, and in analysing it to draw conclusions that can inform practice. At the end of the process the teacher will have a better understanding of some aspect of the teaching and learning in the classroom. So, new knowledge has been produced that should inform future teaching.

Personal or public knowledge

However, this does not mean such a teacher should feel obliged to try to publish the findings. The teacher's personal research has led to new *personal* knowledge: knowledge of real value to professional work. This does not *in itself* make the findings a new potential contribution to *public* knowledge. Even if the personal knowledge could be made explicit (for personal professional knowledge is often at a tacit level, although the research process helps make this explicit), and conceptualised in terms of a wide and relevant literature review, it is still likely that the teacher's study will be judged to have very limited significance in the public domain. (It is by no means *impossible* that a classroom teacher may discover something quite novel that should be brought to wide attention, but most practitioner research does *not* lead to such outcomes.)

As teachers, we should be very familiar with this distinction, because it is at the very heart of our professional work. After all, a great deal of school learning involves individuals developing new (personal) knowledge that is already widely known. In many school subjects, a significant part of the teacher's job is to help learners discover or appreciate or reconstruct well-established public knowledge. The lack of originality of this new knowledge certainly does not take away from its importance to the learners. We appreciate the value of one more human being able to solve quadratic equations, or having an understanding of key conditions that facilitated the industrial revolution.

From this perspective, if the purpose of a teacher's research is purely professional development as a classroom practitioner, and much of the research involves evaluating existing ideas to find 'what works here?', or 'how can I solve this problem/address this issue in my professional practice?', then there would be little value in any kind of formal write-up. Indeed, as suggested above, a great deal of time spent documenting the research could probably be used in more productive ways.

So the two key ideas here are:

- purpose of research – just for my own professional development?
- forms of knowledge – private or public knowledge?

However, the two scenarios discussed here represent the ends of a scale or continuum. Teacher research is often intended only for use within the classroom where it is carried out. But, this is not always the case.

Question for reflection

Can you think of any appropriate audiences for teacher-research beyond the teacher him or herself?

Audiences for teacher research

There are a good many reasons why a teacher may wish to share research with others: some of which are considered here. As the purpose of research is a key consideration when deciding *if* and *how* to report research, these different reasons lead to different advice on sharing your research with others.

So, teachers may share research because:

- they are required to demonstrate research competence (e.g. if taking a formal academic qualification such as the PGCE or a higher degree);
- it is school policy (e.g. the school requires new staff to undertake a research project during their first year in school, see McLaughlin et al., 2006);

- teaching is a collegiate activity (and so colleagues may share their findings, e.g. within the department);
- research is supported (by the school; by an external sponsor);
- they wish to support the advocacy of a new policy (e.g. persuade the department to change policy);
- they feel their experiences may be valuable to others in the profession/they wish to contribute at a professional level.

There are obviously many possible variations and graduations in these options. We shall here consider a number of possible audiences a teacher could have for their research, and the type of report likely to be indicated in each situation. A key issue will also be the basis upon which the research is undertaken. A busy classroom teacher inherently has little incentive to spend time and effort in *reporting* (as opposed to carrying-out) research: the incentive normally comes from likely future 'rewards': a qualification, promotion, increased status in the subject association, seeing one's work in print. Often these are uncertain rewards even with considerable effort and perseverance.

The informal group

An informal research group, within a department, across a school, or among a group of local schools is potentially a very powerful mechanism for supporting professional learning. Such groups lack formal structures, with members' strong interest in topics acting as impetus for attendance and contribution. The lack of formality also provides flexibility. It may be that simply discussing experience and sharing evidence over coffee is the extent of procedure. This allows members to find out what works in other classrooms in the same or similar institutional contexts, and also provides extra eyes and minds to make suggestions and observations. Such groups can also act as useful sounding boards for those who have to present more formal accounts of their work elsewhere.

The department

Persuading the department to make changes or move in a particular direction may be difficult – even for the Head of Department. Arguing from evidence, and showing that proposed ideas can work in the school, can be very important. Depending upon the formality of procedures (and the level of cohesion and collegiality involved) a written paper may be an appropriate instrument *to make a case*. This is more likely to be appropriate at whole school level, where talking to some sort of discussion paper may well be an accepted way of making the case for changes to policy or procedures.

In the context of the school or department, discussion papers are normally expected to be brief and 'to the point'. This is not always the case – (see the comments on sponsored research, below), but generally short papers with bullet points and clear summaries of the research evidence are likely to have more impact. A teacher involved in making a case in this way should look to produce a concise summary of the argument, but be prepared to answer questions to provide any additional background when presenting the case (at a departmental or staff meeting for example). Colleagues are only likely to be convinced by an argument that seems to be well thought-out and based on a careful analysis of relevant evidence: they are however unlikely to have time to commit to reading a lengthy, detailed account.

The sponsor

Sponsors provide money for school research, and usually expect to see outcomes that suggest their money has been well used. A sponsor may well specify the form of report that needs to be undertaken as a condition of funding. So, for example, when government funding in the UK supported 'Best Practice Research Scholarships' (BPRS) there were minimum expectations in terms of an outline of the form the report must take. Reports had to be submitted to a central website so that other teachers could learn from the research. However, the level of detail required was insufficient for this purpose, so that some BPRS reports often provide minimal information to suggest the relevance of the research to other contexts.

BPRS funding was available for a wide range of project areas that teachers might wish to research. Other sponsors may wish to find very specific research, or at least (like the National Academy for Gifted and Talented Youth, NAGTY) offer funding to explore a particular topic. The sponsor's requirements in terms of a report are likely to be tailored to their purposes in offering the money. NAGTY is charged with researching and supporting teaching and learning for those classed as 'gifted and talented' in schools and colleges, so funds teacher research only when it is targeted at that group of students.

When the government decided not to continue to offer BPRS, it was expected that the money would become available to schools to target their own research. Some schools already had established research policies and funds, and so had traditions of sponsoring their own staff to undertake research. Such sponsorship often takes the form of a small reduction of teaching load, with the expectation that the released time will be used to undertake the research. Schools may give an open agenda to teachers to suggests projects that would be useful, or they may have priority themes, or allocate money via a departmental structure.

Sometimes schools may have specific research they wish to see undertaken, and so ask staff to work to a pre-existing brief. When teaching in further education, I was commissioned by my college to undertake a project exploring the use of value-added indicators. The project had set aims, and it was clear from the outset what form the outcomes had to take. My other research projects as a school and college teacher had followed my own research interests. Taking on commissioned research meant following someone else's agenda, but led to being paid a fee for the time and research skills employed.

The professional journal

Professional journals are published by subject associations, and their editors are usually keen to publish material written by practising classroom teachers. These journals vary in the extent to which they are set-up along the lines of an academic journal or a magazine. Articles are normally peer-reviewed, but using somewhat different criteria to academic journals. Editors of professional journals are often interested in publishing accounts of classroom work that might be of interest to other teachers. Practitioner research may often be ideal as a basis for such articles.

A key advantage (for the busy teacher) of writing for a practitioner journal rather than an academic journal – apart from the increased likelihood that some teachers may actually read what you have written – is that the criteria for accepting articles tend to be less demanding. It is difficult to generalise, but many professional journals will publish articles which:

- are shorter (e.g. 2000 words perhaps, cf. typically 5000 words for an academic journal);
- are written in a more conversational style (as that makes them more readable);
- have limited conceptualisation (as they do not expect a significant preamble setting out the issues around the topic: it is preferred that articles 'get to the point' to keep readers' interest);
- have limited use of literature (reference to a few key readings, not a literature review);
- are provocative or speculative (so that they encourage discussion and response from readers);
- are less rigorous (accepting illustrations from classroom practice without considering such issues as sampling bias, etc.)
- are interesting rather than novel (preferring to offer articles across a range of topics, than worry about originality).

The last point is particularly pertinent in view of the discussion earlier in the chapter about the nature of knowledge that derives from teacher research.

A professional journal might be very interested in an account of teacher research that exemplifies an important idea in teaching the subject:

- if it is written in a lively way (e.g. includes personal anecdote);
- if it offers some good illustrative material (photographs, snippets of student dialogue, etc.);
- if it makes clear recommendations to other teachers; and
- if the journal has not published an issue on that theme or topic for a while.

So where the academic editor asks 'does this tell us something new?', the professional editor may instead ask 'does this say something we have not had said for a while?'. The academic journal will publish many articles on the same topic as long as each adds to the literature, and will happily reject papers that do not meet quality standards no matter which topic they are on.

The professional editors want to keep the content fresh, and will need to revisit topics to make sure that there is balance in the contents list. No tone of criticism is implied here, as these are exactly the types of criteria likely to produce journals that busy classroom teachers will subscribe to, and find time to read. Articles may often be very well written and be engaging and thought-provoking.

The academic journal

Academic journals rely for their status upon readers having confidence in the editorial procedures involved in handling manuscripts. In particular, editors send submissions to experts in the topic for comment, and are guided by these referee reports in making decisions about publication. International research journals with good reputations reject most submissions they receive. Those papers that are accepted are nearly always returned to authors with a list of requirements from the editor based upon referees' comments: 'we may be interested in publishing your paper if you can satisfy us you have met the criticisms of the referees…'. In other words, even a 'positive' response from an academic journal is usually an invitation to undertake a lot more work before possible publication. On submitting a revised 'manuscript' the author will often be expected to offer a point-by-point response to referees' comments.

To get that far, the submission must be seen to meet basic quality criteria. The need for some level of originality has already been mentioned, but referees and editors also need to be convinced that the research has been thoroughly and expertly undertaken. Their concerns when evaluating submissions are likely to be very similar to the assessment criteria that university examiners (who are of course often the same people) will be applying when judging research at masters and doctoral levels for students undertaking PGCE, MA, MEd, MPhil, etc. qualifications.

The academic project report or thesis

Higher degrees normally involve the production of a long (perhaps twenty thousand words, sometimes much longer) dissertation on a topic that has been studied in particular depth. Students undertaking research for a higher degree in education are expected to write-up a report of their projects in the form of a thesis: in other words, a well-developed *argument*, making their case.

Student teachers working towards a PGCE will usually be expected to undertake some kind of classroom-based research project which will be much smaller in scope than a masters dissertation or doctoral project. However, this will usually need to be written-up as a research report, albeit a more modest one (e.g. 8000 words).

There are clearly differences between institutions and courses, and of what is expected at different levels. For example, a PhD project normally has to demonstrate the type of originality expected of a published research report, where a masters project would also need to be rigorously carried out, but would not usually be expected to have such a high level of originality. There are also important differences in style: so that in some instructional contexts more discursive or personal modes of writing are acceptable. A PGCE project may be expected to be like a mini-masters study, offering a taste of the full research experience, or it may be that some aspects of the research process are being emphasised at this level.

It is obviously important for any student to obtain and carefully read all information about the expected nature and format of the report, and the assessment criteria that will be used to judge it. It is also useful to know if a fairly formal 'traditional' research report is expected, or whether something that gives a more authentic feel for the actual personal response to the research experience is encouraged. Certainly at masters level and above, reading good theses from previous years is very helpful.

In view of the differences in requirements between different levels, and between institutions, it is not possible to offer comprehensive guidance for writing-up a student research project. That caveat notwithstanding, in the next section I will offer an overview of a fairly 'safe' way of reporting an empirical research project that should satisfy the requirements of most academic courses.

Indeed, this basic plan provides a suitable outline for writing for publication in academic journals as well. Although the requirements of writing for academic journals are rigorous, they parallel what university examiners are likely to be looking for in project reports. A good thesis at masters level, for example, might well translate into a worthy submission for an academic journal. This same structure may also serve as a template for preparing an oral presentation to a research conference such as the annual meeting of BERA (the British Educational Research Association).

Question for reflection

Consider that people who read your research reports will be critiquing them in the same way that you have approached your reading – asking the kinds of questions highlighted earlier in the book. Jot down a list of criteria that you consider to be useful for evaluating research reports you read. How will you ensure that your own research writing will meet your own expectations as a reader?

The teacher as research writer

Writing-up research formally, as a report to a sponsor, a course assignment, or for publication, requires the author to adopt a different style and structure that may not be familiar from other writing. One of the best ways to appreciate good writing is critical reading: reading other researchers' accounts and evaluating the strengths to aspire to, and the weaknesses to avoid.

In Section 2 three useful analogies were suggested that can help us understand the role of the author of research reports. These are author *as story-teller*, *as advocate*, and *as teacher*. That is, effective educational research writing can be seen in terms of:

- The literary analogy;
- The legal analogy;
- The pedagogic analogy.

The literary analogy

A good research report has a narrative that leads the reader through 'the story' of the research. It can be read from start to finish by an attentive reader, without constantly having to check back or read ahead. The reader knows what kind of story is being told, and where the story is going, during reading.

The legal analogy

The author of a research report makes knowledge claims, and must be able to substantiate them. The author needs to make the case by a careful, logical argument, drawing upon convincing evidence.

The pedagogic analogy

The author is a communicator, charged with informing readers about the research. This is a form of teaching. Just as classroom teaching is planned, with careful attention to the structure of the subject matter, and due weight given to students' existing levels of knowledge, so must research writing be planned. The author-as-teacher provides a structure, with suitable use of advanced organisers and reinforcement, and appropriate examples to illustrate key points, and makes sure that the account both makes explicit connection to relevant information the reader already knows, and provides any essential background needed to make sense of the report.

Effective classroom practitioners will already have all the requisite skills for taking on these roles from their day-to-day work, and should be confident of being able to write as story-teller, advocate and (of course) teacher.

Writing-up research: making your case

Any reader who has worked through this book in a linear fashion should already have a good feel for what a satisfactory project write-up must do, and must look like. Chapter 5 presented a series of questions that we might ask to evaluate research studies. The task of the student writing up research for an academic assignment is to prepare a report that would satisfy the same criteria that we apply when critically reading research. Certainly when it comes to research writing, the dictum should be 'expect of others, as you must be prepared for them to expect of you'.

The key feature of a research report is that it makes its case through a logical chain of argument. As we saw in Section 1, the research process has a logic, where decisions are made sequentially, and each stage of the process builds on what has gone before, and prepares for what will come later:

- identify focus;
- conceptualise existing literature;

- develop research questions;
- identify appropriate paradigm for developing knowledge sought;
- identify suitable methodology to answer research questions;
- identify sample, data collection instruments, etc.;
- collect data;
- analyse data;
- formulate findings to answer research questions;
- relate back to initial focus – draw out implications of research.

The research report should reflect this logic, and set out the argument so that the reader can appreciate why key decisions were made, and how the research makes up a coherent study. This sequence will be developed as the basis for a writing plan. However, it would be foolish to pretend that real research is quite as neat as this description may suggest. Among the common objections to following such an 'ideal' prescription, the researcher might well argue:

- 'I'm doing action research (AR), so my work is cyclic, not linear';
- 'I'm doing grounded theory (GT), so my design is emergent, not planned at the start';
- 'my research went wrong, so I don't have a case to make!'.

These possibilities will be explored below, after considering our 'default' writing plan.

Setting-up your writing plan

A useful way of thinking about writing a research report is to consider entering into a dialogue with your reader – the supervisor, examiner, journal referee or editor for example. This is the type of dialogue you are already familiar with from your own critical reading of research. Of course, this is a dialogue separated in time and space: *the authors must anticipate and answer the reader's questions before they are asked.* Many students new to writing-up research find this more difficult than it sounds – like most new skills it takes time to develop competence. The most common error (also often made by inexperienced teachers in the classroom) is to forget to include information that you are familiar with and taking for granted, but which needs to be made explicit if your argument is to be sensible and convincing.

Almost certainly your research report will need drafting and redrafting. You will need to become critical in reading your own drafts, and spotting the omissions, contradictions, lack of clarity, etc. This means being able to read as your audience will – without the benefit of the vast personal context you bring to your reading. If you are writing a report as a university requirement, then you will almost certainly have a research supervisor who will be prepared to read and comment on your draft. It is important to make use of this resource, but that means planning your writing to give plenty of time for your supervisor to 'turn around' the draft whilst there is still time for you to respond to any criticisms.

You will know that *as a reader* it is helpful if the author seems to be answering your questions in the order they occur to you – thus the importance of setting out a logically sequenced argument. It is also useful to use signposts, such as subheadings, which help lead your reader through the logic of your case. Clear subheadings such as 'findings', 'description of sample' and so forth may not seem very imaginative, but they do offer useful signposts for your reader.

Let us consider then, the typical form of the dialogue between the researcher, and the examiner or other audience for the research report. Clearly there is some potential for overlap and flexibility in where some information would occur in the report, but the following plan acts as a useful guide.

A model for writing-up

What is this study about?

Writing up research is not like mystery writing, where the longer you keep the audience guessing, the better. Quite the converse, the aim is to persuade – to make a case – and so it is important to offer the reader an immediate 'hook' on which to 'hang' the story you have to tell. Indeed, it is usual in research to preface your study with an abstract that 'gives away the ending' before the story even begins – this is discussed further below. (Even though the abstract appears at the start, it may be sensible to write it last of all.)

Your reader should know enough about educational research so that a short introductory statement sets up appropriate expectations about what is to come. We might think of this as activating a schema, providing the foundations for developing a conceptual framework for making sense of the paper. Remember, even if your reader is an expert in the field, they are still a learner when it comes to reading about *your* project.

There is no universal rule about how long the introduction should be, nor what exactly it should contain, but I would suggest that when reporting classroom-based research the introductory section should be fairly brief, covering three areas that the reader will find useful:

- topic;
- approach;
- context.

It helps the reader to have an early indication that the general conceptual area being explored is differentiation, learning about chemical reactions, the use of teacher questioning, peer assessment, pupils' explanations in history, or whatever.

It is probably also very sensible to outline at the start something about the type of study being presented, i.e. this paper will report:

- a small AR study based upon my own teaching;
- a case study of the forms of pupil interaction in a single lesson;
- a small scale evaluation of the usefulness of a learning style questionnaire.

It is also useful to provide some basic context about the research, e.g., 'this study was undertaken during my Year 10 geography lessons, whilst I was on professional placement at an 11–16 school in a small town in the midlands'.

Although it is likely that all the information in this section is either explicit or implicit later in the report, this still provides the basics to make a reader feel psychologically comfortable that they have a 'feel' for where your account will be taking them.

So what do we already know about this?

Having introduced the study in very general terms, it is usual to then offer the reader a review of the literature. The literature review is intended to offer a conceptualisation (yours) of the field where you are undertaking your research (see Chapter 3), to show that your thinking is influenced by existing scholarship, and that your research question(s) are important and/or pertinent.

Doctoral level students are meant to demonstrate through the literature review that they are aware of all the relevant research in the field, and that there is some sort of 'gap' in current knowledge that the present study is meant to fill. The element of originality is less significant at masters level. It is unreasonable to expect a PGCE student (probably undertaking the project whilst on teaching placement) to provide a comprehensive and exhaustive literature review. At PGCE level, the student will be expected to demonstrate an awareness of key literature and a critical engagement with the literature that is reviewed.

A literature review is more than an annotated bibliography (although such a bibliography may be one way of beginning the review process). A review presents a story about the literature: organising the studies discussed so that it is possible to use them to offer a view of the field. In other words, the literature review demonstrates the author's personal conceptualisation of the field. Critical reading (as exemplified earlier in the book) will allow the weighing-up of the importance of different sources, so that an overall assessment of the state of the field can emerge. The review will justify the author's views by pointing out where a study is considered to have inappropriate methodology, too limited a sample, inadequate controls, poorly phrased research questions, citation of limited evidence, etc., etc.

So what's the issue/problem here?

The literature review leads to the identification of the specific focus of the study. Commonly this will mean setting up one or more research questions that are being investigated in the study. The wording of those questions will reflect key concepts in the field (as understood from the literature review) and the conceptualisation of the field will also provide the justification for why the research is worth undertaking in the particular context discussed in the present study.

Of course, a full-time research student will *select* their research site(s) as indicated by their research question(s). By contrast, for a teacher-researcher, the context will be their own institution, and teaching and learning in one (or more) of their classes.

It is clearly important that the topic being researched is appropriate to the context. This will not be a problem for *genuine* AR, as the identification of the issue/problem provides the impetus for the enquiry. However, when research is undertaken as a course assignment, such as on the PGCE course, it is important to make sure that the research focus is pertinent to the class(es) where the enquiry will be carried out. Following the guidelines offered earlier in this section on *planning* the research should ensure this is the case. However, the researcher still has to ensure this link is made explicit for the reader of the research report.

What are you trying to find out?

This will lead to the specification of the particular research questions being explored in this enquiry. The reader should be clear exactly what the aim of the research is. If there are formal research questions, or a hypothesis to be tested, then these should be stated. If the purpose is the evaluation of an activity, an approach, teaching resources, etc., then this should be specified. The reader will only be able to judge the research decisions made, and the analysis and conclusions offered, if the purposes of the research are made clear early in the report.

How did you go about it (and why?)

Once the background and purpose of the study are clearly presented, the researcher then explains the methodological decisions made in terms of an overall strategy (methodology, see Chapter 4), and the specific techniques employed to collect and analyse data (see Chapters 8 and 9). For higher degree theses, this discussion will normally be expected to start with a consideration of the type of knowledge that is sought, and how epistemological assumptions lead to working in a particular paradigm. At PGCE level, it is normally sufficient to pass-over this stage, and discuss the choice of an overall approach (such as case study methodology), but it is important for the student to check what is expected in their institution at the level of study concerned.

Although the researcher is expected to justify methodological decisions, it is accepted that a range of constraints (and opportunities) may channel these. Pragmatic concerns (such as degree of access to students, and available time-scale) are quite proper considerations, as is personal research strengths: there is little point selecting statistical analytical methods if one lacks confidence and competence in statistics. Being open and honest about such matters is sensible, and should be appreciated by an examiner as long as such concerns do not compromise a coherent approach. It clearly would be inappropriate to avoid statistics if the research question is set up as a hypothesis about the statistical significance of some effect.

What data did you collect?

Before proceeding to look at the evidence collected, it is useful to give the reader an overview of that data. So if questionnaires were used, the reader should know

| 1. The researcher, not the reader, bears the burden of analysis: the researcher should analyse the data and present the findings from the analysis. | 2. The researcher should assure the reader that findings are based upon a competent analysis of suitable and sufficient evidence. |

FIGURE 10.1

(for example) that 27 questionnaires were issued to the class, and 24 were completed, with three students unable to complete before having to move to another lesson. If a sample of students were interviewed, the reader should know that five interviews were held with pairs of pupils in the class, each interview being 10–15 minutes in duration. Potentially relevant features of the data collection process should also be described: for example that the interviews were held during the lunch hour in a familiar classroom with no other students present. If informants make up samples of a larger group (as when interviewing some students in a class) then the sample should be described, and the basis for selecting the sample should be explained.

What did you find out (and how do you know?)

The findings section is potentially very problematic for any researcher. In writing-up this section there is a need to carefully balance two key responsibilities which are shown in Figure 10.1.

Responsibility 1 in Figure 10.1 tells us that we should not be presenting a catalogue of data, but the results that derive from the careful analysis of that data. The examiner will not have the time to read through the raw data, and the analysis is a key part of the research process. Responsibility 2 tells us that an account which reports the methods of data collection and analysis to be used, and then presents the findings, often leaves the reader feeling somewhat cheated, feeling that they are being asked to trust the researchers' honesty and competence too much.

The solution to this dilemma is slightly different in the case of academics writing academic papers for publication, and students writing academic assignments for university courses. In the former case, there is usually a default assumption that the researcher is competent (they normally hold a doctorate in the field or a related area), and the journal has a premium on space. In the latter case, a large part of the purpose of the assignment or thesis is to allow the unproven researcher to demonstrate competence. The student still has to work within word–limits, but usually has considerable freedom in *appending* supporting material to the assignment or thesis.

In both cases, it will be expected that the findings section of the report draws upon the evidence base collected during the research to illustrate the claimed findings. Quantitative data analysis is actually less problematic in this respect, as it is usually quite simple to present enough numerical information (in tables and charts) to allow any reader to check the reasonableness of findings. Qualitative data presents more of a problem, as such material as lengthy interview transcripts, or class sets of student work, does not readily lead itself to being presented economically. However, an authentic account would normally still *draw upon the data to illustrate the findings*. For example, if the author is claiming that student interviews demonstrated three main classes of pupil attitudes to regular class tests, then one or two interview extracts may be presented to exemplify each of the categories.

The format of findings presented depends very much on the type of data collected. Descriptive statistics (as deriving from a simple questionnaire for example) may be displayed in tables and simple charts. Inferential statistics are normally presented in tables that cite calculated statistics and associated levels of probability. (And more complex statistical analyses may be presented through a variety of graphical forms of representation.)

Where the data is interview dialogue, classroom dialogue, student written work, etc. it is likely that the findings will be in the form of prose. These will likely take the form of a model (e.g. a typology) or theory that describes or explains patterns in the data. Where various slices of data have been collected, the researcher needs to decide whether to present the findings from the different forms of data separately, and then integrate them, or present the overall findings drawing upon the triangulated data.

When submitting a university course assignment it is usual practice to make use (and sometimes extensive use) of appendices to help bridge the gap between data collected and the findings of the analysis. So it may well be appropriate to append a range of different materials (see Box 10.1). It is usually acceptable to also submit other media, for example data on CD or tapes, etc.

Box 10.1   Examples of typical contents of appendices to research reports

Appendices to research reports could include:

- sample questionnaires;
- sample interview transcripts;
- transcripts of classroom dialogues;
- photocopies of students' work;
- photographs or stills from digital video-recordings of students at work (subject to permission being available);
- photographs of displays or models put together by the students.

Where the main text of an assignment draws upon small extracts from the collected data to provide evidence that illustrates the findings, the appendices may be used to present evidence of competence in analysing data. For example, appending a transcript of an interview shows an examiner the care and detail with which the original recording has been transcribed. (Of course, the examiner seldom has the time to check it against the recording, but by providing the evidence it allows that possibility.) If the findings of a study claim that most of the class used anthropomorphic language when describing how electrons moved around an electrical circuit, then the findings may note that evidence was found in work from 18 out of 26 students, and quote one or two examples. Appending the set of accounts from the class would allow the examiner to look through and see that the examples quoted were representative of what was found among a larger number of students.

So, as we saw when considering some of the studies discussed earlier, a good research report does not just offer the final outcome of analysis, but offers enough of a taste of the data and its analysis to give us confidence in the analytical process. The authors' job is to *make the case*, not just report the verdict. The report should present enough evidence to make a *persuasive* case.

So what?

The findings report what was actually found. The researcher's final job is to explain how these findings may be used. In particular, near the start of the report an issue, problem or research question was defined. It is important to clearly show how the findings relate back to this initial concern. It is also important to discuss how the present findings fit into the wider field, in terms of the initial review of literature. The consequences for teaching and learning in the research context should be discussed, as well as the extent to which the present findings may have wider significance (in the department, school, elsewhere?)

As the research discussed developed from a consideration of the existing literature, it is appropriate to briefly consider whether further research is indicated in the light of the present findings. (For teacher-researchers this is likely to be limited to consideration of the particular research focus in the present professional context, especially if the enquiry has not yet 'solved' the identified problem. See the comments on AR, below pp. 188)

Do I want to read this study?

Having finished your report, you should finalise your abstract. The abstract is placed at the start of the report, and is a brief overview of the whole project, including the findings. Abstracts are normally very short, e.g. 150–200 words, and so only outline the main points. Abstracts have an important role in research, as decisions to obtain and read particular studies are often based upon reading the abstract (which is often available more widely than the full report).

Give your sources

A full bibliography is placed at the end of the research report, followed by the appendices separately numbered (or lettered) to allow them to be readily referred to in the main text.

TABLE 10.1 Overview of the structure of a research report

Do I want to read this study?	Abstract – gives an overview of the issue, context, methods and findings
What is this study about?	Introduction – sets scene, introduces focus, context, type of enquiry
So what do we already know about this?	Literature review – developing a personal conceptualisation of the research field/topic
So what's the issue/problem here?	Setting for study – explaining the link between the literature and the current context for the research
What are you trying to find out?	Establishing the specific research questions, hypothesis or aim of the enquiry
How did you go about it (and why?)	Methodology – rationale for the selection of methodology and particular data collection and analysis techniques
What data did you collect?	Specifying the sample or providing an inventory of evidence collected
What did you find out (and how do you know?)	Findings – the results of analysing the data collected in the study, supported with illustrations from the evidence-based practice
So what?	Discussion: conclusions and implications – how do the findings relate back to the initial concern, and what are the implications of the research for the research context, other contexts, further research?
Where did you get your background information?	References – alphabetical lists of literature cited, giving full bibliographic details
Where's the evidence?	Appendices: supporting evidence – sample data, and sample analyses presented to demonstrate authenticity of account and competence in analysis

Difficulties with the model structure for a research report

Although university regulations and most journals do not require papers to fit a single formal format when reporting research, the type of structure outlined above is familiar to those judging the research, and helps present the 'story' of the research and 'make the case'. As summarised in Table 10.1, this structure offers the reader answers to the key questions they would pose if talking to you about your research.

There may be good reasons to modify this structure in particular cases. However, research reports are a genre of writing, and as with any genre the reader comes to the text with expectations about what to find. Confounding those expectations may act as an impediment to communicating your research story, and so to convincing the reader of the strength of your case.

What about action research (AR)?

At first sight the type of structure being recommended may seem inappropriate for reporting action research (AR). After all, a key characteristic of AR is its cyclic nature, and so any linear reporting structure will not do justice to the research. As suggested in Chapter 7, an AR study may be unsuitable for fulfilling the academic requirements of some university courses, because the *balance of* evidence needed to inform professional decision-making may not readily provide the *weight of* evidence required to justify findings in a thesis.

Where an AR approach *is* considered a suitable basis for a course project, writing-up will present a challenge. A masters level student undertaking a project with several cycles of action and evaluation will find it difficult to readily report the project within the structure recommended here. The structure would certainly seem to fit with one cycle of the action-research process, but the student would need to discuss with the supervisor how best to represent the research in the thesis.

For PGCE students adopting 'action-research flavoured' projects it is likely that time will only allow one cycle of the AR process, in which case the structure given above can be used subject to little or no modification.

What about grounded theory (GT)?

A genuine GT study presents a real challenge to the structure suggested. In this case the research plan is emergent, and there is a constant interplay between data analysis and 'theoretical' sampling of new data. However, it would still be possible *in retrospect* to present the report in the form suggested, making it clear it does not represent the chronological story. That is, the report may focus on 'the context of justification', more than 'the context of discovery' (see Chapter 5).

However, when done thoroughly, the very processes of GT lead to the writing-up of the research as 'a grounded theory'. A masters level student who is genuinely following this approach will be led to a suitable form of research report by the analytical methods employed.

As GT is an open-ended commitment in terms of sampling and time needed for analysis, it is a dangerous choice of approach for a higher degree student, and should only be attempted with strong support. It is almost inconceivable that a PGCE student could develop GT within the constraints of a course assignment, so this is unlikely to be an issue on such courses. It is certainly possible to borrow some analytical techniques from FT to search for emergent patterns in data, but from within a more tightly bounded research plan than could be reported within the structure modelled above.

Research that 'goes wrong'

Finally, a few words about research that 'goes wrong'. There is a lot that can go wrong in research. A failure to collect data relevant to the stated research question could be a serious impediment to writing a thesis for a higher degree. However, with proper supervision, such problems should be avoided. Failure to learn what one hoped to learn is unfortunate, but may be perfectly understandable – after all, research is by its nature an uncertain process. It may still be possible to write up an account of what was intended, what was undertaken, and what was learnt from the process, which offers something of value to the reader – if only at the level that one approach to a problem may be usefully discounted.

In terms of PGCE assignments, demonstrating the ability to plan an enquiry, and collect and analyse appropriate data is more important than answering the initial research questions. If the outcome of the research was to find that the data collected did not offer a clear pattern that could guide future practice, then so be it. An honest explanation of how analysis of the available evidence leads to this conclusion would be credit-worthy and appreciated by an examiner, whereas an attempt to conjure-up some form of definite answer that is *not* supported by evidence would be intellectually dishonest *and* suggest the author does not understand what they are doing. The former case is a failure of the research, but demonstrates key research skills; the latter is a failure of the researcher and is more likely to lead to a failure in the assignment.

Indeed, as the examples of published studies discussed in this book have illustrated well, in research we seldom get clear answers from single enquiries, especially at first attempt. But our failures may teach us something about what to do next, and where and how. This is all part of the research process, and of learning what it means to truly adopt research-based practice.

Little by little …

The teacher-researcher should be reassured that most of the published studies discussed in this book can be considered to be flawed. It is inevitable that educational research studies fail to build a complete chain of evidenced argument based *purely* on valid, reliable interpretation of data collected. Most studies are undertaken with small, non-representative samples, in limited contexts; or use simplistic concepts, categories or typologies that derive from previous studies and can only partially reflect the complexity of educational phenomena. Often studies use evidence that is indirect (inferring behaviour from self-reports; assuming informants can offer accurate and honest accounts of their beliefs and ideas), or are heavily reliant on the interpretations of the researchers in making sense of interviews, observations and other data.

Educational processes are complex, and seldom fully described or explained by single studies. Research in education is therefore both iterative and incremental, with studies building upon, and trying to overcome the limitations of previous research. The community of researchers slowly builds up knowledge that might be considered valid and reliable (ERP1), or authentic and trustworthy (ERP2). The practitioner researcher may feel that their contribution is necessarily quite limited in the wider context, but this may often be so for professional researchers as well. In the narrower, but very relevant, context of their own classes, however, the teacher can often use research to make a very real difference to the teaching and learning that is so important to their own students.

Bibliography

Aldridge, D.P. (2006) 'The limits of master narratives in history textbooks: An analysis of representation of Martin Luther King, Jr.' *Teachers College Record*, 108(4): 662–686.

Avis, J., Bathmaker, A-M., Kendal, A. and Parson, J. (2003) 'Conundrums of our own making: Critical pedagogy and trainee further education teachers', *Teacher Development*, 7(2): 191–209.

Bassey, M. (1992) 'Creating education through research', *British Educational Research Journal*, 18(1): 3–16.

Baszanger, I. and Dodier, N. (2004) 'Ethnography: Relating the part to the whole' in D. Silverman (ed.), *Qualitative Research: Theory, Method and Practice* (2nd Edn), pp. 9–34. London: Sage Publications.

BERA (2000) *Good Practice in Educational Research Writing*. Southwell, Notts: British Educational Research Association.

BERA (2004) *Revised Ethical Guidelines for Educational Research (2004)*. Southwell, Notts: British Educational Research Association.

Biddle, B.J. and Anderson, D.S. (1986) 'Theory, methods, knowledge and research on teaching', in Wittrock, M.C. (ed.), *Handbook of Research on Teaching* (3rd Edn), pp. 230–252. New York: Macmillan.

Biddulph, M. and Adey, K. (2004) 'Pupil perceptions of effective teaching and subject relevance in history and geography at Key Stage 3', *Research in Education*, 71: 1–8.

Bruner, J.S. (1987) 'The transactional self', in Bruner, Jerome and Haste, Helen (eds), *Making Sense: The Child's Construction of the World*, pp. 81–9. London: Routledge.

Bruner, J.S. (1960) *The Process of Education*, New York: Vintage Books.

Button, S. (2006) 'Key Stage 3 pupils' perception of music', *Music Education Research*, 8(3): 417–431.

Calissendorff, M. (2006) 'Understanding the learning style of pre-school children learning the violin', *Music Education Research*, 8(1): 83–96.

Carr, W. and Kemmis, S. (1986) *Becoming Critical: Education, Knowledge and Action Research*. Lewes: The Falmer Press.

Coffield, F., Moseley, D., Hall, E. and Ecclestone, K. (2004) *Should We be Using Learning Styles? What Research Has to Say to Practice*. London: Learning and Skills Research Centre.

Cohen, L., Manion, L. and Morrison, K. (2000) *Research Methods in Education* (5th Edn), London: RoutledgeFalmer.

Corrigan, G. and Taylor, N. (2004) 'An exploratory study of the effect a self-regulated learning environment has on pre-service primary teachers' perceptions of teaching science and technology', *International Journal of Science and Mathematics Education*, 2: 45–62.

DfES (2002) *Framework for Teaching Science: Years 7, 8 and 9, Key Stage 3 National Strategy*. London: Department for Education and Skills.

DfES (2003) *Excellence and Enjoyment: A Strategy for Primary Schools*. London: Department for Education and Skills.

Driver, R. (1989) 'Students' conceptions and the learning of science', *International Journal of Science Education*, 11 (special issue): 481–490.

Driver, R., Squires, A., Rushworth, P. and Wood-Robinson, V. (1994) *Making Sense of Secondary Science: Research into Children's Ideas*, London: Routledge.

Duit, R., Roth, W-M., Komorek, M. and Wilbers, J. (1998) 'Conceptual change cum discourse analysis to understand cognition in a unit on chaotic systems: Towards an integrative perspective on learning in science', *International Journal of Science Education*, 20(9): 1059–1073.

Edwards, D. and Mercer, N. (1987) *Common Knowledge: The Development of Understanding in the Classroom*. London: Routledge.

Elliott, J. (1991) *Action Research for Educational Change*, Milton Keynes: Open University Press.

Freebody, P. (2003) *Qualitative Research in Education: Interaction and Practice*. London: Sage Publications.

Galton, M., Hargreaves, L., Comber, C., Wall, D. and Pell, A. (1999) *Inside the Primary Classroom: 20 Years On*, London: Routledge.

García-Franco, A. (2005) Multiple representations about the structure of matter, Royal Society of Chemistry, Chemical Education Research Group Seminar, Cambridge, July 2005. Available at www.http://rsc.org/Membership/Networking/InterestGroups/Chemical Education Research/Seminars.asp, accessed 10 March 2007.

Gardner, J. and Cowan, P. (2005) 'The fallibility of high stakes '11-plus' testing in Northern Ireland' *Assessment in Education: Principles, Policy & Practice*, 12(2): 145–165.

Garet, M.S., Porter, A.C., Desimone, L., Birman, B.F. and Yoon, K.S. (2001) 'What makes professional development effective? Results from a national sample of teachers', *American Educational Research Journal*, 38(4): 915–945.

Gilbert, J.K. and Watts, D.M. (1983) 'Concepts, misconceptions and alternative conceptions: changing perspectives in science education', *Studies in Science Education*, 10: 61–98.

Gilbert, J.K., Watts, D.M. and Osborne, R.J. (1985) 'Eliciting student views using an interview-about-instances technique', in West, L.H.T. and Pines, A.L. (eds), *Cognitive Structure and Conceptual Change*, pp. 11–27. London: Academic Press.

Glaser, B.G. (1978) *Theoretical Sensitivity: Advances in the Methodology of Grounded Theory*, Mill Valley, CA: The Scoiology Press.

Greenbank, P. (2003) 'The role of values in educational research: the case for reflexivity', *British Educational Research Journal*, 29(6): 791–801.

Hallam, S. and Ireson, J. (2005) 'Secondary school teachers' pedagogic practices when teaching mixed and structured ability classes', *Research Papers in Education*, 20(1): 3–24.

Hammersley, M. (ed.) (1993) *Controversies in Classroom Research* (2nd Edn), Buckingham: Open University Press.

Hardman, F., Smith, F. and Wall, K. (2005) 'Teacher–pupil dialogue with pupils with special educational needs in the National Literacy Strategy', *Educational Review*, 57(3): 299–316.

Harrop, A. and Swinson, J. (2003) 'Teachers' questions in the infant, junior and secondary school', *Educational Studies,* 29(1): 49–57.

Hennessy, S., Ruthven, K. and Brindley, S. (2005) 'Teacher perspectives on integrating ICT into subject teaching: Commitment, constraints, caution, and change', *Journal of Curriculum Studies*, 37(2): 155–192.

John, P. (2005) 'The sacred and the profane: Subject sub-culture, pedagogical practice and teachers' perceptions of the classroom uses of ICT', *Educational Review*, 57(4): 471–490.

Keogh, B. and Naylor, S. (1999) 'Concept Cartoons, teaching and learning in science: An evaluation' *International Journal of Science Education*, 21(4): 431–446.

Kinchin, I.M. (2004) 'Investigating students' beliefs about their preferred role as learners', *Educational Research*, 46(3): 301–312.

Kind, V. and Taber, K.S. (2005) *Science: Teaching School Subjects 11–19*. London: Routledge.

Kuhn, T.S. (1977) *The Essential Tension: Selected Studies in Scientific Tradition and Change*, Chicago: University of Chicago Press.

Kuhn, T.S. (1996) *The Structure of Scientific Revolutions* (3rd Edn). Chicago: University of Chicago. (First edition published 1962.)

Kuiper, J. (1994) 'Student ideas of science concepts: alternative frameworks?', *International Journal of Science Education*, 16(3): 279–292.

Kvale, S. (1996) *InterViews: An Introduction to Qualitative Research Interviewing*. Thousand Oaks, California: Sage Publications.

Lakoff, G. and Johnson, M. (1980) The metaphorical structure of the human conceptual system, *Cognitive Science*, 4: 195–208.

Limerick, B., Burgess-Limerick, T. and Grace, M. (1996) 'The politics of interviewing: power relations and accepting the gift', *International Journal of Qualitative Studies in Education*, 9(4): 449–460.

Lyle, S. (1999) 'An investigation of pupil perceptions of mixed-ability grouping to enhance literacy in children aged 9–10, *Educational Studies*, 25(3): 283–296.

Macaruso, P., Hook, P.E. and McCabe, R. (2006) 'The efficacy of computer-based supplementary phonics programs for advancing reading skills in at-risk elementary students', *Journal of Research in Reading*, 29(2): 162–172.

McClune, B. (2001) 'Modular A-levels – who are the winners and losers? A comparison of lower-sixth and upper-sixth students' performance in linear and modular A-level physics examinations', *Educational Research*, 43(1): 79–89.

McIntyre, D., Peddar, D. and Ruddock, J. (2005) 'Pupil voice: comfortable and uncomfortable learnings for teachers', *Research Papers in Education*, 20(2): 149–168.

McLaughlin, C., Black-Hawkins, K., Brindley, S., McIntyre, D. and Taber, K.S. (2006) *Researching Schools: Stories from a Schools–university Partnership for Educational Research*. London: RoutledgeFalmer.

McNiff, J. (1992) *Action Research: Principles and Practice*, London: Routledge.

Medawar, P.B. (1963/1990) 'Is the scientific paper a fraud?', The Listener, 70, 12.9.63, reprinted in P.B. Medawar, *The Threat and the Glory*. New York: HarperCollins.

Muijs, D. (2004) *Doing Quantitative Research in Education With SPSS*. London: Sage Publications.

National Research Council (2002) *Scientific Research in Education*. Committee on Scientific Principles for Educational Research. Washington DC: National Academies Press.

Novak, J.D. and Gowin, D.B. (1984) *Learning How to Learn*, Cambridge: Cambridge University Press.

Petri, J. and Niedderer, H. (1998) 'A learning pathway in high-school level quantum atomic physics', *International Journal of Science Education*, 20(9): 1075–1088.

Phillips, D.C. (1987) *Philosophy, Science and Social Enquiry: Contemporary Methodological Controversies in Social Science and Related Applied Fields of Research*. Oxford: Pergamon Press.

Phillips, D.C. and Burbules, Nicholas C. (2000) *Postpositivism and Educational Research*, Oxford: Rowman & Littlefield.

Pollard, A. and Filer, A. (1999) *The Social World of Pupil Career: Strategic Biographies through Primary School*, London: Cassell.

Pope, M. and Denicolo, P. (1986) 'Intuitive theories – a researcher's dilemma: Some practical methodological implications', *British Educational Research Journal*, 12(2): 153–166.

Powney, J. and Watts, M. (1987) *Interviewing in Educational Research*, London: Routledge & Kegan Paul.

Pring, R. (2000) *Philosophy of Educational Research*, London: Continuum.

QAA (2001) The framework for higher education qualifications in England, Wales and Northern Ireland – January 2001, Quality Assurance Agency for Higher Education. Available at http://www.qaa.ac.uk/academicinfrastructure/FHEQ/EWNI/default.asp, accessed 3 October 2005.

Ravitz, J.L., Becker, H.J. and Wong, Y.T. (2000) *Constructivist–Compatible Beliefs and Practices among US Teachers, Teaching, Learning, and Computing: 1998 National Survey Report #4*, Center for Research on Information Technology and Organizations University of California, Irvine and University of Minnesota, July 2000.

Reynolds, D. (1991) 'Doing educational research in Treliw', in Walford, G. (ed.), *Doing Educational Research*, pp. 193–209. London: Routledge.

Rogers, L. and Hallam, S. (2006), 'Gender differences in approaches to studying for the GCSE among high-achieving pupils', *Educational Studies*, 32(1): 59–71.

Sade, D. and Coll, R.K. (2003) 'Technology and technology education: Views of some Solomon Island primary teachers and curriculum development officers', *International Journal of Science and Mathematics Education*, 1: 87–114.

Sagarra, N. and Alba, M. (2006) 'The key is the keyword: L2 vocabulary learning methods with beginning learners of Spanish', *The Modern Language Journal*, 90(2): 228–243.

Schwandt, T.A. (2001) *Dictionary of Qualitative Inquiry* (2nd edn). Thousand Oaks, California: Sage Publications.

Solomon, J. (1993) 'Four frames for a field', in Black, P.J. and Lucas, A.M. (eds), *Children's Informal Ideas in Science*, pp. 1–19. London: Routledge.

Strand, S. and Demie, F. (2005) 'English language acquisition and educational attainment at the end of primary school', *Educational Studies*, 31(3): 275–291.

Strauss, A. and Corbin, J. (1998) *Basics of Qualitative Research: Techniques and Procedures for Developing Grounded Theory*. Thousand Oaks: Sage Publications.

Taber, K.S. (1992) 'Girls' interactions with teachers in mixed physics classes: results of classroom observation', *International Journal of Science Education*, 14(2): 163–180.

Taber, K.S. (1994) 'Student reaction on being introduced to concept mapping', *Physics Education*, 29(5): 276–281.

Taber, K.S. (2000a) 'Finding the optimum level of simplification: The case of teaching about heat and temperature', *Physics Education*, 35(5): 320–325.

Taber, K.S. (2000b) 'Case studies and generalisability – grounded theory and research in science education', *International Journal of Science Education*, 22(5): 469–487.

Taber, K.S. (2000c) 'Multiple frameworks?: Evidence of manifold conceptions in individual cognitive structure', *International Journal of Science Education*, 22(4): 399–417.

Taber, K.S. (2001) 'Shifting sands: A case study of conceptual development as competition between alternative conceptions', *International Journal of Science Education*, 23(7): 731–753.

Taber, K.S. (2002) '"Intense, but it's all worth it in the end": The colearner's experience of the research process', *British Educational Research Journal*, 28(3): 435–457.

Taber, K.S. (2003) 'Examining structure and context – questioning the nature and purpose of summative assessment', *School Science Review*, 85(311): 35–41.

Taber, K.S. (2006) Beyond Constructivism: the Progressive Research Programme into Learning Science, *Studies in Science Education*, 42, pp. 125–184.

Taber, K.S. and Student, T.A. (2003) 'How was it for you?: The dialogue between researcher and colearner', *Westminster Studies in Education*, 26(1): 33–44.

Tan, D., Goh, N.K. and Chia, L.S. and Taber, K.S. (2005) Development of a Two-Tier Multiple Choice Diagnostic Instrument to Determine A-Level Students' Understanding of Ionisation Energy. Singapore: National Institute of Education, Nanyang Technological University. Available at http://www.educ.cam.ac.uk/eclipse/Tanetal(2005)Ionisation Energy.pdf

Taylor, A., Lazarus, E. and Cole, R. (2005) 'Putting languages on the (drop down) menu: Innovative writing frames in modern foreign language teaching', *Educational Review*, 57(4): 435–455.

Tobin, K. (1990) 'Teacher mind frames and science learning', in Tobin, K., Kahle, J.B. and Fraser, B.J. (eds), *Windows into Science Classrooms: Problems Associated with Higher-level Cognitive Learning*, pp. 33–91. Basingstoke: Falmer Press.

Tobin, K., Kahle, J.B. and Fraser, B.J. (1990) *Windows into Science Classrooms: Problems Associated with Higher-level Cognitive Learning*, Basingstoke: Falmer Press.

Tomlinson, P. (1989) 'Having it both ways: Hierarchical focusing as research interview method', *British Educational Research Journal*, 15(2): 155–176.

Treagust, D.F. (1995) 'Diagnostic assessment of students' science knowledge', in Glynn, S.M. and Duit, R. (eds), *Learning Science in the Schools: Research Reforming Practice,* pp. 327–346. Mahwah, NJ: Lawrence Erlbaum Associates.

Tripp, D. (2005) 'Action research: A methodological introduction', *Educação e Pesquisa*, 31(3): 443–466. Available at http://test.scielo.br/pdf/ep/v31n3/en_a09v31n3.pdf

TTA (2003) *Qualifying to Teach: Professional Standards for Qualified Teacher Status and Requirements for Initial Teacher Training*, Teacher Training Agency: London.

Walford, G. (ed.) (1991) *Doing Educational Research*, London: Routledge.

Watts, M. (1983) 'A study of schoolchildren's alternative frameworks of the concept of force', *European Journal of Science Education*, 5(2), 1983: 217–230.

White, R. and Gunstone, R. (1992) *Probing Understanding*. London, The Falmer Press.

Whitehead, J. (2000) Living standards of reflection, research and renewal, keynote address for the Ontario Educational Research Council Conference, Toronto, 7 December 2000. Available at http://www.bath.ac.uk/~edsajw/writing.shtml, accessed 4 April 2001.

Wong, M. (2005) 'A cross-cultural comparison of teachers' expressed beliefs about music education and their observed practices in classroom music teaching', *Teachers and Teaching: Theory and Practice*, 11(4): 397–418.

Yin, R.K. (2003) *Case Study Research: Design and Methods* (3rd Edn), Thousand Oaks, CA: Sage.

Ziman, J. (1991) *Reliable Knowledge: An Exploration of the Grounds for Belief in Science*, Cambridge: Cambridge University Press. (First published 1978.)

Index